THE STRONG

(A DAY TO DAY HISTORY OF THE BIGG

BATTLE OF BRITAIN 15TH JULY TO 31ST OCTOBER

BY M S MORGAN

Copyright © 2020 by M S Morgan.

All Right Reserved.

No part of this publication may be reproduced, distributed, or transmitted in any form or by any means, including photocopying, recording, or other electronic or mechanical methods, or by any information storage and retrieval system without the prior written permission of the publisher, except in the case of very brief quotations embodied in critical reviews and certain other noncommercial uses permitted by copyright law.

Table of Contents

Chapter 1 The build-up and the battle of the convoys

Chapter 2 The build up to Eagle Day

Chapter 3 Adler Tag! (Eagle Day)

Chapter 4 The hardest day

Chapter 5 The attacks continue

Chapter 6 Towards a change of tactics

Chapter 7 Towards Battle of Britain day

Chapter 8 A battle of attrition

Chapter 9 The month of fighter battles

Chapter 10 The end of the battle

Postscript

Appendix A: 32 Squadron pilot profiles

Appendix B: 610 Squadron pilot profiles

Appendix C: 79 Squadron pilot profiles

Appendix D: 72 Squadron pilot profiles

Appendix E: 92 Squadron pilot profiles

Appendix F: 74 Squadron pilot profiles

Appendix G: Battle of Britain top scoring pilots of Biggin Hill

Appendix H: Roll of Honour, pilots killed while based at Biggin Hill

Sources used in this book

Introduction

This is the third book in a series I have written about Fighter Command in Kent during World War II. I have lived in Kent for nearly thirty years having settled in the county due to my work commitments, but I was originally from the North of England.

Those of you who have read my other books on Gravesend and West Malling, will know that I have had a long interest in the Royal Air Force and tried to become a pilot myself, but a minor medical condition meant the RAF doctors thought otherwise!

I attended the RAF Officers and Aircrew Selection Centre (OASC) in the 1980s when it was based at Biggin Hill. Like the other candidates, I could not fail to feel the history of my surroundings. The old hangars (replaced after the Battle of Britain), the barrack blocks, guard house and store buildings had changed little from the war. The Memorial Chapel was a building all candidates had to attend, not compulsorily, but if you had a genuine interest and wanted to be a pilot……well you just had to pay your respects while at Biggin Hill.

Sleeping in a four-man room in the barrack blocks while under-going testing, meant that your mind wandered as you drifted off to sleep. Biggin Hill was and still is the most historic airfield in Britain. One dark foggy evening while returning to our barracks we were surprised to see a De Havilland Rapide in RAF livery taxying past the site. I still wonder to this day if we were seeing things as it was too foggy for a 1930's machine to fly.

Sadly, the RAF no longer maintains a base at Biggin Hill, the OASC having now moved to the RAF College at Cranwell. Even the annual Air Fair has been curtailed. However, the Heritage Hangar on the far side of the airfield now maintains and flies several Spitfires, a Hurricane and even a Messerschmitt 109E. To some extent this visible history is even more poignant today. In the Spring and Summer months, the Spitfires can be regularly seen flying around the county of Kent. If you are lucky you might see more than one of them at once.

Some of the most famous names in the Battle of Britain flew from Biggin Hill. 'Sailor' Malan is probably the biggest, but there was also Peter Brothers, Mike Crossley, Brian Kingcome, 'Dimsey' Stones and Don Kingaby to name just a few. Their squadrons are some of the most famous in the Royal Air Force with 'The Tigers' of 74 Squadron, 32, 92, 72, 79 and 610; all carrying the burden of defending the South East and the capital city. But all this came at a cost: they lost 36 pilots killed during this period with countless others wounded and hospitalised, many with terrible burns which required pioneering plastic surgery at East Grinstead hospital under Sir Archibald McIndoe.

Some of the greatest photographic images of the Battle of Britain were taken of Biggin Hill squadrons. 32 Squadron on readiness at Hawkinge and the Spitfires of 610 Squadron in formation over the English Channel, are often used in books and television programs. An image of Keith Gillman, a 32 Squadron pilot posted missing over the Channel during the battle became iconic. His image unnamed at the time, was used on recruiting posters for RAF aircrew during the war. Only a few people were aware that this member of 'The Few' had died in 1940. It is a lasting tribute to his and the other pilots sacrifices.

Which brings me to this book. Although Gravesend and West Malling were important airfields, Biggin Hill was the big one. The airfield was so busy during the summer of 1940 with the various squadrons passing through it, that the research and writing was clearly going to be time consuming.

As with my earlier books, I have researched the National Archives, RAF records, Luftwaffe records and other histories and biographies. Pulling together the various aspects and views while cross-referencing them is time consuming, but I believe this creates a chronological history covering the personal successes and losses.

This book may not be earth shattering in terms of new revelations, but it pulls things together so that anyone can read a concise history of what went on at Biggin Hill between mid-July and the end of October 1940. Many other books have concentrated on a squadron, or a single pilot. While they are valued texts and well-worth a read, they very rarely cover the squadrons operations like a diary. Some books have covered a certain base, but they have concentrated on a longer period, such as the whole of the war. As a result, they become less personal and I believe often detract from the human face of the story.

I would like to thank Simon Parry at WW2images.com for kindly allowing me to use their images in this book.

I hope this book as with my earlier volumes, will pull the facts together to give a fuller more human read. I hope you enjoy the book.

Luftwaffe ranks and their RAF equivalent:

Flieger (Flgr)...............Aircraftman 2nd Class (AC2).

Gefreiter (Gefr)..................Aircraftman 1st Class (AC1).

Obergfreiter (Obgfr)................Leading Aircraftman (LAC)

Hauptgfreiter (Hptgfr).....................No RAF equivalent.

Unteroffizier (Uffz).........................Corporal (Cpl).

Unterfeldwebel (Unfw).....................No RAF equivalent.

Feldwebel (Fw)..Sergeant (Sgt).

Oberfeldwebel (Obfw)..................Flight Sergeant (F/Sgt).

Stabfeldwebel (Stfw).........................Warrant Officer (WO).

Leutnant (Lt)......................................Pilot Officer (P/O).

Oberleutnant (Oblt.)...............................Flying Officer (F/O).

Hauptmann (Haupt.)............................Flight Lieutenant (F/L).

Major (Maj.) ....Squadron Leader (SQL).

Obersleutnant (Oberstlt)..................Wing Commander (W/C).

Luftwaffe Structural Organisation:

- **Staffel** – A Staffel consisted of nine aircraft and was roughly the equivalent of a RAF squadron.
- **Gruppe** – A Gruppe was made up of three Staffeln (plural of Staffel) and were number accordingly. A full group including the Stab flight would number 30 aircraft.
- **Stab** – The Gruppe had a Stab or headquarters flight of three aircraft.
- **Geschwader** – The Geschwader was made up of three Gruppen and their Stab plus its own Stab of four aircraft. In total the Geschwader would number up to ninety-four aircraft

Luftwaffe Unit Designation:

- **JG** – an abbreviation of **Jagdgeschader** (Fighter Wing), was the fighter equivalent of the Geschwader and were number accordingly e.g. Jagdgeschwader 26 (JG26). The third Gruppe of the Geschwader would be listed as 3/JG26.
- **KG** – an abbreviation of **Kampfgeschwader** (Bomber Wing), they were also numbered accordingly e.g. Kampfgeschwader 53 (KG53). The first Gruppe would be listed as 1/KG53.
- **ZG** – an abbreviation of **Zerstorergeschwader** (Destroyer Wing) – in the summer of 1940 attributed to ME110 units e.g. Zerstorergeschwader 26 (ZG26). The second Gruppe would be listed as 2/ZG26.
- **(F)** – Refers to a Long-Range reconnaissance unit.

Chapter 1.

The build-up and battle of the convoys.

After the British Expeditionary Force had been evacuated from Dunkirk, there followed a period of calm. The RAF licked its wounds and sort to replace pilots and aircraft lost over the continent. The Supermarine Spitfire had made its operational debut and given the Luftwaffe something of a surprise in terms of its abilities, while the Hawker Hurricane continued its steady work.

At the same time the Luftwaffe, who had more losses of their own than many people acknowledge; were also making good their losses.

The RAF pilots based in the South East of England, and those at Biggin Hill made regular patrols over the English Channel and Kent. The Luftwaffe rarely appeared, and when they did, they often beat a hasty retreat back to France.

32 Squadron were long-time residents of Biggin Hill, and they flew Hawker Hurricane Mk. I's, with the squadron code 'GZ'. They were a regular RAF unit and had a long and respected history.

By the 2nd July 1940, 32 Squadron were joined at Biggin by 610 (County of Chester) Squadron of the Auxiliary Air Force. These pre-war volunteer reservists flew Supermarine Spitfire Mk.1's bearing the code 'DW' and they were to be the perfect foil for 32 Squadron.

In early July, the two squadrons were engaged on endless patrols over the convoys transiting the Dover Straits. There was some contact with the Luftwaffe and even some losses but compared with the coming weeks; this was a quiet period. The patrols were however quite relentless and boring.

32 Squadron regularly flew down to RAF Hawkinge near Folkestone. As a forward base this prevented delays in transiting down to the Channel. The fighters could have their fuel tanks topped up and they could therefore spend more time on patrol. In Nick Thomas's biography of 32's Flight Lieutenant Peter Brothers, Brothers remembered sitting with the other pilots at Hawkinge awaiting the order to scramble. The head of Fighter Commander Sir Hugh Dowding arrived one day and when he spoke to the pilots, Brothers gave him a piece of his mind about how pointless the patrols were. Whether his words had any impact is officially unknown, but the next day the patrols were stopped.

On the 14th of July, 32 Squadron was sent forward to RAF Manston near Margate in Kent. Like Hawkinge this was a forward operating base, but it was always suspectable to attack and strafing by enemy fighters. In fact, over the course of the Battle of Britain it was hit time after time.

Between 2:50pm and 4:15pm both 32 and 610 Squadrons were ordered to patrol over the convoys in the Channel. The convoy was attacked by Junkers 87 Stukas and the Hurricanes intercepted them. At the time the BBC's Charles Gardiner was making a running commentary of the events. This would become one of the most iconic war reports, but it was tinged with a some-what jingoistic attitude which today seems rather blasé and even ridiculous. It was more like the FA Cup final or an Ashes Test match at Lords than a deadly combat. (It is well worth listening to on You Tube). With hindsight we now know that the RAF did lose a pilot who died of his injuries later that day. The pilot from one of Kenley's squadrons was seen parachuting into the Channel, but the BBC's Charles Gardiner stated that it was a single crewed Stuka pilot who had baled-out! Why a Stuka would be single crewed is another matter.

However, events really started to gather pace for 32 and 610 from the 15th of July onwards.

At 4:25am the pilots of 32 Squadron who had been woken from their slumbers by their batmen with a cup of hot tea, flew in squadron strength down to RAF Hawkinge from Biggin as the dawn brightened.

Squadron Leader John Worrall led Flight Lieutenant Peter Brothers, Pilot Officers John Gardener, John Proctor, Rupert Smythe, Victor Daw and 'Polly' Flinders; Flight Sergeant Guy Turner, Sergeants Dennis Ashton, Bernie Henson and Leonard Pearce. Making up the final place in the formation was Sub-Lieutenant Geoffrey Bulmer who was attached from the Fleet Air Arm. They arrived at Hawkinge at 4:45am and after refueling and another cup of tea, Peter Brothers led four pilots aloft on a Channel patrol at 5:05am. They returned at 6:40am without incident.

Fifteen minutes after the first flight had left, Squadron Leader John Worrall led another five off on a patrol. They also returned at 6:40am without sighting the enemy.

After a good breakfast at their dispersal area, the squadron returned to Biggin Hill taking off at 8:45am. The remainder of the 15th was quiet with practice flights and servicing work on the aircraft of both squadrons. 610 appear to have not carried out any combat flights or patrols on the 15th according to their records, but as we shall see these could be misleading due to the hectic pace of operations in the coming weeks.

On the 16th of July, both squadrons remained on the ground at Biggin Hill. 32 Squadron's Sergeant Dennis Ashton however was on the move. With the Italians threatening the island of Malta, he joined nine other pilots and set sail on the aircraft carrier HMS Argus. They flew their aircraft from the carrier on to the island before engaging the Italians who sought to bomb the small island into surrender.

On the 17th of July, 610 Squadron remained fairly in active. 32 Squadron however after a misty start to the morning, were dispatched at 12:20pm down to Hawkinge. A full squadron of twelve aircraft led by Squadron Leader Worrall arrived at the forward base, but they remained on the ground until 3:00pm when Worrall led, Pilot Officers Rupert Smythe, Keith Gillman, Flight Lieutenant Mike Crossley, Sergeants Edward Bayley and John Proctor back to Biggin Hill. However, they were quickly recalled and landed back at Hawkinge after just ten minutes.

The Luftwaffe were active, but 32 were not having any luck. At 4:10pm Mike Crossley and Sergeants Bayley and Proctor scrambled after a raider but having failed to make contact with the enemy they returned to Hawkinge at 5:55pm.

Shortly after they took off, Squadron Leader John Worrall took off and flew alone back to Biggin Hill. At 4:25pm

Flight Lieutenant Peter Brothers led the remainder of the squadron when they were scrambled after another raid. The raiders however saw the approaching Hurricanes and dived into a cloud bank. The result was that 32 lost contact and were recalled by the controller to base. Despite having no actual combat, Flying Officer John Humpherson had to make a forced landing at Dungeness due to an oil problem. He was not injured in the landing and returned by road to the base.

At 6:25pm 32 Squadron returned to Biggin Hill minus the one Hurricane and all without firing their guns in anger.

The next day the 18th of July started bright and sunny with Flight Lieutenant Mike Crossley leading two other Hurricanes up on a dawn patrol at 5:15am.

At 7:35am Peter Brothers led four other Hurricanes up in a scramble after a reported raider. No enemy aircraft was sighted, and they returned at 8:05am. It is likely this was a lone weather reconnaissance aircraft which the Luftwaffe regularly dispatched to gauge the conditions over southern England before they unleashed their air armada. Often flying at high altitude and often undertaken by the Junkers JU86 high altitude bomber, the chances of interception were low.

At 9:37am 610 Squadron were scrambled from Biggin Hill with twelve aircraft led by Flight Lieutenant E. B. Smith. Enemy aircraft were reported to be approaching Ramsgate from between Calais and Dunkirk. The squadron must have scrambled very quickly as they met 9 - 12 Messerschmitt 109E's of JG51 about 10 miles from the French coast.

There was three layers of cloud mid Channel and this caused visibility problems for both sets of pilots. As a result, very little actual combat took place, the 610 Squadron Operations

Record Book reporting that only two pilots fired their guns, and one aircraft was seen going straight down. Sadly, this is believed to have been 25 years old Pilot Officer Peter Litchfield, who was reported as missing from this action in DW-T (P9452). It is probable that he was victim of Hauptman Horst Tietzen of 2/JG51 who claimed a Spitfire north of Calais at 10:00am. Litchfield was quite an experienced pilot and had already destroyed three German aircraft. 152 Squadron had also been involved in the action, but no Messerschmitt's were lost. 610 returned to Biggin Hill and were not in action again for the rest of the day. 32 also remained inactive for the rest of the day before both squadrons were released for the day.

Peter Litchfield's body was never recovered, and his name is recorded on the RAF Memorial at Runnymede Panel 9.

The pilots often attended the White Hart in Brasted on the road between Sevenoaks and Westerham. Large parties were held there and went on late into the night. While the pilots and the officers held their parties at Brasted, the ground crews used The Old Jail in Jail Lane on the boundary of Biggin Hill's airfield. The ground crews working long hours after the pilots had been released, would often only have time to nip through the boundary fence to the local pub for a quick pint. The next day would see the start of the hectic action for 32 and 610 Squadrons.

It is worth noting that 141 Squadron, flying Boulton Paul Defiants were attached to Biggin Hill at this time, but were operating from the new airfield at West Malling near Maidstone. The headquarters staff of 141 Squadron worked out of Biggin Hill as the parent sector and airfield.

The Defiant was an unusual two seat fighter with no forward firing guns. Instead, it had a power operated gun turret behind the pilot with 4x .303 Browning machine guns. Unfortunately, the aircraft was too unwieldy for day combat against the more agile ME109's and they suffered heavy losses.

On the 19th of July 1940, twelve Defiants were moved to the forward airfield at Hawkinge. At 12:32pm, nine of the aircraft were scrambled and headed out over the Channel before being vectored to 5,000 feet to the south of the nearby town of Folkestone. Unfortunately, 141 Squadron met sixteen Messerschmitt 109E's of JG51 over the sea. Within a few minutes six Defiant's and most of their two-man crews for heading into the sea. It was only the timely intervention of 111 Squadron's Hurricanes that prevented the complete annihilation of the squadron. Four pilots and five gunners were killed, the gunners being trapped in the close confines of their powered turrets.

Three aircraft returned home, but gossip spread quickly with many at Biggin Hill, believing the entire squadron had been wiped out. Ground crews from 32 and 610 Squadrons who were desperate for spare parts, descended in a ghoulish manner to take parts from the remaining Defiants at Biggin Hill. It was only when the RAF Police stopped them that the stripping stopped.

The squadron would later be withdrawn from the fight and became a very proficient night-fighter unit; the Defiant being a much more accomplished night fighter.

At 12:55pm 610 Squadron sent two flights totaling six aircraft on a patrol over Hawkinge and Dymchurch. No enemy aircraft were sighted, and they returned to base and landed at 2:20pm.

While they were away, 32 Squadron sent twelve Hurricanes from Biggin hill down to Hawkinge at 1:45pm. However, Flight Sergeant Turner in P3144 had engine problems and returned to Biggin Hill. He swapped his aircraft for another and followed his colleagues to Hawkinge.

At 3:30pm Stuka dive bombers were approaching Dover harbour and 32 Squadron were scrambled from Hawkinge to stop the JU87's which were escorted by Messerschmitt 109E's.

The ensuing combat lasted for some time and at 4:25pm Flight Sergeant Guy Turner in his replacement Hurricane was shot down and suffered serious burns near Dover. His Hurricane crashed at Hougham and it is likely his victor was Unteroffizier Mayer of 3/JG51 who claimed a victory at this time. Turner was rushed to the Union Road hospital in Dover before being transferred to East Grinstead Hospital and treatment by the plastics pioneer surgeon Sir Archibald McIndoe.

Six 32 Squadron pilots made claims, but none were confirmed. A few ME 109's was lost but attributed to pilots from pilots from 64 and 43 Squadrons.

In his combat report, Squadron Leader John Worrall (Green 1) said they had intercepted about five JU87 Stukas at 6,000 feet. They were escorted by a dozen Messerschmitt 109E's. Green section was attacking the dive bombers when the ME109's attacked red section. Worrall found himself underneath two 109's and climbed after them. He fired a quick burst and damaged one 109 and bits flew off its port wing. As he closed in to finish off the Messerschmitt, a Spitfire appeared and followed the 109 down, getting in the line of fire for Worrall who did not press the gun button.

Pilot Officer Keith Gillman a member of Green section saw the 109's dive and picked out the number two in the formation. He fired three bursts at the fighter which dived away vertically towards the sea. He claimed it, but it was not unconfirmed.

Yellow 1 was Pilot Officer Rupert Smythe. In his combat report he stated that a section of ME109's passed over him as they attacked red section. He pulled the nose of his Hurricane up and fired two bursts at a 109. He then attacked the 109's formation leader and saw his bullets entering the wings of the ME109. The engine cowling then flew off, but he was unable to follow as another 109 attacked him.

The newly commissioned Bernard Henson saw a 109 on his section leader's tail near Dover harbour. Henson opened fire but could not gain any hits. He then saw a Stuka diving for the harbour and dived after it. As the JU87 pulled out of its dive, Henson opened fire and as the aircraft turned away, he pulled inside it and opened fire again. This caused smoke to emit from it as it headed back to France. Henson chased after the Stuka and opened fire again, but he only saw tracer bullets flying over his own wings as a fighter attacked him from behind. Henson pulled away and as his assailant climbed away, he looked around to see what had happened to the Stuka. He spotted a large splash in the sea and claimed a JU87 destroyed and a damaged ME109.

Peter Brothers also claimed a ME109E destroyed in the same action. The squadron returned home and were not in action again that day.

The morning of the 20th of July started off with morning haze. This curtailed the early morning flying at Biggin Hill.

At 12:45pm John Worrall led ten Hurricanes down to the forward airfield at Hawkinge. The aircraft landed at 1:05pm, but immediately seven of them were scrambled to investigate raiders near Dover.

Red section spotted three Messerschmitt 110's about to bomb the harbour and attacked them. The 110's were dive bombing from 8,000 feet before attempting to escape back to France at low level. Flight Lieutenant Mike Crossley and Pilot Officer John Proctor shared a ME110. Crossley stated in his combat report, "We gave chase and over-took him 12 miles out from Dover. When within 800 yards he started to zig-zag slightly, increasing in intensity as I approached. At about 400-500 yards he tried a burst of tracer to which I replied with a short burst…." Crossley says he then saw the 110 hit the sea while he tried to avoid the attention of another 110. However, he must have been mistaken as no ME110 is recorded as being lost at that time and location.

At 2:45pm three Hurricanes of 32 Squadron flown by Flight Lieutenant Mike Crossley, Pilot Officer John Proctor and Sergeant Ed Bayley took off to investigate raid X44 which was at 5,000 feet. However, when they found the target, it was a friendly aircraft with its IFF (identification Friend or Foe transmitter) switched off or faulty, so the Hurricanes returned to base.

At 5:40pm Squadron Leader Worrall and Flight Lieutenant Peter Brothers led Flying Officer John Humpherson and Sergeants John Higgins and Leonard Pearce up from Hawkinge as Green section. They were to patrol over Dover, when they were made aware by control of enemy aircraft approaching at various heights from 10,000 to 20,000 feet. Fifteen minutes later at 5:55pm, Flight Lieutenant Mike Crossley led Pilot Officer Proctor, Sub-Lieutenant Geoffrey Bulmer and Sergeant Ed Bayley aloft to join Green section.

The two Hurricane formations linked up and headed off towards a point, east of Dover where a convoy had another formation of enemy aircraft heading for it. The enemy formation consisted of about fifty Messerschmitt 109E's, ME110's and Junkers 87 Stukas.

While 32 Squadron had been taking off from Hawkinge, 610 Squadron had scrambled three sections at 5:45pm. They were vectored towards Folkestone, where the convoy code named 'Bosom' was already under attack.

32 Squadron attacked the dive bombers while fending off their fighter escort. They were to make a number of victory claims against the raiders, but no losses consistent with their claims can be found. They attacked just as the Stukas started their dives.

Squadron Leader Worrall fired at one, and despite having throttled back, he still over-took the JU87. He then turned back and fired at another Stuka but had to break off when a ME110 attacked him. As the dive bombers finished their bombing runs, Worrall tried to attack another but this time he was attacked by a ME109 and just managed to get away. As he looked around, another MR109 hit him hard and he felt bullets striking the armour plating behind his seat. Two heavy thumps announced the arrival of two cannon shells, one in the Rolls Royce Merlin engine and another in the gravity tank. Worrall's Hurricane GZ-H (N2532) started to splutter, and he dived away but the engine stopped. Worral made a forced landing about half a mile from Hawkinge. He scrambled out unharmed as the aircraft caught fire at 6:20pm. It is possible his victor was Oberfeldwebel Illner of the 4/JG51 who claimed a Hurricane at this time and rough location.

It is believed the squadron had fought the ME109's of JG51 and lost Sub Lieutenant Geoffrey Bulmer in N2670 when he was shot down over the sea at about 6:00pm. It is unclear whether he baled-out or not, but the victor was probably Oberleutnant 'Pips' Priller from JG51. Yorkshireman Geoffrey Bulmer's body was never recovered, and his name is on the Lee on Solent Fleet Air Arm memorial. There is now a road called Bulmer Court in his honour on a new housing estate at Biggin Hill.

Flight Lieutenant Mike Crossley in his combat report reported sighting twelve 109's and a 'string of JU87's'. He saw one ME109 moving round in front of him, so he gave it a three second full deflection burst. Crossley said the 109 went straight down into the sea about a mile south of Dover harbour. He also reported seeing a Stuka crash into the sea about two miles out of Dover.

Pilot Officer John Proctor reported shaking a ME110 off Mike Crossley's tail, while Sergeant Edward Bayley stated that at 4000 feet, he spotted five ME110's. He rolled over and attacked the nearest machine from just 100 yards. He opened fire with a five second burst and the 110 turned over and dived into the sea. Bayley followed it down, but he saw no survivors.

Sergeant Bayley also claimed to have damaged a ME110 over sea, while Peter Brothers claimed to have destroyed a Messerschmitt 109. In his combat report, he said he was off Folkestone and attacked a 109 setting it on fire. He moved on to a second 109, but he was attacked by two more head-on. A third 109 moved onto Brothers tail while a fourth attacked him from the side. He concentrated on firing at the two head-on 109's, which flew over the top of his cockpit canopy, before turning to the starboard side and fired at the side attacker. Brothers later claimed the one he set on fire as destroyed but it was not confirmed.

Sergeant Leonard Pearce claimed a ME109 damaged, while Sergeant William Higgins claimed a 110 destroyed, but this was not confirmed even though he claimed it had hit the sea and sank near a destroyer. Higgins was attacked and sustained glass splinter wounds to his face after being attacked by Hauptman Horst Tietzen of 1/JG51.

A review of Luftwaffe losses finds a 1/JG51 and a 2/JG51 ME109E shot down, although the times cannot be determined. Four JU87 Stukas returned to base with damage but none were lost. No ME110's was lost or damaged.

This naturally begs the question, did 32 Squadron over claim? It is possible the pilots saw bombs striking the water and mistook them for crashing aircraft, but what of their claims to have seen 'their' aircraft crash? It is possible they had also fired at an aircraft already fired upon by another squadron and those pilots were given the credit.

610 Squadron were also engaged with the same raid. Pilot Officer Geoffrey Keighley in DW-S (N3201) was hit by a Messerschmitt 109E and wounded in the leg at 6:30pm. He managed to bale-out and his Spitfire crashed at Wootton, Lydden near Canterbury, Kent. He is said to have been shot down by Oberfeldwebel Schmid of JG51, but it may also have been Leutnant Michael Sonner of 3/JG51. This being his third victory.

No one from 610 was able to make a serious claim, but an unknown pilot is said to have damaged a 109 at 6:00pm near Dover.

The two squadrons returned to Biggin Hill that evening and a well-earned rest and a drink or two in the pubs!

The next day was the 21st of July and started off cloudy with thundery showers. As a result, 610 was not engaged and although 32 Squadron sent three flights of three Hurricanes forward to Hawkinge, they all returned that morning.

The weather continued to be unsuitable for flying operations and the Luftwaffe failed to make an appearance over the south east of England. There was some action over the Isle of Wight, but it did not involve the Biggin Hill squadrons.

The 22nd of July started with cloud once again. 32 Squadron sent fighters down to Hawkinge and they made a patrol at about 10:00am, but they were recalled again. The poor weather at least allowed the shipping in the English Channel to pass through unmolested. 32 returned to Biggin Hill in the early afternoon and remained on the ground for the rest of the day.

610 Squadron took no part in the flying that day. This was probably due to them having been assigned on the 22nd to RDF (Radar) trials with a Bristol Blenheim bomber between the Cap Gris Nez and Dieppe.

The 23rd July started off poorly once again in terms of the weather over Kent and the English Channel, before it improved in the afternoon, but it was too late for any aerial activity. 32 Squadron continued on their daily routine and sent nine Hurricanes down to Hawkinge.

There followed two patrols, one for twenty minutes over Hawkinge and another at 5:50pm, when six Hurricanes went to investigate a radar plot. Nothing was found before they returned to their home airfield at Biggin.

The 24th of July started off cloudy with slight to moderate rain fall. Visibility was only 8 to 12 miles and clouds varied with 2/10 at 400 feet and 4/10 at 1000 feet. However, despite these conditions there was some aerial activity by the Biggin squadrons.

At 5:05am three 32 Squadron Hurricanes flown by Mike Crossley, Pilot Officer Victor Daw and Sergeant Edward Bayley took off. However, the weather conditions were so poor that they were recalled after just five minutes.

At 5:30am, Flight Lieutenant Crossley led six Hurricanes off on a convoy escort over the Channel. They did not see or meet any Luftwaffe aircraft and landed at RAF Hawkinge where they were re-fuelled and the pilots had breakfast. The same six aircraft carried out another patrol over the same convoy at 7:20am, but the enemy were not sighted, and they returned to Biggin Hill at 8:40am. 32 Squadron remained on the ground after this as the weather was too poor.

At 11:12am 610 Squadron sent nine Spitfires of Red, Blue and Green sections to patrol over Dover at 12,000 feet. Flight Lieutenant John Ellis (blue leader) and led Flight Lieutenant Edward Smith (who was acting Squadron Commander), Flying Officer William Warner, Pilot Officer Douglas Wilson and Sergeants Claude Parsons, Horatio Chandler, Peter Else, Norman Ramsay and Stanley Arnfield. They came across three Messerschmitt 109E's flying in the opposite direction some 3,000 feet above them and John Ellis fired successive bursts of fire at one ME109, which dived vertically for the sea pouring black smoke. In his hand-written combat report Ellis stated,

"I had to use full throttle to catch the enemy aircraft the remaining two sections got left behind. The formation on 109's broke up on being attacked and I sighted one of them. I opened fire at 200 yards on the first burst and he immediately rolled on to his back and dived vertically, he then pulled out and proceeded to climb practically vertically. He carried out this maneuver four times and each time I got in a good burst while he was climbing. Throughout, these evolutions bluish-white smoke was coming from a point about a foot from each wing tip". He fired at it one more time and it spiraled down through the cloud layer at 3000 feet. It is possible this was Hauptman von Houwald the Gruppen Commander of 3/JG52 who was killed or Leutnant Werner Bartels of Stab 3/JG26. He was shot down and force landed while being badly wounded, after being hit by a Spitfire with a deflection shot near Dover. Bartels came down at North Down near Margate.

610 Squadron did not realise how lucky they had been. The Second Gruppe of JG26 led by Hauptmann Noack was below them, but Noack thought there were thirty Spitfires above them and broke away with his Gruppe (see JG26 War Diary volume one by Donald Caldwell). To make matters worse for JG26, Noack was killed in a crash landing upon his return to France.

Flight Lieutenant Ed Smith (red leader) sighted nine to twelve ME109E's below him. They were in line abreast heading towards his flight. He opened fire causing one to dive away emitting smoke. Sergeant Chandler also claimed a ME109E. In his combat report he states,

"I dived below and attacked from underneath allowing deflection. As the range decreased the effect of the fire became apparent, damage to the aircraft with pieces falling off. I stalled and spun down through the cloud. He claimed a Vought Chance V156 destroyed". Clearly his aircraft recognition was not up to scratch. The French Air Force had used these prior to the invasion and Chandler probably thought they were flown by German pilots.

The 7th Gruppe of JG52 had lost two pilots Oberleutnant Fermer and Gefreiter Frank off Margate around this time. Both pilots were killed and are likely to have been the aircraft shot down by Smith and Chandler. 610 Squadron returned without incurring any losses and landed at 12:10pm.

On the 25th of July the weather improved slightly, although there was a fair amount of cloud and limited visibility.

At 4:35am Flight Lieutenant Mike Crossley led nine Hurricanes from Biggin Hill to Hawkinge. However, Flight Lieutenant Peter Brothers returned after just five minutes with engine problems in N2921. After a bit of magic from the air mechanics he flew it down to join the others at 6:30am.

That morning 32 Squadron flew a couple of sorties over the Channel, but the enemy were not seen.

At 12 noon 32 Squadron sent nine aircraft off to patrol over the convoy proceeding down the English Channel. At 12:46pm they encountered eight Messerschmitt 109E's at 22,000 feet over Dover. Mike Crossley attacked one and claimed it as destroyed, but it was not confirmed. Pilot Officer Victor Daw (P3677) was hit by one of the 109's and wounded in the leg. He managed a forced landing near Dover at 12:50pm and was taken to the hospital under Dover Castle. The remainder of the squadron landed safely at 1:15pm.

At 2:58pm 610 Squadron scrambled nine aircraft from Hawkinge led by Squadron Leader Smith. From their hill-top position over-looking Folkestone and the Channel, they had seen the dive bombers even before they had taken-off. As they approached the convoy, which was off Dover and Folkestone, a large formation of enemy aircraft was sighted. 611 Squadron were just below 610 Squadron as they approached the enemy. Smith led 610 against the 109's leaving 611 to deal with the Stukas. 64 Squadron were also in attendance.

As the Spitfires attacked, twenty JU87 Stukas were still dive-bombing the ships with a formation of about fifteen ME109E's above them at 12,000 feet.

John Ellis attacked a 109 and reported to have shot it down in flames. This was confirmed by his numbers 2 and 3. In his combat report, John Ellis described attacking the leading 109 and firing four or five bursts at him over five minutes of combat. He then ran out of ammunition as the 109 was on fire and emitting smoke. The 109 spiraled down and appeared to be out of control.

Sergeant Else also attacked a 109 and caused it to 'fall out of control' after he opened fire. Flying Officer Fred Gardiner in DW-O (R6595) shot at another 109 and claimed hits, but he was then wounded when an unseen assailant fired at him. He managed to return to base, but his aircraft was badly damaged and he was taken to hospital. Pilot Officer Stanley Norris also claimed to have sent a 109 down out of control.

Unfortunately, Squadron Leader Smith DW-A (R6693) was hit badly and after extricating himself from the battle flew home but crashed at Hawkinge when he stalled attempting a landing at 3:40pm. Sadly he was killed in the subsequent crash. The rest of the squadron landed back at base at 3:50pm.

610 Squadron were the victims of JG26 led by Major Adolph Galland who claimed a Spitfire over Dover harbour, while Leutnant Gerhard Muller-Duhe, Oberleutnant Georg Beyer and Leutnant Josef Burschgens of 7/JG26 all claimed Spitfires over Dover at this time. Although JG26 appear to have been the Luftwaffe victors, the victims of 610 Squadron appear to have been JG52 who lost four 109's in combat with Spitfires off Dover. While Smith's claim was a confirmed victory, the other 610 pilots victory claims were not confirmed.

At 4:20pm Mike Crossley led nine Hurricanes from 32 on a patrol over Tenterden. Within minutes they were vectored towards a raid over Folkestone and Dungeness at 12,000 feet, but they were unable to locate the raiders and were directed onto another possible raid. Failing to locate this raid as well, they returned to base at 6:00pm.

At 6:37pm 610 Squadron now led by Flight Lieutenant John Ellis, sent seven Spitfires to patrol over the convoy off Folkestone. Upon arrival they spotted about fifteen aircraft bombing the escorting destroyers. According to their combat reports the squadron was soon heavily engaged and making claims against ME109's. Ellis later reported that while on patrol he saw a destroyer being bombed two miles out to sea. He did not see the actual bombers, but he saw twenty ME109E's at 7,000 feet. Ellis ordered the squadron to attack them and he fired at the rear most 109. The 109 formation did not break up and he formed the opinion that they had taken them by surprise. The Messerschmitt he fired at turned on to its back and plunged towards the sea out of control. John Ellis climbed into the cloud above and saw a 109 hit the sea. He believed this to be 'his' 109 and claimed it as destroyed.

Ellis hid in the cloud so that he could see below him, but he could enter the cloud to escape the enemy. He soon spotted another section of four 109's in line astern and attacked the last fighter. He fired emptying all his .303 ammunition into the 109 which, "Fell out of the sky burning furiously and hit the sea".

Flight Lieutenant Smith who was Red 1 saw twenty to thirty ME109's south east of Dover. He fired at one ME109E and an unknown aircraft, both of which disappeared into the clouds.

Pilot Officer Stanley Norris hit a 109 which emitted white smoke and then flames from an area near the cockpit. It spiraled down and was enveloped in further flames before it hit the sea and left burning fuel on the surface of the water.

Sergeant Horatio Chandler attacked a 109 from astern and although he believed the pilot knew he was behind him, the 109 took no violent evasive maneuvers and dived for the French coast evading the Spitfire pilot.

Pilot Officer Douglas Wilson claimed a ME109 on fire and said he saw it crash into the sea. Other 610 Squadron pilots also made claims, but analysis of the Luftwaffe records finds that only five 109's where lost between Dover and Folkestone on this day and therefore the pilots must have been mistaken.

As I have mentioned in my previous books, over-claiming by fighter pilots on both sides of the Battle of Britain was endemic. Very often more than one pilot fired at the same target and they both claimed the victory, while bomb bursts on the sea or ground could be misconstrued as a crashing aircraft.

610 Squadron returned and landed at 7:19pm without any casualties of their own. This completed the action for 610 Squadron on the 24th of July.

At 7:30pm 32 Squadron were scrambled once again and vectored towards aircraft off Dover. None were encountered and they returned to base and an end to flying for the day.

It had been a busy and hectic day, but the following day had light rain which allowed them some rest. The pilots relaxed and some went to the mess bar, but unfortunately, the sun came out and 32 Squadron was recalled to readiness. 32 were sent up with some of the pilots probably slightly worse for wear, but thankfully no enemy aircraft were encountered. In his biography of Peter Brothers (Hurricane Squadron Ace), Nick Thomas cites Brothers recalling the event and that they were none too pleased.

On the 27th of July, the Operation Training Units (OTU's) who had been hard at work training new Spitfire and Hurricane pilots, sent several new faces to 610 Squadron.

Pilot Office Eric Aldous arrived from 9 FTS. Pilot Officers Claude Merrick and Donald Gray and Sergeant Robert Beardsley arrived from 15 SFTS at Chipping Norton and Pilot Officer Ken Cox, Sergeants Cyril Bamberger, Edward Manton, Peter Willcocks, William Neville arrived from 5 OTU at Aston Down. Finally, Pilot Officer Frank Webster arrived from 6 FTS at Sealand. The quality and levels of training varied considerably, but the shortage of pilots meant they were all welcome additions.

At the same time, Sergeants Raymond Gent and Sidney Whitehouse arrived at 32 Squadron from 5 FTS at Sealand with Tony Pickering. However, these three new pilots were so under-trained, that Squadron Leader John Worrall sent them immediately to 6 OTU at Sutton Bridge for further training on Hurricanes. The three pilots would return to the squadron on the 27th of August, a day before 32 moved north to Acklington in Northumbria for a rest. The three were therefore passed on to 501 Squadron at Gravesend.

The weather had however improved with a cloudy day becoming cloudy with thundery showers at midday. 32 Squadron remained on the ground but on stand-by until at one minute to midnight. Pilot Officer Douglas Grice was sent up after a raid, but he failed to make contact with it in the dark and landed back at Biggin Hill at 1:25am.

The next morning Biggin Hill was covered in a morning fog which slowly cleared to give 5/10ths cloud at 2,500 feet with decent visibility.

At 1:00pm 32 Squadron sent Peter Brothers with Pilot Officers 'Gubby' Grice, Alan Eckford, Keith Gillman, Rupert Smythe, Proctor and Gardiner, together with Sergeants Henson, Pearce, Higgins and Bayley down to Hawkinge. They arrived at 1:10pm to find a Fox Film unit at the base. They took a series of black and white photographs of the pilots and their Hurricanes awaiting a scramble. They became some of the most iconic images of the Battle of Britain and one is contained within this book.

At 2:15pm the squadron was ordered to patrol over Hawkinge below the cloud base, but no enemy aircraft was sighted, and they landed on the airfield at 3:10pm.

At 5:45pm 32 Squadron was scrambled from Hawkinge and directed to climb to 15,000 feet. Various raids had been seen by the RDF chain, but no aircraft made contact with the patrolling Hurricanes. As a result, 32 were sent back to Biggin Hill and landed at 6:30pm for tea.

At 8:15pm, 610 Squadron who had remained at Biggin Hill all day, was scrambled and vectored to patrol over Dover at 10,000 feet. No Luftwaffe aircraft arrived, and they returned to Biggin at 9:10pm.

After a light tea 32 squadron had remained on stand-by and were scrambled once again at 8:35pm, this time being vectored towards a raid approaching Dungeness. However once again no contact was made, and they returned to Biggin Hill and landed at 9:25pm before being released for the night.

The Luftwaffe was mainly operating over the English Channel and the ports and rarely ventured over land at this time. The 28th of July had been busy for the two Biggin Hill squadrons, but they had no contact with the Luftwaffe.

Monday the 29th of July 1940 started with fair to fine weather and good visibility. As such, it was expected the Luftwaffe would mount several raids against the south of England and any shipping in the Channel.

At 7:50am Flight Lieutenant Peter Brothers led eleven Hurricanes of 32 Squadron aloft from Biggin Hill. They were initially directed towards Hawkinge, but they were re-directed to the Dover and Deal areas. After patrolling for about forty minutes, they landed at Hawkinge to refuel at 8:50am without seeing the Luftwaffe.

At 12:50pm the same eleven Hurricanes flew a patrol over the Channel and returned to Biggin Hill at 1:20pm, once again without seeing any enemy aircraft. These flights were symptomatic of fighter pilots at that time. They flew on the edge of their nerves knowing that contact with the enemy was likely with death a possibility; but in many cases their scramble or patrol was fruitless.

As the 32 Squadron Hurricanes were taking off from Hawkinge, 610 Squadron were scrambled from Biggin Hill and vectored towards Dungeness. Ellis led twelve Spitfires to the area where 'B' Flight was ordered to land at Hawkinge, while 'A' Flight was ordered to intercept raid number 49 off the coast of Dungeness.

'A' Flight soon spotted a Dornier 17 which immediately dropped its bomb load into the sea and headed for France. Four Spitfires jostled for position and fired all their ammunition into the Dornier, which shed various pieces as it dived at speed for the coastline. The pilots mentioned in their combat reports the high speed of the bomber which necessitated them opening of the throttles to full power.

Flight Lieutenant Smith reported firing two or three bursts from high above and astern of the Dorner, before allowing his numbers two and three to follow him into the attack. The fourth Spitfire then made an attack and Smith saw its bullets hitting the wing of the bomber and the engines started to smoke. Smith himself made a further attack but the bomber, which was now just above the surface of the sea continued to fly on.

Sergeant Stanley Norris fired all his ammunition into the Dornier and reported that the rear gunner continued to fire at him. He was hit in the leading edge of the port wing and the bullet entered the wheel bay, puncturing the tyre on one of his wheels leading to a hairy landing.

Sergeant Ron Hamlyn also fired all his ammunition into the Dornier in four bursts and noted serious damage to the aircraft, but it continued on its way. With no ammunition left the four Spitfires flew home. The Dornier 17 is believed to have been from Stab KG2 which landed with 60% damage at St. Inglevert with Leutnant Hunger wounded.

There was no further flying in squadron strength that day according to the two squadrons Operational Record Books and they were eventually stood down for the night.

However, in his book 'Hurricane Squadron Ace', Nick Thomas records that Peter Brothers having been scrambled with the other pilots of 32 Squadron, claimed to have shot down a Messerschmitt 109E into the sea. No parachute was seen. This victory he says was confirmed, but the ORB's do not report it, the combat report cannot be found or that of any other pilot for that time. A check of Luftwaffe loss records also finds only one 109 to have been lost on this day. That was a 6/JG51 machine which crash landed outside at the Cap Blanc Nez near Calais. Two other JG51 machines returned to base and made crash landings.

Christopher Shores and Clive Williams credit Peter Brothers with the victory in their book 'Aces High'. It has to be acknowledged, that administration officers and staff were under pressure to fill in the Operations Record Book's and keep them up to date. To do this during this hectic period was particularly onerous. The same applies to pilot's trying to keep their own logbooks up to date. While there is no corroborative evidence as such, we must respect the claims of Peter Brothers as he may be just confusing his dates.

At 9:40pm, Stanley Norris of 610 Squadron was ordered to patrol a line, but no enemy aircraft were seen so he returned to base only 15 minutes later.

Tuesday the 30th was quite cloudy. RAF Biggin Hill had a visit from Air Chief Marshal Sir Ludlow-Hewitt, Inspector General of the RAF that day.

Before he arrived, 32 Squadron were up very early and at 4:45am and Flight Lieutenant Peter Brothers led eleven Hurricanes to Hawkinge. Within a few minutes of their arrival, red section consisting of Pilot Officers Rupert Smythe, Douglas Grice and John Proctor were scrambled to investigate raid X13. No contact was made, and they all returned to Hawkinge for breakfast.

Over the next two hours 32 Squadron launched aircraft from Hawkinge four times without meeting the Luftwaffe.

At 8:30am 610 Squadron were sent down to Hawkinge. While 'B' Flight landed at 9:10am, 'A' Flight were vectored towards 'bandits' mid Channel between Cap Gris Nez and

Dungeness. Yet again, no contact was made, and they joined the others landing at Hawkinge.

The Luftwaffe remained on the ground due to the cloudy conditions along the French coast and no further action was seen on the 30th.

Wednesday the 31st of July started off with misty conditions before turning into a fair day. There was no flying in the morning with the pilots remaining on stand-by, but at 12:55pm 32 Squadron headed in squadron strength from Biggin Hill to Hawkinge.

That afternoon the squadron was scrambled twice at 2:40pm and 4:10pm but no contact was made with the enemy as the raids failed to materialize from being just RDF plots.

At 5:30pm 32 Squadron were scrambled and vectored towards another raid, this one consisting of six Heinkel III bombers and a number of escorting fighters. However, as 32 started to approach the formation, it immediately turned and headed back towards the French coast at Le Touquet. The squadron were unable to interfere and returned to Biggin Hill although two of their number landed at Hawkinge.

There was even less action for 610 Squadron. They made only one operational flight when Flight Lieutenant Smith led Sergeants Hamlyn and Parsons on a patrol at 6:20pm towards Dungeness. The weather however was so poor, that they returned after just five minutes and landed safely at Hawkinge.

Although the weather at the end of July had been poor, the fact that convoys were no longer steaming through the Dover straights had given the Luftwaffe another victory. They had in effect cleared the English Channel of British shipping and they patrolled the area without seeing too much of the RAF; even though the British fighters were being scrambled unsuccessfully to counter the Luftwaffe. The weeks to come would become more aggressive and deadly.

Chapter 2
The Build-up to Eagle Day.

After the attacks upon the convoys in July 1940, which were now only permitted to enter the Straights of Dover during the hours of darkness; the Luftwaffe would soon be ordered to destroy the RAF as a prelude to an invasion.

The 1st of August 1940 started with some cloud, but it was generally fine and as the day progressed, the visibility extended to 12 miles by the evening.

At 8:20am 32 Squadron dispatched eleven Hurricanes led by Peter Brothers down to Hawkinge. They arrived after the usual twenty-minute transfer time and refueled upon landing.

At 9:30am Pilot Officers Grice, Proctor and Sergeant Bayley took off for a patrol over Dungeness. No enemy aircraft were sighted, and they returned to Hawkinge and landed at 10:00am.

At 11:20am and 11:50am, 32 Squadron sent up flights after raiding aircraft, but on each occasion no contact was made with the Luftwaffe. In the evening, the squadron returned to Biggin Hill in separate flights. No further flying took place that day.

The 2nd of August was similar in terms of weather to that on the first. 32 Squadron sent eight Hurricanes to Hawkinge at 4:45am.

At 5:15pm Pilot Officer Douglas Grice was scrambled to intercept a lone aircraft over the airfield, but he failed to make contact with it. In all probability, it was the early morning high altitude weather reconnaissance by the Luftwaffe. The aircraft, often a JU86 high altitude machine with a pressurized cockpit, flew far too high for a Hurricane to intercept and after an hour of trying, Grice landed at 6:15am.

At 7:15am Pilot Officers Rupert Smythe, Keith Gillman and Sergeant Henson took off after raid E21 which was at 15,000 feet over Folkestone. They were unable to intercept it and returned to Biggin Hill at 8:15am. It was clear that any high-level raiders could not be intercepted in time by aircraft scrambling from Hawkinge or Manston.

While the three pilots were chasing the raider, Flight Lieutenant Peter Brothers led the rest of the squadron after another raid, but again no contact was made with the enemy. They too returned to Biggin Hill and landed at 8:45am.

There was no further activity, and the squadrons were stood down later that day. The weather was such that the Biggin Hill pilots must have thought the war was passing them by. However, as we now know, the Luftwaffe was gathering its strength and replacing its losses before launching its main onslaught in mid-August.

The next few days remained quiet for Biggin Hill. On the 3rd of August, 32 Squadron sent the obligatory twelve Hurricanes down to Hawkinge and they flew various sorties, until they returned to Biggin that evening at 6:30pm.

At 9:50pm Pilot Officer Douglas Grice flew a night patrol over Canterbury, but no enemy aircraft were seen. When he landed, he nearly crashed at Biggin due to the poor airfield lighting. (Biggin like many day-fighter stations, was not fully equipped for night operations and relied on goose neck paraffin lamps being placed to mark the runway).

On the morning of the 4th of August, there was fog which took some time to clear. The mechanics started the engines of the aircraft and warmed them up just like every morning, before topping up their fuel tanks. By late morning, the fog started clear which allowed some flying by 32 Squadron.

At 11:40am 32 sent twelve Hurricanes to patrol over Hawkinge at 8,000 feet. They were vectored on to a possible raiding aircraft, but this turned out to be a single Spitfire. The squadron therefore landed and refueled at Hawkinge at 12:30pm. They flew a number of afternoon sorties from Hawkinge which were uneventful before they returned once more to Biggin Hill.

At the same time 610 Squadron appear to have also been inactive and their records show no details of actions.

Although the operational flying was some-what mundane, 32 Squadron did receive three new recruits. The RAF had been receiving numerous 'recruits' in the form of pilots who had escaped the German forces in Poland, France, Belgium, Czechoslovakia and other conquered nations. As a result, three new pilots arrived from 6 OTU at Sutton Bridge. The three Polish Pilots were Pilot Officers Boleslaw Wlasnowalski, Jan Pfeiffer and Karol Pniak. Their names appeared to be so unpronounceable, that they were given the names Vodka, Fifi and Cognac. They would soon become integral parts of the squadron.

On the 5th of August there was continued flying from Hawkinge by 32 Squadron, especially over the small convoys that tried to scuttle through the Dover Straights before the Luftwaffe could attack them.

The 6th of August dawned with better weather, but Pilot Officer Jan 'Fifi' Pfeiffer embarrassed himself and 32 Squadron by failing to get airborne in V7205 and went straight through an airfield boundary fence and into a small wood at Biggin Hill. The accident was deemed to be due to rough handling of the throttle and he was sent back to the Operation Training Unit for further training.

However, Pfeiffer was not the only accident-prone Pole. Boleslaw Wlasnowalski was given tuition on the Hurricane by the experienced Pilot Officer 'Polly' Flinders, only for him to open the throttle too much and to again hit the boundary fence, cartwheeling into the garden of an adjacent bungalow. In the book 'RAF Biggin Hill', the author Graham Wallace, says that Pniak was so angry at this afront to Polish pride that he beat the fire tender and ambulance to his stricken colleague and after ensuring he was alive, set about him to such a degree that he needed to go to the sick bay!

One piece of good news was the award of a Distinguished Flying Cross to Squadron Leader John Worrall. This was primarily for his leadership of a squadron which had to this point claimed forty-three aerial victories.

The 7th of August again saw a number of patrols without any contact with the Luftwaffe. However, these patrols could be nerve straining with the pilots expecting to be bounced at any time.

On the 8th of August, the weather was fine and a large convoy CW9 code name 'Peewit' once again tried to slip through the English Channel. At dawn on the 8th, they were attacked by Kreigsmarine E-Boats, while the Luftwaffe sent out a large formation of JU87 Stukas to try and sink the fleet. They were escorted by about one hundred and fifty Messerschmitt 109E's.

610 Squadron's Spitfires were scrambled together with 41, 64 and 65 Squadrons and engaged the Luftwaffe over the convoy. Despite their best efforts, three ships were sunk, and four Spitfires were lost, with one pilot being killed. 610 Squadron made no victory claims but had no casualties of their own. As the convoy proceeded down the Channel further attacks were made leading to the loss of 13 Hurricanes and 1 Spitfire. Most of the pilots were killed.

32 Squadron had sent twelve Hurricanes to Hawkinge at 5:05am and at 11:40am they were scrambled to intercept raid E36 which was approaching Brighton. They climbed rapidly and could see the enemy aircraft, but they did not actually engage them and returned to base empty handed.

The 9th of August saw the arrival at 32 Squadron of another overseas pilot. This was Pilot Officer the Comte Rudolphe de Grunne from Belgium who arrived from No. 7 OTU at Hawarden near Chester. He was a real novelty having flown Messerschmitt 109's for Hitler's Condor Legion in the Spanish Civil War. As such, he was well-aware of the ME109's abilities and the Luftwaffe fighter tactics. His prior knowledge, experience and advice was very much appreciated by 32 Squadron's pilots!

The day had started with over-cast conditions with 8/10ths cloud at 1,500 feet. However, this started to disappear, and conditions became fairer with visibility of between seven and ten miles.

At 1:05pm, Flight Lieutenant Peter Brothers and Flight Lieutenant Mike Crossley led twelve Hurricanes of 32 squadron to Hawkinge. At some point they appear to have made a standing patrol which is not recorded in the Operational Record Book, as Peter Brothers records that at 4:55pm while at RAF Manston; they were scrambled after reports of two Messerschmitt 109's near Dover. No contact was made with the enemy and they then returned to Biggin Hill landing at 5:25pm.

Elsewhere 610 Squadron were not having any better luck.

That evening at 9:15pm Mike Crossley of 32 Squadron, was scrambled alone after a German raider. He climbed to height and chased a bomber from Chatham following RDF directions. He pursued it all the way to Dover without any success and returned to base at 9:55pm without actually seeing it.

The lull in operations was a bit of a surprise to all the pilots but with hindsight, we now know that the Luftwaffe were about to be set loose with an all-out attack on the RAF and its airfields. Adler Tag (Eagle Day) as the Luftwaffe high command would call it, was just around the corner.

The 10th August 1940 was over-cast with slight rain in the morning. Initially cloud was complete at between 600-900 feet; but this later changed to 5/10ths at 2000 feet with good visibility.

At 7:45am Pilot Officers John Pain and Peter Gardener of 32 Squadron were sent off to patrol a line between Gravesend and Tenterden, before being directed towards a raider who was taking the opportunity to hide in the cloud layer. After about seventy-five minutes they returned to base without seeing the raider.

At 8:30am the squadron flew to Hawkinge and landed and refueled. However, with no sign of the enemy they returned to Biggin at 1:20pm.

Later at 4:55pm the whole of 32 Squadron flew to Hawkinge and then made two patrols but again no enemy aircraft were sighted, and they returned home.

Sunday the 11th of August would be much busier with better weather all day.

At 5:05am Mike Crossley led twelve Hurricanes of 32 Squadron down to Hawkinge. At 7:40am they were ordered to patrol Hawkinge at 15,000 feet and as they patrolled between Deal and Dover, they encountered a formation of ME109's. Nine of them attacked from head on, while another three dived on them from above and behind. A large formation of over thirty Messerschmitt 110's of EprGr 210 escorted by the 109's was briefed to attack

Dover harbour between 8:00am and 8:30am; and this appears to have been part of that raids escort. 74 Squadron who would later occupy Biggin Hill themselves were on the ground at RAF Manston refueling when they received the order to scramble and join 32 Squadron in the air over Dover.

Pilot Officer Tony Barton later stated in his combat report, that three 109's dived on them from behind. Making the classic slashing attack they opened fire and sped away down to the left of the Hurricanes. Barton gave one a short burst of machine gun fire and saw bits fly off the 109 as it flew past, before hearing over the R/T that there were eight others. He lost sight of the machine he fired at and later claimed it as damaged. The squadron managed to extricate themselves without losses or causing losses, before returning home at 9:05am.

32 Squadron had become embroiled in a combat with ME109's from JG2 who lost a number of aircraft to the Spitfires of 74 and 64 Squadrons in this action.

At 10:05am 32 Squadron was again scrambled and led by Mike Crossley with Peter Brothers. However, Brothers who was flying N2921 returned to Biggin Hill with engine problems. The squadron were directed to a position over Dover at 24,000 feet, but no enemy aircraft were encountered.

Flying Officer Peter Gardner (Green 1) somehow managed to lose the rest of the squadron and at 4,000 feet over Dungeness, he spotted a small formation of five ME109E's. In his subsequent combat report, he stated that the fighters were in line astern just above a layer of cloud. He closed in astern of the final fighter and fired off a three second burst which caused several bits to fall off it. The ME109 seemed to stagger before falling away through the clouds. He followed it down, but all he saw was three other 109's heading for France. This would only be classed as a damaged.

610 Squadron were also busy. That morning they flew under the command of Squadron Leader Ellis to Hawkinge. After refueling, they took off at 10:46am to patrol over the English Channel. Red section was directed to break away and investigate an enemy aircraft on the water below them while the remainder acted as top cover.

Red section spotted a Heinkel 59 seaplane flying low over the surface of the sea just off Calais. These aircraft with Red Cross markings were declared by the Luftwaffe to be air sea rescue aircraft, but there was no doubt after one was captured, that they were also interested in the convoy movements. Listening stations had also picked up radio transmissions to this effect from them.

Flight Lieutenant Edward Smith opened fire and reported that his tracer fire could be seen entering the Heinkel 59 which made several gentle turns to avoid his fire. It eventually settled on the water. Flying Officer Douglas Wilson then spotted a number of enemy patrol boats off Cap Griz Nez. At some point a general melee appears to have ensued, as when the squadron returned to Biggin Hill, Flight Sergeant John Tanner (R6918 DW-D) and Sergeant

William Neville (R6630 DW-X) were both missing. 25 years old Tanner's body would be washed up on the shore near Calais where he would be buried. 26 years old Neville was never found. Claims were made by Hauptmann Hrabak and Oberfeldwebel Hier of 4/JG54 at this time for two Spitfires off Calais.

This sad incident is compounded further when post-war analysis identified the fact that the Heinkel 59 was actually rescuing the three-man crew of an RAF Blenheim which was shot down at about 11am that morning by Oberfeldwebel Grosse of 3/JG52. One RAF NCO was injured, but whether that was from the fire of Grosse or Ellis is unclear.

Both 610 and 32 Squadron returned home for lunch and remained on the ground for the rest of the day.

The Luftwaffe was now building up for Eagle Day and raids on the RDF stations intensified causing the radar coverage to fail. As a result, RAF Fighter Controllers had to keep fighters on standing patrols and rely on the Observer Corps. Despite this, the two Biggin Hill units were not engaged again that day.

On the 12th of August, 610 Squadron were given the role of dawn readiness with all twelve Spitfires available for operations. By 5:30am the pilots had checked their Spitfires, they had been 'run-up' by the ground crews and flying helmets and parachutes had been carefully positioned on the aircraft for a quick scramble. Although the pilots did not know it, the Luftwaffe was en route as they ate their breakfast at dispersal. Newly promoted Squadron Leader John Ellis allocated the pilots to their sections on the black board at dispersal and they awaited developments.

At 7:00am the RDF stations started to plot a large build-up of enemy aircraft over the Pas de Calais. By 7:20am Observer Corps members had spotted the Luftwaffe as it headed towards Dover across the Channel and informed headquarters. They in turn told the sector stations. The first wave introduced a new Luftwaffe tactic and they dropped smoke cannisters in a bid to form a smoke screen, but this was not very effective.

At 7:31am, 610 Squadron were scrambled from Biggin Hill and ordered to intercept a raid approaching Dungeness. When the controller called Ellis (call sign Dog Rose leader), he correctly advised that nine aircraft were heading their way. In fact, various formations made the raid a large and widespread one, spread along the Channel coastline. The Observer Corps post on Dover Castle had sighted the raid at 10,000 feet and it spread from Deal down to Dungeness.

As 610 Squadron approached a formation of nine Heinkel 111's in three 'vic' formations with ME109's as an escort at 16,000 feet, they readied themselves for combat. The pilots turned on their gun sights and rotated the ring around their gun buttons to a position in which the guns would fire.

The Luftwaffe were at that time attacking the RDF stations at Rye, Dover and Dunkirk near Canterbury. As 610 had left the airfield the station Tannoy system called 32 Squadron's pilots to readiness.

1/JG26 led by Hauptmann Kurt Fischer had been escorting the bombers to Lympne when they saw 610 Squadron and dived on them from out of the sun.

Squadron Leader Ellis in his combat report states that he first noticed the enemy when he saw a stick of bombs falling out at sea off New Romney. 610 Squadron were at 10,000 feet so they climbed quickly towards the bombers who were heading for Rye and probably the RDF station. As the 610 Squadron formation was closing in, a formation of ME109's came down out of the sun and attacked them. Ellis states that the controller had told them another squadron would deal with the escort leaving 610 to deal with the bombers, but something went wrong. An almighty dog fight ensued, and the bombers were left unmolested.

Ellis picked out a 109 and fired at it, as it dived away registering hits on it. Ellis climbed back up to 15,000 feet and spotted another climbing 109 which he attacked. The 109 went into a spin as he emptied his ammunition into him. This caused the spinning ME109 to go down slowly with a slowly ticking over engine and Ellis believed he was out of control. John Ellis then returned to base to claim two victories and another probable. He was credited with two destroyed 109's and a probable.

Other sections of JG26 joined the fray and there was soon a whirling dogfight above the coast of Kent.

Pilot Officer Kenneth Cox (Blue 3) lost his leader and turned to see a 109 on another Spitfires tail. This was Brian Rees. Cox opened fire and the 109 went down out of control confirmed by a grateful Brian Rees. Another 109 appeared in front of Ken Cox who fired off the rest of his ammunition without result. Cox was awarded a victory.

Pilot Officer Constantine Pegge (Yellow3) became detached from the rest of the squadron and climbed to 23,000 feet. He then saw six ME109E's in a circle about 3,000 feet below him. He dived down and opened fire on one 109 which erupted in smoke and flames before he dived away. He climbed again up to 23,000 feet and now saw just five ME109E's in a circle below him. He attacked another one which went into a spin. He returned home and claimed two 109's destroyed both of which were confirmed.

Various other claims were made by Pilot Officer Rees (a probable 109), and Sergeant Chandler (a damaged 109). However, it was not all one sided and Flight Lieutenant E.B.B. Smith (K9818 DW-H) was hit by cannon shells in the cockpit. He felt his Spitfire shudder as the cannon shells felt struck his machine. He later reported that the engine stopped dead and the cockpit filled with smoke, before small flames started to flicker from behind the instrument panel. These soon grew in intensity and he knew he had to abandon the Spitfire.

Smith tried to open the canopy, but it was stuck and would not move. As the flames intensified, he could feel his face and hands start to burn. The Spitfire was full of flames and choking smoke, but Smith still had the clarity of mind to think that his aircraft was diving away too fast. He therefore fought against the dive and the flames, slowing the aircraft enough for the canopy to free itself. He rolled the aircraft over and fell out, tumbling before deploying his parachute with burns to his face and hands. He landed in the Channel off New Romney suspended by his Mae West. The cool sea water managed to ease his burns somewhat before he was picked up by a patrol boat and taken to hospital in Dover. (Many burned aircrew would be grateful for the emersion in the salty water as it was found to assist in the healing process).

Sergeant Gardner chased a ME109 all the way back to France and claimed to have shot it down in flames into the sea. As he headed back to England, he saw another Spitfire fighting with a 109 and joined in the scrap. He claimed to have damaged this 109, which he claimed must have had a very experienced pilot due to his flying ability. The 109 headed back to France with an idling engine and leaking glycol.

Gardner then reported tangling with another ME109 over Lympne at 10,000 feet and was damaged himself when debris from the 109 hit his canopy. He pulled up alongside the 109 and saw the lifeless slumped pilot in the cockpit before it fell way earthwards.

Pilot Officer Fred Gardiner was damaged (R6806 DW-N) and he was slightly injured over New Romney by a 109. His fuel tank was punctured and the aircraft although it returned was written off. Another machine was also damaged.

The Messerschmitt 109's where from Adolph Galland's JG26, with claims being made by Leutnant Ruppert and Unteroffizier Hogel of 3/JG26.

610 Squadron returned to Biggin Hill where the Intelligence Officer 'Spy' de la Torre took down their combat reports while the pilots snatched a quick sandwich and a mug of tea. However, it appears that JG26 only lost Oberleutnant Freidrich Butterweck from 1/JG26 at this time and there may have been an element of overclaiming by the squadron's pilots.

At 1:35pm 32 Squadron moved forward to their forward operating base at Hawkinge from Biggin Hill. The squadron arrived flying all the way at low level. After having their fuel tanks topped-up, they were ordered at 2:30pm to make a patrol in squadron strength between Dover and Hawkinge at 8,000 feet, but no Luftwaffe aircraft were seen. The Hurricanes returned to be refueled once again, the whole squadron being refueled in just fifteen minutes. There was no time to hang about on the ground as a raid could destroy them in minutes.

At 4:50pm 32 Squadron were scrambled and ordered to patrol above Hawkinge at 10,000 feet. As they took off, they saw over Dover thirty to forty Dornier bombers with a similar number of ME109's as an escort at 12,000 feet. Despite the best efforts of the anti-aircraft guns, the Hurricanes flew through the barrage to attack the bombers.

The squadron attacked the bombers before the 109's intervened and various combats took place between Dover and Whitstable to the north.

Mike Crossley in his combat report said, "We climbed and attacked almost head on, and became mixed up with 109's". He said he fired at a Dornier but did not see the damage. He then attacked a 109 and fired a three second burst at it. There was a flash of flame and it went down on fire with smoke pouring from it.

Red 2, Pilot Officer John Proctor carried out a quarter attack on a Dornier when a number of 109's attacked him. He managed to evade them and followed the formation towards Whitstable where he managed to get 'up sun' of a 109. He attacked and a five feet long section of the starboard mainplane flew off. The 109 flicked onto its back and started to dive away. Proctor was then attacked by other fighters, but as he had expended all his ammunition, he broke off and headed home. The ME109 was credited as being probably destroyed.

Pilot Officer Rupert Smythe was flying as Yellow 2 and attacked a Dornier before he was attacked by a ME109E. He reported later that anti-aircraft guns had opened fire, and this caused one Dornier 215 to become separated from the formation. He attacked this aircraft, firing a four second burst which caused the port engine to catch fire, before side slipping towards the sea off Dover and Deal. He was later awarded a victory.

Pilot Officer Karol Pniak attacked a Dornier firing several bursts before he had to break off and engage the escort. He was attacked by a 109 from above and managed to out-turn his adversary. He then turned inside the 109 and onto its tail before opening fire. The 109 started to spiral down and Pniak followed firing occasionally at the machine which started to emit a lot of smoke. He broke off the dive at 3,000 feet and lost sight of the 109 which was cited as a probable victory.

Flying Officer John Humpherson sent another one spinning away after a piece flew off its tail north east of Margate. He was awarded a probable victory.

Flying Officer Grice made two head-on attacks against the Dornier's using all his ammunition but only caused damage before he returned home.

32 Squadron lost Pilot Officer Tony Barton in N2596 when he was shot down over Dover and bailed out. The aircraft crashed near Hawkinge, but Barton was not hurt and was back at Biggin that night recounting his experience at the bar over a pint or two.

As the squadron tried to reform, Flight Lieutenant Mike Crossley thought he was joining two Hurricane's, but they were in fact Messerschmitt 109's over the Channel. As he realized they were 109's he closed-up to the rear most machine and opened fire from 250 yards, A six second burst caused a red flash and a fire behind the cockpit before it dived away on fire.

The squadron eventually returned home at 6:10pm. Initially they tried to land at Hawkinge, but it had been hit hard by the raid while they were up, but some of 32's pilots were so short of fuel, they had to land among the bomb craters. There were about twenty unexploded bombs lying on the airfield, but after carefully landing, the aircraft were refueled and rearmed while the others went home to Biggin Hill.

The pilots at Hawkinge had just got out of their cockpits, when a small formation of twin-engine bombers flew across the airfield. The pilots stood and watched as the ground crews dived into the nearest slit trenches. They soon followed them as the bombers fired at the Hurricanes, but miraculously did not inflict any damage.

It had been a successful day's fighting for both 32 and 610, but the airfield was still operational, and the squadrons were in fine spirits.

Chapter 3.

Adler Tag! (Eagle Day)

The 13th of August 1940 was Eagle Day. The day Herman Goering decided he would destroy the RAF on the ground and in the air. The day was mainly over-cast with 8/10th to 9/10th cloud cover at 2-4,000 feet. Visibility varied from 4 to 12 miles.

At 5:10am a large formation of Luftwaffe bombers took off from France and started to head for the RAF airfields they were to destroy. However, due to the poor weather, the attack was cancelled. Despite this cancellation, poor communications led to seventy-four Dornier's of KG2 and sixty ME110's of ZG26 continuing on their way.

Matters took a turn for the worse for the Luftwaffe when the ZG26 Messerschmitt 110's received a recall order via their R/T, but the bombers carried on. The problem was that they had differing and incompatible radio sets. The Dornier's carried on alone.

At 6:30am the RDF chain identified the incoming bombers and tracked them. The Hurricanes of 601, 43 and 87 Squadrons were scrambled as well as the Spitfires of 64 Squadron. Biggin Hill's 32 and 610 Squadrons remained on the ground at readiness. In the next hour various airfields across Sussex, Hampshire and Dorset were to be attacked, causing a number of casualties.

At 8:40am 32 Squadron was scrambled to deal with raid X25 but made no contact and landed at Hawkinge at 9:05am.

At 9:40am Squadron Leader John Worrall led Flight Lieutenant Mike Crossley, Pilot Officers Douglas Grice and John Proctor plus Sergeant Edward Bayley on an interception of raid X41, but again no contact was made. They returned to Hawkinge at 10:00am and were refueled before being scrambled again at 10:55am and ordered to patrol above the airfield at 5,000 feet. No enemy aircraft were sighted, and they landed once again at 11:35am.

The remainder of the squadron under Flying Officer John Humpherson were ordered up at 11:00am after raid X37, but this was located and found to be a returning RAF Bristol Blenheim light bomber, which had carried out a bombing mission against the invasion barges being gathered on the French and Belgian coastline.

At 12:45pm the situation continued when the squadron were ordered to patrol above Hawkinge once again, but again nothing was seen of the Luftwaffe. It seemed the massed raids were passing by the Biggin Hill squadrons. At 1:20pm 32 Squadron landed back at their home base.

At 4:55pm 32 squadron were sent to Hawkinge once again. The RDF chain had identified what was formation of JU87 Stukas and their Messerschmitt 109 escort near Dungeness. Their target was we now know, to have been the Shorts aircraft factory at Rochester, but they could not locate it and headed for RAF Detling, a Costal Command airfield near Maidstone. As well as 32 Squadron, 56 Squadron's Hurricanes were also scrambled from North Weald.

For 32 Squadron, Flying Officer Gardner developed engine trouble and returned to base. Sadly 32 Squadron missed the JU87's as did 56 Squadron. The Stukas attacked the poorly defended airfield causing havoc, killing 68 personnel including the station's Commanding Officer on the ground and injuring many others. The fuel dump and several Bristol Blenheim's were destroyed or damaged in what was a very costly raid.

That evening, 32 Squadron returned to Biggin Hill. 610 had remained on the ground all day.

Eagle Day had cost the RAF thirteen aircraft with four pilots killed and two others wounded. The RAF squadrons claimed numerous victories with well-over one hundred claimed. We now know the Luftwaffe actually lost, thirty-one aircraft (5x 109's, 5x Dornier 17's, 1x Heinkel III; 6x Junkers 88's, 9x ME110's, 5x JU87 Stuka's) with many others returning with damage.

The Luftwaffe had taken a severe pounding on Eagle Day, but they would return in numbers on the 14th of August and throughout the next month.

The 14th was a fair day with some cloud when at 5:30am Squadron Leader John Worrall led 32 down to Hawkinge from Biggin Hill. After they arrived, Pilot Officer Gardener was sent off on a lone weather patrol at 6:30am which was completed without incident. While he was away, John Worrall led six Hurricanes on a patrol, but no enemy aircraft were encountered. Later at 8:30am the squadron returned directly to Biggin Hill.

At 11:40am RDF stations started to location numerous enemy aircraft approaching the coastline. As a result, Fighter Command brought several squadrons including 32 and 610 to readiness.

At 11:50am a number of the other squadrons were scrambled and positioned by controllers to meet the incoming raiders. The main raid consisted of eighty plus Junkers 87 Stukas, ME109's and ME110's of EprGr210. At noon, the ME109's shot up the barrage balloons over Dover before 65 Squadrons Spitfires arrived to drive them off.

At noon 610 was scrambled in squadron strength and led by Flying Officer William Warner they headed towards Manston, but they were re-directed to Dover. When they arrived, they joined 65 Squadron in attacking the ME109's and the Stukas who were also now present and aiming to bomb shipping in the harbour. The Messerschmitt 109E's were from the much feared JG26 and were led by Major Adolph Galland. The three Gruppen involved had some exceptional pilots and Galland, Munchenberg and Schopfel claimed a Hurricane each in this action, while a number of others claimed to have shot down seven more Spitfires.

Sergeant Ronald Hamlyn was leading 610's Yellow section when he saw Red section attack the Stukas. Four ME109's dived upon red section and Hamlyn attacked these fighters, he opened fire on one which started to emit smoke and dived away. Hamlyn did not see it crash as he was also attacked. He did report seeing another 109 crash, but it was not the one he had attacked. He therefore claimed a ME109 as damaged.

Sergeant Stanley Norris who was a member of Red section reported attacking the Stukas in his own combat report but near Folkestone at 15,000 feet. As he attacked the rear-most JU87 and opened fire, it went down bellowing smoke and flames on its back. The Stuka formation broke up and Norris dived down to see another formation of Stukas and ME110's over Dover. Norris selected a JU87 this time on the edge of the formation and when he opened fire this too, fell away emitting smoke and flames. He then fired at another one which he damaged. Norris claimed two destroyed and one damaged.

The Luftwaffe in fact only lost one JU87 Stuka in the encounter. Oberleutnant G. Ramling and his NCO gunner of 10/LG1, were reported as missing off Folkestone and were possibly the one shot down by Norris. One other returned to base with damage and a wounded gunner.

Sergeant Norman Ramsay claimed a Messerschmitt 110 destroyed while Pilot Officer Rees claimed a probable Stuka near Hawkinge.

Only one Messerschmitt 109E appears to tally with the squadrons claims and this was that of Oberfeldwebel George Weiss of 9/JG52. His body was washed up at Broadstairs on the 24th of October some two months after his last flight.

However, 610 Squadron had Sergeant Bernard Gardner shot down in K9947 (DW-M). He made a forced landing at Wye in Kent after being shot in the arm by a Messerschmitt 109E. He was quickly taken to Ashford hospital. It is believed he was shot down by Leutnant Burschegens of 7/JG26, being Burschegens fourth victory.

While this action was under way, the ME110's attacked RAF Manston and hit four hangars and three Bristol Blenheim's on the ground.

610 Squadron returned to base at 1:00pm and refueled and re-armed to await their next scramble.

Meanwhile, 32 Squadron had been scrambled at 12:30pm and six Hurricanes headed for Dover to join in the fray.

Pilot Officer Rupert Smythe who was leading Yellow section spotted a group of ME109's circling over Dover at 16,000 feet. He attacked two 109's and chased one which started to break up as he opened fire. The ME109 crashed into the English Channel with the wounded pilot, Feldwebel Gerhard Kemen of 1/JG26 managing to escape just in time. He was later picked up by a boat to become a prisoner of war. The other ME109's then attacked Smythe and his Hurricane was hit in the glycol tank and he had to withdraw before his engine overheated.

In the same incident Pilot Officer Boleslaw Wlasnowalski was in V7223 and had to force land near Dover. This was his first combat flight in the United Kingdom, and he managed to make his way back to base by road to fly again.

The rest of 32 had followed the first six Hurricanes off ten minutes after their take off. They too made their way towards the action around Dover and became engaged with the Luftwaffe. At 1:30pm Pilot Officer Tony Barton force landed at RAF Hawkinge after combat with the ME109's, but he was unharmed.

As the Luftwaffe withdrew back across the English Channel, the RAF squadrons returned to their bases. 610 and 32 were not called upon again that day and were allowed to repair their machines and rest.

The 15th of August 1940 had fair weather with good visibility and would be another very active day for Biggin Hill's two squadrons. Both 32 and 610 had been at fifteen minutes readiness since just before dawn. However, neither squadron was called upon until the afternoon and most pilots sat around sleeping, reading, playing cards or just listening to music.

At 11:30am JU 87 Stukas attacked the airfields at Hawkinge and nearby Lympne. Luckily for Biggin Hill's squadrons they were at their home base at the time as they were called to readiness. 501 and 54 Squadrons tried to intervene, but they were successfully driven off by the Stukas escort. The RDF stations at Dover, Rye and Foreness were all dive bombed and temporarily put out of action causing problems for the controllers.

Half an hour later twelve Messerschmitt 110's attacked RAF Manston and killed sixteen airmen as well as destroying two Spitfires on the ground.

At 12:43pm 610 Squadron were scrambled and directed towards Manston. However, they ran into and attacked twenty-five Dornier 17's and their 109 escort just ten miles south east of Biggin Hill. Pilot Officer Ken Cox claimed a probable ME109 and two others were damaged by Sergeants Stanley Arnfield and Douglas Corfe.

At 12:55pm, 32 Squadron was directed to fly to the recently bombed airfield at Hawkinge.

At 2:15pm the RDF chain that was still functioning, backed up by the Observer Corps but was under extreme pressure due to constantly changing raids. They identified another build-up of enemy aircraft of the English Channel. This time 32 Squadron were scrambled and rather than head out over the Channel, they were directed towards Essex and on towards Harwich. A formation of JU87 Stuka's attacked RAF Martlesham Heath in Suffolk and 32 and various other squadrons were tasked with defending the airfield. However, when 32 arived, there were no dive bombers for 32 Squadron to engage and they ended up challenging the remains of the 109 escort.

During the course of this operation Pilot Officer Boleslaw Wlasnowalski shot a ME109 down. He was just off Harwich at the time and upon sighting the fighters he climbed and attacked one from behind. The 109 pilot saw him and turned to try and get behind the Hurricane, which was a classic mistake. The high-speed fuel injected 109 was perfect for high-speed slashing attacks, but against the Hurricane and the Spitfire, it could not turn tight enough. Wlasnowalski tucked in behind the 109 and with a well-aimed five second burst, hit the fighter hard. It started to burn and dived towards the sea. It is believed having examined Luftwaffe loss reports, that the enemy 109's where from JG51 and the aircraft shot down was possibly that of Feldwebel Stiegenberger of the 5th Gruppe. He crashed into the sea off Margate, where he was rescued by the local lifeboat and detained.

The pilots of JG51 claimed a number of victories in the area at that time, Feldwebel Arthur Haase and Oberleutnant Josef 'Pips' Priller of the 6th Gruppe, claiming a Hurricane each. This was Prillers 11th victory, but he would go on to score 101 victories against the RAF and the USAAF including 68 Spitfires in that number.

One of the victims of Priller and Haase was Pilot Officer Douglas 'Grubby' Grice in Hurricane GZ-C. He was shot down in flames off Harwich and his fuel tank was struck and the cockpit filled with smoke and fumes. A 109 turned and made an instinctive shot hitting the Hurricane. With the Hurricane started to burn and fearing an immediate explosion, Grice baled-out successfully and landed in the sea. He suffered burns to his face and hands but like so many other burned pilots, the salt-water would assist his later recovery. A rescue launch picked Grice up out of the sea and took him to a Royal Navy hospital.

Despite his victory, Wlasnowlaski became a victim himself. His Merlin engine suddenly died and it unclear whether he was hit by debris or enemy bullets, but he had to make a forced landing in a field near Harwich. He was unharmed and made the long road journey back to his base in Kent.

The two squadrons returned to base to refuel and re-arm with 32 landing at Hawkinge.

At 5:20pm 32 Squadron were scrambled again with Squadron Leader John Worrall leading nine Hurricanes towards an incoming raid off Selsey Bill, but Pilot Officer Tony Barton had to return to Biggin Hill as his aircraft was defective.

The squadron spotted a formation of Junkers 88 and Dornier 17 bombers, with an escort of Messerschmitt 109's and 110's. Mike Crossley attacked a section of three JU88's who were lagging behind the main formations, firing half of his ammunition into a JU88 which left the formation and made off in a slight dive towards the south east, with its port engine smoking. He was then attacked himself by a fighter and had to break off the chase. Climbing again he made a beam attack on another bomber, firing the rest of his ammunition into it and causing the port engine to catch fire.

Flying Officer Humpherson also claimed a share in a Junkers 88 destroyed, seeing it crash west of Chichester. 32 Squadron eventually broke off the engagement and headed home. Sergeant Henson ended up with a bullet through his crank case and had to land at RAF Tangmere in P3522. LG1 had lost a number of its JU88's in this action, but it is difficult to link individual claims to actual victories.

At 6:43pm 610 Squadron were scrambled and ordered to intercept a formation heading for their own airfield at Biggin. They attacked twenty-five Dornier 17's with numerous ME109's at 14,000 feet.

Pilot Officer Cox was Blue 2 and attacked a 109 on his port side. He turned towards it and made an attack from astern. He hit him three times and the Messerschmitt went into a vertical dive before Cox lost sight of it. Ground crews at Biggin Hill reported a 109 at this time diving straight into the ground near the airfield. However, a review of Luftwaffe and crash reports cannot locate a possible match for this claim.

Elsewhere, Acting Flight Lieutenant Warner claimed a probable ME109 near Maidstone at 6:50pm, this may have been the 109 of Uffz. Friedrich Niedermaier of 9/JG54 who baled-out when he was shot down. His machine crashed to earth at a farm near Cranbrook, Kent. Sergeants Douglas Corfe and Stanley Arnfield also claimed 109's as damaged.

It was around this time that Biggin Hill's ground crews got their first real sight of the enemy, when a formation of Messerschmitt 110's passed on their way to another target (believed to have been Croydon). As the air raid siren wailed its long continuous notes the formation thundered by apparently oblivious of the close proximity of Biggin on the bump.

Seven minutes after 610 left Biggin at 6:50pm, 32 Squadron were scrambled yet again, this time against a raid heading for Croydon. As the pilots took off, they could see smoke rising from the initial bombing of Croydon. A formation of up to twenty Junkers 88's and Dornier 17's with an escort of 110's and 109's was sent to attack the airfield when 32 set off across the short distance towards them.

As 32 Squadron arrived overhead, the Messerschmitt 110's where dive bombing the airfield. 111 Squadron who were based at Croydon had been scrambled and had engaged the Luftwaffe as 32's pilots were arrived. The Junkers completed their attack, but the Dornier's had diverted to bomb RAF West Malling which was then still a relatively new airfield without its own squadrons.

Mike Crossley shot down a Dornier 17 reporting in his combat report that he closed in and knocked some pieces off it. Red three Sergeant Henson, attacked the same aircraft and the bomber started to turn away to starboard sharply. Squadron Leader Mike Worrall also fired at this Dornier and the port engine was now on fire. The bomber crashed according to Worrall somewhere east of Sevenoaks, while other reports said it was at Plaxtol near Borough Green.

Sergeant Bernard Henson claimed a Dornier 215 (actually a DO.17) over Selsey Bill, while Pilot Officer John Humpherson reported a probable ME109E. His combat report noted that he had seen about six ME109's in line astern. He went in to attack the rear-most machine, but as he did so, another one appeared and made a beam attack upon him. As this 109 broke away in front of him, it allowed him to open fire at just 100 yards distance. Henson gave a long twelve second burst, using up most of his ammunition which shot away a large piece of the Messerschmitt's radiator, causing it to spew out glycol and immediately lose air speed.

Pilot Officer John Pain claimed a probable 109 over Croydon having fired repeated bursts at one which started to emit smoke and dived away. Mean-while Sergeant Pearce shared a Dornier 17 with Sergeant Dymond of 111 Squadron near Redhill. In fact, this was actually a ME110 from Stab/Erp.Gr 210. The aircraft came down at Nutfield airfield (now Redhill) at 7:15pm, with Unteroffizier Werner the gunner being captured, and the pilot Oberleutnant Fiedeler killed.

Another ME110 of 2/Erp.Gr 210 fell to Squadron Leader John Worrall and Flight Lieutenant Mike Crossley. This aircraft crashed at Ightham in Kent with the pilot Leutnant Ortner baling out injured and being captured. The gunner Obergefreiter Lohmann was killed.

Virtually every pilot in 32 Squadron made at least one claim. This included a small training flight they maintained at Biggin Hill to assist the squadron. Flight Lieutenant Humphrey Russell and Pilot Officer 'Polly' Flinders both took off using the flights spare Hurricanes and they both made claims over or near Croydon.

Flinders claimed a Messerschmitt 109 probable near Caterham and Russell a ME110 destroyed. Flinders probable was actually confirmed and the ME109E of Leutnant Marx of 3/ErpGr210 which crashed at Frant in East Sussex, ten miles to the south east of Caterham was his likely victim.

One of the Polish pilots Pilot Officer Karol Pniak also made claims. He stated in his combat report, "I attacked a Do. 17 at 11,000 feet which turned over Croydon. I opened fire from 200 yards, I fired several short bursts from astern and the Do. 17 began to smoke. I saw him glide down with much thick black smoke coming from him. When I climbed up, I saw an

ME109 which was attacking a Hurricane. I attacked him from astern …….. he 'planed down' zig-zagging with thick black smoke. I was then attacked head on by a ME109, I fired but I had run out of ammunition".

Karol Pniak was awarded two probables. The raid on Croydon had caused some damage to the airfield, but the attackers had sustained heavy losses. 32 and 610 Squadrons returned home, thankfully having lost no pilots on a day the Luftwaffe would call 'Black Thursday'. RAF Biggin Hill had surprisingly not received a visit from the Luftwaffe bombers unlike Croydon and West Malling, but their time would come.

The 16th of August started fair with some cloud, but this would disperse by evening leaving visibility of between 4 and 6 miles. The early morning was therefore quiet, but at 11:10am 32 Squadron sent Squadron Leader John Worrall and five other Hurricanes up to patrol above their home airfield. After fifty minutes they landed without seeing the enemy.

It was at this point in time, that elected local representatives of the people started to bombard the airfield in their own indomitable way. With hindsight now, it is unbelievable that they asked the Station Commander Group Captain Grice, to ensure the bombers were intercepted elsewhere as they were jettisoning their bombs in the local area!!!

At 12:15pm the squadron again led by John Worrall were directed to take off and patrol over Dover at 10,000 feet. RDF and the Observer Corps had identified a large formation of over one hundred Dornier 17's and their ME109 escort, heading across the Channel. They were about to cross the coast between Folkestone and Brighton when 32 attacked with the Hurricanes of 54 and 56 Squadrons, as well as 64 Squadron's Spitfires. The raiders started to split up for different targets when Squadron Leader Mike Crossley, Pilot Officer Gardner and Belgian Pilot Officer De Grunne claimed a ME109 each.

Mike Crossley (Red 1) stated in his combat report that he saw a battle between about five machines over Dover. Two ME109's broke off and headed for home, but he selected the port hand side machine and opened fire with a quarter attack. A thick puff of black smoke came from the 109 which wobbled and dived on his back before recovering again and hitting the sea about two miles off Folkestone.

De Grunne as Red 2, saw Mike Crossley attack the 109 and saw it dive into the sea. De Grunne therefore attacked the second 109 which turned sharply. He closed to within just forty yards of the 109's tail before firing two bursts of two seconds each. He over-took the 109 and saw the pilot slumped forward in the cockpit. He therefore turned in behind it and fired another burst which caused the engine to start emitting black smoke and it dived into the sea. The pilot was not seen to bale-out.

Pilot Officer Gardner claimed his 109 to have been destroyed near the Goodwin Sands off Deal. A number of Messerschmitt 109E's were lost that afternoon from various Gruppen but is impossible to link these losses to individual victory claims.

When they landed, 32 Squadron found that Squadron Leader John Worrall had been posted as Senior Sector Fighter Controller at Biggin Hill. Mike Crossley would be promoted and take over as the new CO of 32 Squadron.

At 4:15pm Squadron Leader John Ellis led 610 Squadron aloft from Hawkinge where they had been positioned. They were directed by the Fighter Controller to intercept an in-coming raid over Dungeness.

At 25,000 feet they encountered a formation of some thirty Junkers 88's and an escort of twelve Messerschmitt 109E's. The visibility was very hazy with a layer of thin 10/10th cloud below them.

John Ellis stated in his combat report, that due to the poor visibility the squadron broke into flights. He led his flight into attack with Red section attacking the rear of the bomber formation, while two aircraft from Yellow section tried to divert their 109 escort. The bomber formation split up and Ellis dived after one firing at it and causing it to emit smoke. He would later claim this as damaged.

Sergeant Stanley Arnfield and Pilot Officer Donald Gray claimed a damaged and probable ME109 each. Arnfield claimed that his bullets had hit the 109 in the cockpit area. However, Gray lost his radio when he was hit by fire from another 109, but his aircraft (L1036 DW-D) returned to base without sustaining any further damage.

610 Squadron then became embroiled in another scrap with a formation of Heinkel III's and ME110's of ZG76 off Dungeness. Acting Flight Lieutenant William Warner (in R6802 DW-Z) was shot down and killed by a ME109 off Dungeness at 5:15pm. Again, due to the numbers of claims and losses on both sides it is impossible to link claims to incidents or losses. Warner's body was unfortunately never recovered, and his name is on the Runnymede memorial.

Mean-while at 4:40pm, 32 Squadron was scrambled from Biggin Hill as a large formation of JU88's, ME110's and ME109's entered the vicinity of the airfield. Twelve Hurricanes led by new CO, Squadron Leader Mike Crossley were straight into the fray and attacked the bombers head on. Crossley would later claim a Junkers 88 destroyed near Sevenoaks. In his combat report he stated that after attacking head-on, he singled out a straggling formation of three more JU88's. He opened fire at one JU88 which caught fire and started to go down in a spin witnessed by Pilot Officer John Pain. Crossley then opened fire at a Messerschmitt 110 causing the port engine to catch fire and the machine to dive away steeply. It appears neither aircraft crashed as no losses in the area at that time can be identified. A number did return home to France with varying degrees of damage and thus was more likely result in both cases.

Flight Lieutenant Peter Brothers was leading 'B' flight and he stated in his combat report, that he dived, firing all the way through the JU88's without success. He eventually chased and caught up with a ME110 cruising behind a JU88 and emptied his eight Browning machine guns into it. The port engine started to smoke badly, and it hit the sea about twelve miles south of Brighton. The two-man crew of the aircraft from 3/ZG76 were rescued from the sea by the German air sea rescue service and returned home to safety.

It is interesting that in his biography of Brothers, Nick Thomas cites Brothers having a note in his flying logbook, stating that it was actually a Junkers 88 of the 2nd Gruppe of KG76. 2/KG76 actually flew Dornier 17's so this is probably a mistake on his part. 2/KG76 had an entirely different aircraft to the ME110 or the JU88 and lost no aircraft that day. We do know from other records that the location of his crashed claim was in fact that of the ME110 of 3/ZG76.

Elsewhere, Red 2 and Red 3 Pilot Officer Tony Barton and Sergeant Edward Bayley also engaged the formation. Barton was chasing a JU88 at 15,000 feet when several 109's appeared overhead going northward. Thinking they were about to attack him, he turned to the right and found what he described as a 109 making a half-hearted dive at him. The 109 'shot-up' in front of him in a climbing turn to the right; and Barton opened fire managing to turn inside the enemy fighter. He continued firing and bits flew off the 109 and white smoke appeared from its underside before it 'wobbled' and turned over. Barton then carried out exactly the same attack on another 109 with similar results. He later claimed two 109's as probably destroyed somewhere to the south south east of Biggin Hill.

Ed Bayley joined in the full-frontal attack on the bomber formation and then a further head-on attack upon two ME110's who were escorting the JU88's. He gained hits on one machine which entered a defensive circle with the other 110 before it dived away vertically for the cloud layer below.

Sergeant Leonard Pearce also attacked the 109's damaging one, but the debris hit his own Hurricane and knocked off the panel covering the four Browning machine guns on a wing. He found that this made his aircraft hard to control but he managed to extricate himself from the action and returned home.

Pilot Officer De Grunne also claimed a Messerschmitt 109 destroyed in the Biggin Hill area, but it is impossible to link this to an individual loss.

32 Squadron broke off and landed back at Biggin Hill almost immediately at 5:45pm with no losses of their own. That evening they managed to entertain a Luftwaffe Hauptmann at their dispersal who claimed he was a ME110 pilot. The NCO gunner was more talkative and still thought the Luftwaffe would be victorious. The pilot was a little condescending, especially when viewing the dispersal and its various trophies (bits of shot down Luftwaffe aircraft). I have been unable to positively identify these men, but I believe they could have been Oberleutnant Urban Schlaffer and Obergefreiter Franz Obser. They were from 9/ZG76 and force landed after combat with fighters at Lee Farm, Clapham Wood, Sussex at 5:45pm.

Both men were unharmed and captured. Schlaffer was the Staffel Captain and therefore may have just been promoted to Hauptmann.

The Luftwaffe over the past few days had given their all, but so too had the RAF squadrons. That evening there was little activity and the Biggin Hill pilots could relax while the ground crews worked tirelessly to repair and service the Spitfires and Hurricanes. However, Lord Haw Haw that evening on his radio program 'Germany Calling' told Biggin Hill that they would soon be visited by the Luftwaffe like Croydon. In time Lord Haw Haw's predictions would come true.

The next day there was a pause in aerial activity for the Biggin Hill squadrons and for Fighter Command as a whole. The reasons would soon become apparent on the 18th August. A day soon to be known as the 'Hardest Day'.

Chapter 4.

The Hardest Day

Sunday the 18th of August 1940 dawned with fair weather and 7/10th cloud at 1,000 feet. Visibility was about twelve miles. No one knew that morning, but this day would become known as 'The Hardest Day'; a day of intense aerial fighting for both sides with many losses. As dawn broke, both of Biggin Hill's squadrons were at readiness and expecting raids.

By 11:55am KG1 and KG76 dispatched a large force of bombers to attack the RAF airfields to the south of London. In addition to the main bomber force, they sent nine Dornier 17's of 9/KG76 on a low-level attack to RAF Kenley. The idea was for a pin-point raid to be carried out before a high-level raid totally destroyed the base. The low-level raiders would be unescorted by Luftwaffe fighters and would fly across the Channel at low-level, navigating their way via railway lines to Kenley. The high-level raid would be made up of twelve Junkers 88's, twenty-seven other Dornier 17's and an escort of twenty-five ME110's (from ZG26) and twenty ME109E's (from JG51).

To cover this raid and to act as a diversion, JG3 and JG26 sent a force of fifty to sixty ME109's on a free hunt (Frei Jagd) over the north Kent coastline and along the Thames Estuary.

Kampf Geschwader (KG1) sent sixty Heinkel III's with forty ME109E's as an escort to bomb Biggin Hill in a bid to put the sector airfield out of action.

At 12:55pm Fighter Controllers reacted to the massing formations and sent 17, 54, 56, 65 and 501 Squadrons to the Dover and Canterbury areas; while Biggin's 32 and 610 Squadrons were scrambled to join 615 and 64 from Kenley to deal with the raiders heading their way. The Hurricanes of 111 Squadron were also scrambled from RAF Croydon.

32 Squadron's twelve Hurricanes climbed for height as the raiders headed for their home base at 15,000 feet. The two large formations heading for Biggin Hill and Kenley were soon confusing the fighter controllers as the two airfields are only a few miles apart. As a result, the various RAF squadrons attacked aircraft from both formations.

610 Squadron followed 32 into the air with fifteen Spitfires and started to climb for height. Mean-while Squadron Leader Mike Crossley positioned his Hurricanes near Sevenoaks ready

for a head on attack upon the bombers. 32 Squadron flew straight into the Dornier's hosing them down with machine gun fire as they swept past them. Crossley in his combat report, later said he saw a lone Junkers 88. This was in fact a Heinkel III of the 1st Gruppe KG1 piloted by Leutnant Rudolf Ahrens. Crossley attacked the bomber in a quarter attack and after about five seconds there appeared to be an internal explosion. Bits flew off the bomber and the undercarriage flopped down with the starboard engine smoking. The bomber ejected ten small bombs over the countryside before it crash-landed at Snargate on Romney Marsh at 1:40pm. Ahrens was injured, and one crew man was killed. In fact, the aircraft had been attacked by numerous Spitfires and Hurricanes before Crossley delivered the coup de grace. Crossley also attacked a ME110 head-on and damaged that.

Despite the confusion both airfields were hit, Kenley being especially hard hit with the low-level raiders of KG76 causing damage to the hangars and grounded aircraft.

Sergeant Bernard Henson attacked the Dornier formation and as he singled out one machine, he was hit by return gun fire from another bomber. He sustained a wound to his face but managed to continue his own attack causing the starboard engine of the Dornier to burst into flames. His own aircraft was in serious trouble and his central fuel tank leaked into the cockpit covering him in fuel. Fearing a fire and becoming a human torch, he turned off the engine and the fuel before making a forced landing in a field at Shoreham near Otford, Kent. He was lucky not to have been incinerated.

Pilot Officer Tony Barton claimed a Junkers 88. He reported seeing a long line of bombers and fired at one causing bits of debris to fly from its fuselage. He then fired at its starboard engine causing it to emit smoke and flames. The bomber wobbled and dropped back but Barton did not see it crash. I cannot locate a possible connection within the Luftwaffe loss records and it may have got home.

Flight Lieutenant Russell took aim at a ME110 and watched his bullets 'walk along the fuselage' of the 110, sparkling as they went into the aluminum airframe. The German fighters had a sting in their tail and the rear gunner hit Russell in the left arm and right leg. The Hurricanes cockpit started to fill with smoke, and he decided to bale out. Russell managed to get out and deployed his parachute, but he found that his leg was bleeding profusely. He therefore tried to use his parachutes wire ripcord as a tourniquet, but it was useless, and he could not stem the flow of blood. Russell was lucky when he came down next to the railway line near Edenbridge, where a railway man who had just completed a first aid course was only too delighted to assist him with his new-found skills. Russell was rushed to hospital where they managed to save his leg and his life.

Elsewhere, Sergeant Ed Bayley claimed a Dornier destroyed and a ME110 damaged.

Flight Lieutenant Peter Brothers who led 'B' Flight during the head-on attack, managed to stall his Hurricane which fell away in a spin. As he regained power and control, he saw a

Junkers 88 (he actually called it a Dornier 17, but like many pilots his aircraft recognition was not very good!). Together with Pilot Officer Boleslaw Wlasnowski and as it later transpired, pilots from 615 and 64 squadrons, he shot down the JU88 which crashed in woods near the church at Ide Hill. The crew of Feldwebel Karl Geier from 2/KG76 were all killed. It has been claimed in some reports that this was a Dornier 17 of the low-level attack of 9/KG76 flown by Wilhelm Raab, but we know his aircraft returned home damaged that day.

Pilot Officer 'Polly' Flinders had taken off once again in a training flight Hurricane. He chased a ME110 all the way past West Malling to Detling airfield with the twin-engine fighter doing barrel rolls in a desperate bid to shake him off. The chase continued across Kent to the RDF station at Dunkirk near Canterbury where a 40mm Bofors gun caused damage to the heavy fighter. Flinders closed in and opened fire once again, causing the ME110 to burst into flames and dive into the ground a few miles further on, north west of Canterbury at Harbledown.

Two 110's came down at this time at this location and Flinder's machine was either that flown by Unteroffizier Mai of 1/ZG26 or that of Oberfeldwebel Stange of 1/ZG26. Neither aircrafts crews survived the crash.

After this Flinders also attacked what he thought was a Dornier, but it was in fact another ME110. This one crashed near Godstone and was shared with Sergeant Horatio Chandler of 610 Squadron. Feldwebel Klare and his gunner from 3/ZG26 were killed.

Pilot Officer Alan Eckford of 32 Squadron joined in the head-on attack and after coming out of the other side of the bomber formation he saw the Dornier he had fired at, pull up into a drunken half roll and spin away. The Dornier was that of Oberleutnant Werner Stoldt the head of the 1st Gruppe of KG76. Eckford's rounds had shattered the glazed cockpit and nose. Stodlt was hit but the navigator Feldwebel Johann Beck was miraculously unharmed as was the flight engineer Oberfeldwebel Wilhem Lautersack. As the surviving crew members baled out the Dornier slowly came down in a series of turns until it crashed at Hurst Green near Oxted at about 1:20pm. Three crew men sadly died in the crash while Beck and Lautersack survived their parachute descent. Alan Eckford suddenly found himself in the middle of the escorting ME110's and their cannon fire. The emergency panel on his cockpit canopy (used to ease air pressure in the event of baling out) suddenly flew open and the draught started to pull his flying helmet from his head. He quickly dropped 5,000 feet before regaining control of both his Hurricane and his helmet and headed home.

In addition to Sergeant Chandler's joint claim with 'Polly' Flinders, 610 Squadron managed to get fifteen aircraft airborne in a bid to defend their station. At 31,000 feet they were ordered to attack the escorting Messerschmitt 109E's before hitting the bombers.

Pilot Officer Brian Rees chased a Dornier 17 and fired two long bursts into it. The port engine started to burn, and he followed it down. At this point a 109 attacked him from behind so he calmly throttled back the Rolls Royce Merlin engine and his adversary shot past him. As it over-took him, he fired a long burst into the 109 at very short range. The Messerschmitt turned over and crashed into a wood about ten miles from the airfield. What airfield he was referring to is unclear as no 109's crashed near Biggin Hill.

Squadron Leader Ellis tried to attack two ME109E's, but in his words they seemed intent on escape and he gave up the chase to turn his attention to six Heinkel III bombers in a 'vic' formation. Ellis attacked them over Cranbrook from out of the sun, but their defensive fire was so severe that he broke off and made a further quarter attack. Ellis's machine was slightly damaged by their return fire. The rear most Heinkel dropped back, and he carried out a beam attack on it. The machine in Ellis's words started to move erratically and the port engine was on fire. The bomber hit the sea 7-8 miles off Dungeness and broke up before sinking. Upon checking loss records I cannot identify this aircraft although it was corroborated by Flying Officer Peter Lamb in Ellis's combat report.

Pilot Officer Pegge attacked a ME109 from behind before it spun away on fire. He then attacked a Heinkel III from above and behind at a range of one hundred yards, closing as he fired to just twenty yards. Pieces fell from the fuselage and engines but as he turned to attack it once again, the bomber disappeared. As he returned to Biggin Hill he was preparing to land when he was attacked by a 109 which scored hits upon his Spitfire. He managed to maintain control and was thankful when the Messerschmitt disappeared. When he landed, Pegge hit a small crater and crashed the Spitfire but he was alive.

Pilot Officer Ken Cox (Blue 3) was attacked by 109's. He lost his Squadron Leader and turned to see a 109 on another Spitfires tail. He opened fire and this 109 fell away apparently out of control. In his combat report, Cox states that Pilot Officer Brian Rees confirmed the destruction of this machine. As Cox watched this 109 go down, he saw another one close by and emptied all of his remaining ammunition into it. This also dived away past the vertical and in his opinion, was definitely out of control. However, a check of Luftwaffe losses at that time and place cannot identify any apparent losses. It must therefore be assumed that they both returned home damaged.

Sergeant Peter Else also claimed two Dornier's damaged and Sergeant Stanley Arnfield claimed two ME109's at Edenbridge at 1:15pm and Dungeness at 1:45pm. Again, exact losses cannot be linked to these claims. The experienced seven victory ace, Oberleutnant Helmut Tiedmann of the 1st Gruppe of JG3 sustained radiator damage at 1:50pm in combat with RAF fighters and force landed at Leeds near Maidstone. He managed to evade capture for some twelve hours before being finally detained. He is likely to have been one of these claims.

By 2:00pm both 32 and 610 Squadrons were back on the ground at Biggin Hill. The airfield had been bombed at about 1:30pm, but most of the bombs fell on the nearby golf course, although the airfield had also suffered.

When the fighters had taken off earlier, it became clear to the Fighter Controllers that Biggin was the target. As the sirens wailed ground crew and station personnel dived into the air raid shelters. Bombs fell on Biggin Hill, both across the landing ground and the station buildings. The Motor Transport section was hit but the vehicles had already been dispersed.

A 40mm Bofors gun site had a near miss which killed one of the gun crew. One Dornier 17 came down low, undoubtedly already damaged when the Local Volunteer Force (LDV) opened fire. The aircraft crash landed on Leaves Green near the station by the Bromley road and was used by the media as useful propaganda.

The raid had lasted just ten minutes. It was claimed that a young army officer brought in wounded, came face to face with the crew of the Dornier that had been shot down at Leaves Green. The pilot is alleged to have spat at the injured British officer, but this is likely to have been anti-German propaganda. The pilot of the Leaves Green machine Oberleutnant Rudolf Lamberty and all his crew were themselves injured. The other Dornier's to have crashed nearby had no survivors.

Sergeant Joan Mortimer WAAF had remained at her post in the station armoury throughout the raid. Now it was over, she grabbed a handful of red flags and walked around the airfield pinpointing unexploded bombs for defusing and allowing aircraft to return and land. She was later awarded the Military Medal.

Biggin Hill had about five hundred bombs dropped on it that afternoon. Ninty of them were delayed action devices. Surprisingly, no vehicles or aircraft were lost or damaged in the raid. Two men were killed and three were wounded. It is said that when the craters were filled in and the unexploded bombs defused, they were found to be British bombs left behind in France. The airfield however was soon returned to active service.

The following is a combat report from Gefreiter Willi Wanderer who flew Heinkel III with KG1 on this raid and translated by the author. It gives a good impression of how the Luftwaffe were viewing events:

'After a futile approach on 16th we had to go through the unclearness of the machine at the channel, at last I wanted the desire to be in fullness in a big attack.

"Get up", the first word of the day tore me out of my beautiful dream. The first look after the weather. Clear skies today, it's definitely going to be. Get in the clothes. Sip some hot coffee and quickly to the truck, which brings us to the aircraft. There the squadron captain gave the target -airfield Biggin Hill. The start is postponed due to poor weather. Now it is time to wait. Slowly the hour jerked around, and bombers are called to start.

The necessary equipment, life vest, parachute and oxygen were already laid to a close. To buckle all this and to put it in the machine, lasted only a few minutes and already we rolled to the start. The flight line gave the start signal and already brewed the whole area. I quickly grasped the waving of the ground crew, then the bird hovered with his heavy greetings for England in the air. A flight around the place and course England was recorded. On the approach to the coast, the other squadrons joined. A magnificent picture the whole wing 50 machines.

It soon became serious. I took over the command of the airplane leader, "Install mg". Twice I controlled the two MG's to be sure. For only a few seconds I have time to give a shock to the English fighters. At the French coast, the previously popular hunting ground is nearing us. Now I see to the left and right of us, all the sky full of black dots. It did not last long, the channel shone already deep blue up as the points whirled.

English fighters were to attack. We already saw the need to turn on the breathing mask. In the meantime, a white coast strip became visible of the English coast. Now we expected flak fire, but no shot fell and unmolested we flew on. "The bombs were dropped". A look at the other machines. It was just raining with heavy parcels. Well, there's nothing left. With a hissing intoxication, our bombs had fallen too.

Now a left turn and the goal was to be seen. A black cloud of smoke told us that the bombs had been on target. A single flak site opened fire, but where were we. No English fighter no flak came close to us. Where are the Englanders? - it went through our heads. Nothing was touched and unmolested we set our course home. Not even my machine gun was in action. It was a pity that no Englander had burns on his fur.

In the view of the French coast, we flew lower and now the breathing mask was no longer necessary. The minutes passed quickly to the landing. With many questions, we were assaulted. For us there was only one answer like a practice flight over the sleeping English. No one has experienced such quiet flight. Is that supposed to be the end of Tommy's?'

The Spitfires and the Hurricanes landed back at Biggin Hill with the wind whistling over their now exposed gun ports, the canvas patches applied prior to flight to avoid the guns icing up; having been shot through by .303 rounds.

610 Squadron would not be in action again on the 18th, but at 5:15pm 32 Squadron was scrambled and vectored towards a raid north of Canterbury. Squadron Leader Mike Crossley led nine Hurricanes up from the airfield and towards a raid that was heading for RAF Hornchurch on the other side of the Thames in Essex.

The enemy bombers were escorted a formation of Messerschmitt 109E's of 2/JG51 at and above 12,000 feet. 32 Squadron were joined by a small section of 501 Squadron's Hurricanes from Gravesend. 501 had lost a number of aircraft and pilots that lunch time at the hands of JG26's Oberleutnant Gerhard Schopfel and were not at full strength. The Hurricanes met the enemy force over the Thames off Herne Bay.

As Crossley moved his unit into an attacking position, they were bounced by the 109's. It appears 7/JG26 and 5/JG51 also became involved and a large dog fight developed over the sea.

At 5:35pm Pilot Officer Comte Rudolphe De Grunne the Spanish Civil War pilot was shot down by a ME109 and his aircraft crashed at Ruckinge near Ashford. He was badly burned and after taking to his parachute was taken to hospital. He did claim a probable 109, but this cannot be confirmed.

Squadron Leader Mike Crossley reported being bounced by a dozen 109's but managing to latch on to one. He sent it down on its back in flames. He says he saw the 109 crash near Canterbury and the pilot did not get out. I cannot identify the actual Luftwaffe machine from the records, and it appears that Crossley had actually fired at a ME109 attributed to other pilots. This appears to have been Oberleutnant Walter Blume of 7/JG26 who was also attacked by Pilot Officers Alan Eckford and Karol Pniak of his squadron who were credited with this victory. Blume crashed at Kingston near Canterbury at 5:30pm and was wounded and captured.

Flight Lieutenant Peter Brothers and Pilot Officer Boleslaw Wlasnowski hit another ME109E from JG26 shooting down 22 years old, Leutnant Mueller-Duhe who was killed. He crashed at into a wood at Chilham near Canterbury at 5:30pm. Interestingly both pilots claimed the ME109 came down near Chatham when in fact it was near Canterbury!

Elsewhere, 501 Squadron fought with JG51 and sent two down, including the top ace Hauptmann Horst Teitzen. He had twenty victories and another seven from the Spanish Civil War when he had flown with the Condor Legion.

The losses were not all one direction. 501 Squadron lost Flight Lieutenant George Stoney (killed) while Sergeant Leonard Pearce of 32 was shot down over Canterbury at 5:29pm and baled-out slightly wounded. His aircraft (R4106) came down at Chartham Hatch.

Squadron Leader Mike Crossley after his initial attack was hit over the Medway towns and his Hurricane (N2461 GZ-F) crashed at Wigmore. Crossley baled-out and landed in an allotment at Gillingham unharmed. The local Home Guard took him to the local pub and in his words, "Got me plastered" before he returned to base by road.

It is impossible to identify which Luftwaffe pilots shot down the 32 Squadron pilots, but those pilots that returned to Biggin Hill found that they had to land among the bomb craters and unexploded bombs. Some managed better than others and Pilot Officer Boleslaw Wlasnowski ran into a crater while taxiing back to dispersal.

The Messerschmitt 109's had done their job and the Dornier's were given a relatively free run into Hornchurch where they dropped their bombs. As already stated, Biggin Hill had been bombed on the 18th, damage was light, but this would soon change with further raids.

32 and 610 Squadrons were eventually released with 32 being back at Biggin by 6:30pm. The rest of the evening was quiet, and they went off to rest and have a beer or two.

The impact of the hard days fighting on the 18th of August was a down-turn in operations for a few days.

32 Squadron had lost six Hurricanes and although they could be replaced in a day or two, pilots were much harder to replace. Spitfires with an all-metal air frame were harder to repair than the part fabric covered Hawker Hurricanes. Whereas a bit of canvas and a needle and thread could patch up a Hurricane, the Spitfires needed much more intricate metal and sheet work. As a result, many of the 610 Squadron Spitfires were in urgent need of repair with parts and panels needing replacement not just a patch up. The ground crews worked on tirelessly without sleep into the late-night hours. Just as pilots were tired, so too were the poor ground crews.

On the 19th the weather was decent, but after so much fighting the day before, both sides needed a rest and time to repair and service machines as well as to replace lost and hospitalised pilots.

The Luftwaffe did send over a 'Free hunt' of over one hundred Messerschmitt 109's at about 12:30pm over Dungeness and Dover but overall, the Fighter Controllers kept their squadrons on the ground to avoid unnecessary losses.

Between 1pm and 4pm ME109's strafed the forward airfields at Manston, Hawkinge and Lympne causing some damage and losses. 32 Squadron had been at Hawkinge that morning but had thankfully returned to Biggin before the 109's attacked. Later afternoon they flew back to Hawkinge and made a patrol, but no enemy contact was made again that day.

Over the next few days, (the 20th and the 21st) operations were hindered by occasional showers and rain, but it allowed the squadrons and the airfields to return to full capacity. The poorer weather was welcomed by Biggin Hill as its pilots rested and the ground crews repaired and prepared the aircraft for the next phase of the battle.

Chapter 5.

The attacks continue

Thursday the 22nd of August 1940 started off with overcast weather and continued with low clouds and visibility of six to twelve miles throughout the day.

At readiness since dawn, at 8:25am 32 Squadron's Flight Lieutenant Peter Brothers led six Hurricanes flown by Pilot Officers Karol Pniak, Jan Pfeiffer, Eugene Seghers and Peter Gardener as well as Sergeant Donald Aslin down to Hawkinge.

Five minutes later at 8:30am, Squadron Leader Mike Crossley led another five Hurricanes with Pilot Officers, Rupert Smythe, Boleslaw Wlasnowski, Keith Gillman and Tony Barton on a patrol over a convoy which was travelling through the Dover Straights.

Upon arrival the five Hurricanes led by Crossley patrolled at 5,000 feet, when there were suddenly four huge spouts of water near the convoy. Initially the pilots thought that Luftwaffe bombers had managed to evade them and bomb the convoy, but no aircraft could be seen. Suddenly another four large spouts appeared in the sea. A pilot then noticed flashes from the Cap Griz Nez and in seconds another four splashes appeared. It was large caliber guns firing from the French shoreline. Crossley informed control and about twenty minutes later a squadron of Bristol Blenheim light bombers flew by en route to deal with the guns. No enemy aircraft were seen.

At 9:20am Peter Brothers led his flight from Hawkinge to take over from Crossley's 'A' flight above the convoy. However, despite not seeing the enemy, Pilot Officer Jan 'Fifi' Pfieffer managed to crash land at RAF Hawkinge in P3205 at 10:45am when they returned. He was unhurt.

At 12:40pm the entire squadron was led aloft by Mike Crossley and flew a patrol over the convoy without incident. They were joined on the patrol by 615 Squadron's Hurricanes from Kenley, before landing back at Hawkinge at 1:40pm for a late lunch.

While 32 were on patrol, 610 Squadron took off to patrol over Folkestone. Nearby, 54 Squadron's Spitfires were also on patrol. While at 15,000 feet, 610 were 'bounced' by twenty Messerschmitt E109E's from out of the sun.

The attack was so sudden that 610 hardly had time to react. In fact, only Pilot Officer Gardiner and Sergeant Hamlyn were able to fire off a few shots as the ME109's dived straight through them and into the low-level cloud below. The Messerschmitt's had hit Sergeant Douglas Corfe's aircraft (P6695 DW-P), making it virtually uncontrollable. Corfe tried to make it back to Hawkinge, but he had to make a forced landing in a field near the airfield at about 2:15pm where the Spitfire burned out. Corfe thankfully managed to get out unharmed and returned to the nearby aerodrome on foot.

54 Squadron also tangled with the same 109's and at about 1:15pm they lost Sergeant Collett off Deal. The Luftwaffe did not lose any 109's around this time and area according to their records and neither did they make any claims against British fighters. No claims were made by the pilots of 610 and 54 squadrons either. Is it possible the British squadrons fired at one another, leading to the loss of Sergeant Collett and the forced landing of Corfe? Poor aircraft recognition was rife at the time as was over claiming. There is no evidence to support this, but misidentification was a problem for both sides during the battle.

610 Squadron took no further part in operations on the 22nd of August, but 32 Squadron flew in squadron strength back down to Hawkinge at 5:00pm.

At 5:55pm after having their fuel tanks 'topped-up', Peter Brothers took his flight of five Hurricanes up to escort and lumbering Avro Anson which was spotting for the shore batteries. After thirty minutes on patrol and escort duties, 32 Squadron were vectored by the Fighter Controller on to a formation of about twenty plus Dornier 17's and their escort of ME110's and ME109E's. The slow Anson turned for home as Brothers flight headed towards the enemy.

At 6:35pm the remainder of 32 Squadron were scrambled from Hawkinge to link up with Brothers flight. Together they attacked the bomber formation at just 3,000 feet between RAF Manston and Deal.

Sergeant Don Aslin claimed a Dornier 17 damaged, as did Pilot Officer Rupert Smythe, while Pilot Officer Karol Pniak claimed to have damaged a Dornier which was in fact a ME110. He said he had broken off the engagement with the aircraft's engines smoking; although the Luftwaffe lost no aircraft which match these claims. The eleven Hurricanes returned to Biggin Hill and landed at 7:35pm when they were released for the night.

On the 23rd of August, there was a celebration for Flight Lieutenant John Humpherson of 32 Squadron who was awarded the Distinguished Flying Cross. However, he was soon posted to 607 Squadron as a Flight Commander a week later, on the 30th.

At 5:40am that morning, Squadron Leader Mike Crossley led the whole unit to Hawkinge. At 6:55am eleven Hurricanes minus Pilot Officer Jack Rose who had technical problems, took off on a patrol over the airfield. No enemy aircraft were seen, and they landed after just 20 minutes. Pilot Officer Jan Pfeiffer's poor fortune continued when he had to land P2795 with just one wheel down. He again escaped without injury although his Hurricane needed some TLC.

At 8:15am the remaining ten Hurricanes (minus Rose and Pfeiffer) took off from Hawkinge for another patrol, this time over Dover. Again, no Luftwaffe machines were encountered, but Pilot Officer Rupert Smythe made a forced landing upon his return to Hawkinge in P3900. This was due to engine trouble, but he was unhurt. The aircraft were in urgent need of major servicing and in many cases should have been taken out of line for this work to be completed. This may or may not have been the reason for Smythe's engine trouble, but the aircraft were making a great deal of flights each day with only minor servicing and checks possible between the scrambles.

The rest of the day saw little flying with low cloud, drizzle and poor visibility which hindered any activity. However, the next day would be a very busy one for Biggin's squadrons.

The 24th of August was fair with some low cloud. 610 Squadron were on dawn readiness and at 7:58am twelve Spitfires were scrambled from Biggin Hill to intercept a raid off the south east coast. The squadron ran straight into a large formation of forty plus Dornier 17's and Junkers 88's with an escort of over sixty Messerschmitt 109E's, between 12,000 and 15,000 feet some twelve miles off Ramsgate.

There is some confusion, and it appears that Sergeant Ronald Hamlyn (yellow 2) was one of the very few to actually engage the enemy. How this happened is unclear from his combat report. He reports attacking the formation of Junkers 88's and receiving a large amount of return fire from the various bombers. At 250 yards he opened fire hitting the port engine of one JU88 which crashed into the sea. A Messerschmitt then overshot him, and he throttled back allowing him to fire into the 109 from some 150 yards. The ME109 was hit in the fuselage and turned over and also crashed into the sea according to Hamlyn. I have been unable to locate losses that correspond with Hamlyn's claims and it is possible that neither aircraft actually crashed.

Sergeant Stanley Arnfield in R6686 (coded DW-D) was shot down in this attack and baled out. When he landed, he fractured his ankle and was admitted to hospital in Deal. The rest of the squadron returned to base at 9:00am where despite his report, it appears Ronald Hamlyn's two claims were not confirmed.

At 10:35am Squadron Leader Ellis led 610 up once again. This time they were ordered to patrol over Biggin Hill, before being re-positioned over Gravesend. They were then re-located to the Dover area and after an hour's patrolling they were attacked by a small formation of ME109E's from above.

Sergeant Hamlyn was again in the action and in his combat report he states that after they were attacked, he got on to a 109's tail which fled towards France. As he was chasing this 109, he saw another being chased by two Spitfires before it crashed into the sea off the Cap

Gris Nez. Hamlyn then broke the golden rule of following aircraft across the Channel and chased his 109 over the French coast. He claims he then shot it down and it crashed into a field. (It is impossible to match this claim to individual losses, although the Luftwaffe had a number of ME109's crash land or ditch in the Channel after combat that day). Hamlyn adds that the aircraft he witnessed crash into the sea, was shot down by Flying Officer Peter Lamb (Yellow Leader).

Pilot Officer Eric Aldous was Green 3 and attacked a 109 which he claimed as probably destroyed. He met two ME109's, one almost head-on and managed to get in front of him and slightly above. Aldous fired a number of bursts of machine gun fire into the 109, which started to smoke and dived away. He followed it downwards, but at 3,000 broke off and started his return to base. He was then attacked and slightly damaged in DW-X (R6641) by another 109 before eventually returning home.

Pilot Officer Donald Gray was hit by a 109 and was shot down over Dover. He managed to make a forced landed at Shepherdswell near Dover, but he sustained some wounds and was admitted to the Waldershare hospital. Several claims were made by pilots of LG2, JG26 and JG51, but it is difficult to correctly attribute them to any losses.

The rest of 610 Squadron returned home and landed by noon.

32 Squadron had sent two pairs of Hurricanes up during the morning hours, but no contact was made with the Luftwaffe. At 1:00pm the squadron was ordered to patrol over Dover, but yet again no enemy aircraft were encountered. They landed at Hawkinge to refuel at 2:20pm where they were joined by Squadron Leader Mike Crossley and Sergeant Sidney Whitehouse.

At 2:30pm having had barely enough time to put a few drops of fuel into their Hurricanes, 32 Squadron were scrambled and ordered to climb above Hawkinge to 20,000 feet. As they moved towards Dover harbour they were attacked by a formation of about twelve ME109E's. A major dogfight took place but despite repeated attempts, neither side could inflict any losses on the other. Eventually they broke off and returned to Hawkinge.

The Squadron Operations Record Book is very confusing, and it appears this combat may have been confused by its author as they were scrambled again at 3:45pm and 4:00pm in two sections. This time they tangled with fifteen ME109E's at 10,000 feet over Folkestone. The ORB makes claims for both combats, but the combat reports and diaries appear to show a confused mix of the two incidents. Therefore, the following combat reports and comments are from one or the other actions…

The Luftwaffe had sent a number of formations to bomb the RAF airfields at Hornchurch and North Weald in Essex and eight squadrons, including 32 and 610 were scrambled to meet the raiders.

Pilot Officer Keith Gillman claimed a ME109 over Folkestone, as did Sergeant William Higgins who also claimed to have shot one down with it crashing into the sea off Folkestone. Other pilots made claims of causing damage to several of the 109's.

Flight Lieutenant Peter Brothers claimed to have shot one down with part of its starboard wing coming off before it hit the sea at around 4:00pm, some ten miles south east of Dover. The pilot appears to have been Leutnant Franz Achleitner of 3/JG3 who bailed out and landed in the sea. He was rescued by the Herne Bay lifeboat.

Polish pilot Josef Pniak attacked a Messerschmitt 109 and caused it to emit smoke before he was hit and set on fire. He fought to control his Hurricane as it came down in Dover harbour and he eventually baled-out with a slight injury.

32 Squadron had a number of losses in this action and Mike Crossley was shot down by a ME109 coming down at Lyminge near Folkestone at 4:30pm. Sergeant Eugene Seghers (V6567) a Belgian pilot was shot down by a 109 near Elham and bailed out successfully. He landed by parachute and returned to the unit later that day. It is likely his victor was Oberleutnant Ruppert of 3/JG26, but this cannot be confirmed.

Pilot Officer Rupert Smythe was injured in combat with a 109 over Folkestone in V6568, he managed to land and was admitted to the Royal Masonic Hospital in Hammersmith, London.

Oberfeldwebel Walter Meyer of 5/JG26 also claimed a Hurricane at this time and he is likely to have hit one of the other 32 Squadron losses.

The remains of 32 Squadron returned home and carried out a few minor flights that afternoon and evening, but there was no further combat that day.

At 3:45pm 610 Squadron had also been scrambled with nine aircraft of Red, Yellow and Blue sections ordered to intercept a raid over Gravesend. They engaged some twenty Junkers 88's and an escort of twenty ME109E's off the Isle of Sheppey.

Sergeant Ronald Hamlyn was once again in the thick of the action, this time leading Yellow section. In his combat report he states that as they approached Gravesend at 5,000 feet, they saw anti-aircraft fire over London, so they changed course. At 12,000 feet he sighted the JU88's and turned his section after them. However, he saw a schwarm (flight) of 109's above and attacked them. He fired into one of them with two bursts which caused it to emit smoke and fall away apparently out of control. He then saw tracer bullets passing over his Spitfire and turned sharply to see his number three being attacked by ME109. Hamlyn fired at this 109 and it caught fire, falling away and shedding debris on its way down. Unfortunately, his number three (Yellow 3) was also going down and apparently out of control having been hit by his adversary.

Flight Lieutenant Stanley Norris was leading the squadron at the time and claimed to have shot down a 109, twenty miles north of the Isle of Sheppey. He fired a number of times into the ME109 which went down vertically, leaving a thick trail of black smoke, but he did not see it crash.

Pilot Officer Constantine Oliver Pegge claimed a probable ME109E to the north of Gravesend in the same engagement. In his combat report he said he saw pieces flying off it from the cockpit area and it went into a slow spiral, but he had to leave it due to the attention of other 109's.

Sergeant Baker claimed a ME109 destroyed to the west of Sheppey, but it appears Yellow 3 (seen by Sergeant Ron Hamlyn) going down was Pilot Officer Claude Merrick. He crash-landed L1037 (DW-D) at Fyfield in Essex and was admitted slightly wounded to Ongar Hospital.

Number 56 Squadron had also been engaged in this engagement, and it is impossible to align individual claims and losses. 610 Squadron returned to base at 4:45pm.

Ronald Hamlyn was credited with five victories in a day and would later be interviewed on BBC radio with his victory claims being broadcast around the world. I cannot substantiate the claims as such, and the pilot must be credited as an honest man without other evidence to the contrary. We can also not blame the pilot for being made into a propaganda figure.

While the squadrons were in action, RAF Hawkinge was once again visited in force by the Luftwaffe. The airfield suffered quite heavily from the bombing and this led to Group Captain Grice the Biggin Hill station commander flying down to the airfield to inspect it in the station's Miles Magister trainer. Grice took the Sector Signals Officer Flight Lieutenant Osmond with him.

On the way back, flying at very low-level, they were spotted by two Messerschmitt 109E's who tried to attack them. Grice used every ounce of his experience and flying skills to evade the fighters, turning and side slipping the little trainer. He flew so low he was below the trees. Eventually the 109's probably low on fuel, broke off the chase and the exhausted Grice and the petrified Osmond returned to Biggin Hill.

Their action had not gone unnoticed with the Observer Corps reporting the contest to the Sector Operations room at Biggin Hill, where it was tracked with a certain degree of anticipated doom for the Magister. Little did they know that this was their own station commander and signals officer!

Upon their return Grice went to the operations room to speak with Squadron Leader John Worrall and to get an update on the combat situation. After being given a short briefing, Worrall told Grice that some fool in a Magister had been chased by some 109's. Apparently Grice laughed and admitted that he was the fool.

This brought an end to the fighting on the 24th of August 1940. It had been a hard day for Biggin Hill's squadrons with seven aircraft lost. Thankfully, no pilot's lives had been lost, but a number had to be admitted to various hospitals for treatment. Sadly, the next day would be different.

The 25th of August was mainly overcast with a cloud layer at 2,500 to 4,500 feet. On the 25th things were to change. 32 Squadron received a signal from Fighter Command instructing them to move north to RAF Acklington in Northumberland. 79 Squadron would travel in the opposite direction to replace them.

At 8:25am Squadron Leader Mike Crossley led 32 Squadron from Biggin Hill to RAF Hawkinge. They carried out some local flights, but nothing was seen of the Luftwaffe. In the early afternoon, the squadron returned to Biggin Hill, but at 4:55pm, Crossley led the Hurricanes back to Hawkinge.

At 5:50pm Pilot Officers Alan Eckford and Tony Barton took off on a patrol and according to the Operations Record Book, they were recalled and landed at 6:10pm. However, at 6:15pm the two pilots reported shooting down a Henschel 126 search plane south east of Dungeness.

The Henschel 126 was a high winged two-man spotter plane often used in a similar way to the Westland Lysander to which it bore more than a passing resemblance. Barton reported the aircraft spotting their approach and it dived down to sea level in a bid to escape back to France. Alan Eckford attacked first while Barton kept a look out for the reported 109 escort (where they directed on to this fighter control?). As Eckford broke away, Barton attacked and reported his tracer fire entering the HS126. There was no return fire from the Henschel 126 as he broke off. It appears this aircraft escaped to France as the Luftwaffe did not report any missing that day. In fact, the Henschel 126 is not shown in the official list of victories that Alan Eckford attained during the war.

Within minutes of landing back at Hawkinge, Barton and Eckford were airborne again as 32 Squadron were scrambled and ordered to patrol over Dover. A raid comprising of some twelve Dornier 17's and a fighter escort of about thirty-six ME109E's was approaching from the south at 14,000 feet.

Mike Crossley led the Hurricanes into the attack and shot down a Dornier over the sea. Pilot Officer Jack Rose also reported damaging a Dornier's port engine. However, he was then attacked by a 109 and had his rudder shot away leaving his machine uncontrollable. He baled-out and landed in the sea where he was picked up an hour and a half later and returned to Dover by a patrol boat. He was lucky to survive, as a winter dunking would have certainly led to his death. Mike Crossley then added to his earlier Dornier by claiming to have shot down another 109 into the sea.

Pilot Officer Proctor (Yellow 1) reported that, "A ME109 settled on to the tail of one of our aircraft so I gave him my first burst (four seconds at 250 yards closing to 50 yards, expending the rest of my ammunition at 150 yards) from astern". The 109 dived and climbed before heading for France, but it crashed into the sea four miles south east of Cap Gris Nez.

When the squadron landed, they found that Pilot Officer Keith Gillman was missing in P2755. He was never found. Gillman would become the face of the RAF fighter pilots for the remainder of the war. An anonymous publicity shot of the pilot in his flying helmet and cravat appeared a week later, on the cover of the Picture Post magazine. Many thousands of people would see his image never knowing that this un-named pilot had just paid the ultimate sacrifice a week before.

The squadron returned to base and made no further combat flights. They would travel to Acklington in Northumberland the next day.

At 6:52pm 610 Squadron were scrambled to assist with the defence of Dover. Squadron Leader John Ellis led the squadron to 22,000 feet when they encountered eight to twelve Messerschmitt 109's 5,000 feet above them. 616 Squadron's Spitfires also became involved.

In fact, the entire Geschwader of JG26 was on a free hunt and escort to a raid by bombers on Hawkinge airfield.

Sergeant Robert Beardsley flying as Yellow 3 attacked a 109 at 20,000 feet. He fired a short burst into the cockpit area of the fighter which flicked over onto its back and dived down vertically. It disappeared into the clouds at 7,000 feet but Pilot Officer Lamb confirmed that he saw it crash.

However, the ME109's shot down and wounded Flying Officer Frederick Gardiner at 7:20pm. He bailed out of K9931 (DW-P) and was taken to Waldershare Hospital, the Spitfire crashing to earth at Stoneheap Farm, Northbourne in Kent. The 109's of 3/JG26 were their antagonists and their Geschwader commander Major Adolf Galland claimed a Spitfire at this time and location, while Feldwebel Muller claimed two more. However, JG26 did not lose anyone so it is unknown who Beardsley shot down. 616 Squadron lost two of their Spitfires with one pilot killed and one, Sergeant Wareing captured over France having been chased there by the JG26 Messerschmitt's. Two years later Wareing managed to escape from his prison camp and returned home via Sweden.

Sergeant Claude Parsons was returning home when he saw a green-yellow streak in the water. He circled the downed pilot who had released his fluorescein dye into the water before a boat arrived. This is believed to have been Pilot Officer Rose of 32 Squadron. It is unclear if Keith Gillman had his dye with him. It had been handed out to the pilots of 32 Squadron that very morning and if he had, he might have been found; but his body has never been found and it is more likely that he went down with his Hurricane.

The next morning on the 26th of August the weather was fair with some cloud. 32 Squadron made their way to Ackington in Northumberland.

At 11:42am Squadron Leader Ellis led eleven Spitfires of 610 Squadron on an interception. They engaged eight ME109E's of JG52 over Folkestone which were dropping bombs on the town from 5,000 feet. The combat was hard, and it is believed that other 109's joined the fray as 610 sustained some losses.

Sergeant Peter Else in P9496 (DW-L) was hit by a 109 and slightly wounded. He baled-out and upon landing, he was taken to the Kent and Canterbury hospital for treatment. His Spitfire crashed at Paddlesworth at 12:40pm.

Flying Officer Frank Webster in R6965 (DW-O) was damaged by a ME109 and tried to land his crippled aircraft back at Hawkinge. As he came into land, he lost control and crashed in flames. Sadly, he was killed.

Sergeant Ronald Hamlyn was Yellow 3 and followed his leader into the attack over Folkestone. At about 9,000 feet he saw a ME109E and fired two long bursts into it causing it to emit smoke. The 109 started to lose height and he turned his attentions to another 109. This was coming out of a dive at 3,000 feet. He fired an initial burst but did not notice any results, so he fired a longer burst which caused the cockpit to catch fire and it dived into the sea about a mile off Folkestone. This might have been Feldwebel Ziegler of 3/JG52 who crashed at this location around midday and was rescued but burnt and made a prisoner. However, the Squadron Leader also claimed a 109 at the same time and area. This was confirmed by Pilot Officer Douglas Wilson so Ziegler may have been shot down by Ellis or both men. Wilson also claimed a 109 destroyed, while Sergeant Norman Ramsay claimed a probable 109.

The victorious 109 pilots cannot be identified as JG52 made several claims at this time and they cannot be linked individually to the losses.

Flying Officer Lamb spotted a lone Dornier 17 out at sea and attacked this, claiming to have shot it down. Having checked the records, I cannot identify the exact machine, but KG3 lost a number at lunchtime around the Goodwin Sands and Ramsgate areas.

610 squadron eventually returned to Hawkinge and landed at 12:45pm.

There was no further action on the 26th and 610 Squadron were left as the sole squadron at Biggin Hill awaiting the arrival of 79 Squadron from Acklington.

The 27th of August was a fair day with some cloud and there appears to have been little or no action concerning the Biggin Hill squadrons. The action on this day is a little confusing as the 610 Squadron Operations Record Book makes no mention of flying or combat, but there is a combat report from Squadron Leader John Ellis claiming a ME109E destroyed. It is therefore likely that due to the hectic circumstances, the officer deputed to write the book was distracted or had it been Frank Webster who was killed the day before?

Ellis reports leading the squadron, when they were ordered to intercept a formation of fighter's over Dover at 22,000 feet. As 610 Squadron climbed to 15,000 feet, they saw ME109's above them and below them. This was a classic tactic with the higher staffel ready to bounce the Spitfires if they dived upon the lower unit. Ellis therefore ordered the squadron into two sections, with four aircraft detailed to deal with the higher enemy, while he led the remaining four aircraft down onto the lower formation.

Ellis believed the 109's where bombing Dover, as they could not see any bombers. Ellis fired at one 109 and hit it causing part of its exhaust manifold to fly off and hit his wing. The ME109E then dived into the sea being witnessed by Flying Officer Douglas Wilson. However, Luftwaffe records have no 109's being lost on this day and it is possible this was an incorrectly dated report.

79 Squadron had started their journey down to Biggin Hill, but the fifteen Hurricanes had to divert to Hucknal due to poor weather. They completed their journey arriving later that day at Biggin Hill.

The 28th of August was fair day weather wise and at 8:45am a formation of fifty plus Dornier 17's and over fifty ME109's and 110's was sighted crossing the Channel. 79 Squadron had been ordered down to Hawkinge early that morning and were scrambled with 85, 615 and 264 Squadrons. 264 were flying Defiants and had already been mauled by the Luftwaffe during the battle when at 9:00am, they lost another three to the Messerschmitt's of JG26 over Faversham.

79 Squadron were on their way down to Hawkinge, when they were ordered to intercept and assist the Defiants. Flight Lieutenant Rupert Clerke claimed a probable ME109 and Pilot Officer George Nelson-Edwards a probable Heinkel 111.

79 Squadron managed to escape unharmed from their first combat since their return to the south east. Pilot Officer Tracey reported sighting some eighteen Heinkel 111's and some 109's. Two Heinkel 111's where probably destroyed and Flight Lieutenant Haysom was hit in the glycol tank; but managed to return unharmed. JG26 pilots Leutnant Rysavy and Oberleutnant Losigkeit of 2/JG26 claimed two Hurricanes, one of which was confirmed even though all of 79 Squadrons machines returned home.

At 11:00am, 79 Squadron's 'A' Flight took off to intercept two Heinkel 59's sea planes over the English Channel. These machines were still being used in an air sea rescue mode, but as they also gathered intelligence, the RAF continually sought to shoot them down. 'A' Flight led by Flight Lieutenant Rupert Clerke spotted the two sea planes with an escort of three Messerschmitt 110's. While the others engaged the 110's, Clerke shot down one He59 and forced the other to land on the surface of the sea. Seenotflugkdo/3 lost two Heinkel 59's at this time with one crewman killed and seven others wounded. A couple of E-Boats arrived to rescue the survivors, but they too were shot up by the Spitfires.

At 11:30am 'B' flight was ordered to intercept another Heinkel 59 which they claimed as probably destroyed. 79 Squadron did not know at the time, but the Prime Minister Winston Churchill had been at Dover Castle watching the action out over the harbour and Channel.

At 3:30pm, 610 Squadron were scrambled and vectored towards Dover and Deal. At 18,000 feet they met an estimated twenty Messerschmitt 109's. The 109's were ringed initially by anti-aircraft fire which pinpointed their location to the approaching Spitfires.

610 Squadron swung in behind the 109's and opened fire. Sergeant Ronald Hamlyn was again in the thick of the action as Yellow 1. In his combat report he says he picked out a 109 and attacked it from the rear. After a few bursts of fire, the 109 dived straight down. Hamlyn claimed this as probably destroyed as he saw no smoke or flames coming from the 109. However, Sergeant Edward Manton (Yellow 4) reported seeing it crash inland after catching fire on its way down. Hamlyn reported that the 109's engine cowlings were painted bright yellow as were the wing tips. This machine was almost certainly that flown by Leutnant Landry of Stab flight 1/JG3 which crashed at Church Farm, Church Whitfield just north of Dover. He had managed to bail out injured but died on the 23rd of September 1940. Landry was an Ace with six victories of his own at the time.

Pilot Officer Pegge also claimed a 109 destroyed over Dover. He was Red 2 diving on three 109's with yellow cowlings and wing tips. He opened fire hitting one in the fuselage which caught fire and went straight down being confirmed by Sergeant Claude Parsons. JG3 lost a number of 109's and one of these may have been that which Pegge attacked.

Sergeant Cyril Bamberger also claimed a probable 109 which emitted smoke and dived away, but 610 Squadron lost Pilot Officer Kenneth Cox who was shot down and killed when his Spitfire P9511 crashed at 5:00pm into a house at Stelling Minnis between Canterbury and Folkestone.

By 4:45pm, 610 Squadron had returned to their base and there was no further flying that day.

On the 29th of August, 79 Squadron made no operational flights. 610 were however back in combat once again.

At 2:45pm a large free hunt formation of ME109's and ME110's from JG3, JG26, JG51, ZG26 and ZG76 headed across the English Channel. The formation was estimated to total over six hundred fighters and was a major attempt to entice the RAF into combat. The fighter controllers, clearly unaware that this massive formation contained only fighters, scrambled some thirteen RAF fighter squadrons including 610 at 3:30pm.

85 Squadron and 603 Squadron initially made contact with the formation, but they withdrew when it became clear this was a massive fighter sweep.

610 took off to engage them from Biggin Hill and they clearly expected to find ME110's and Dornier bombers as stipulated in their Operational Record Book. They attacked the formation over Mayfield and Gatwick.

Sergeant Aubery Baker was Yellow 3 (in X4011 DW-O) and reported staying with Yellow 1 who destroyed a ME110. They then split up and he attacked a 110 Jaguar from the rear, port quarter and from underneath. He fired into the engine (port) which started to smoke, and the aircraft heeled over and dived away. Baker then carried out a similar attack on what he thought was a Dornier. This dived away past the vertical, but he broke off as his engine was over-heating. He therefore landed unharmed at Gatwick airfield.

Pilot Officer Eric Aldous (Green 2) attacked with the squadron what he believed were Dornier's. He dived after one aircraft and fired a number of rounds into it, claiming it as damaged.

Sergeant Chandler from Red section also claimed to have damaged a Dornier. Pilot Officer Pegge (Red 2) damaged another 'alleged' Dornier over Mayfield which shed bits as he opened fire; but Pegge had to break off when ME110's intervened.

Sergeant Stanley Norris (Red Leader) attacked twelve Dornier 17's but was forced to evade a ME110 which was part of a formation of fifty fighters he claimed. He managed to get in a few bursts in and the starboard engine of a 110 started to smoke badly. The 110 went into a steep spiral and dived away out of Norris's sight.

Sergeant Robert Beardsley fired at a Dornier from the rear and after two bursts of fire, there was no further return fire from the bomber's gunner. Pieces flew off the Dornier and holes could be seen all over the aircraft. The Dornier then started to make what Beardsley described as short jerky dives and followed it down to the haze where he lost sight of it.

Flying Officer Lamb claimed a 110 destroyed between Tunbridge Wells and Rye, but Sergeant Manton (in R6629 DW-E) was shot down and killed, his Spitfire crashing at Gatwick at 4:00pm. He was later buried at Hawkhurst cemetery.

Despite the claims of 610 Squadron, no ME110's or Dornier's where lost according to Luftwaffe records and no enemy claims were made which matched the loss of Sergeant Manton.

610 Squadron returned to Biggin Hill and were not on the ground long, when they were scrambled once again at 6:00pm. They were vectored towards Folkestone and ordered to patrol over RAF Hawkinge at 25,000 feet.

They soon tangled with a formation of ME109E's just off Dungeness and Sergeants Beardsley and Baker made claims.

Sergeant Beardsley became separated from the rest of 610 Squadron and found himself against six 109's. He delivered a beam attack on one 109 and it went down in a deep diving turn. He was then attacked by the other 109's and managed to escape. He claimed the 109 as a probable.

Sergeant Baker saw a 109 on the tail of a Spitfire and latched onto its tail. His initial short two second burst made the 109 break off its pursuit of the Spitfire. As it turned away, he followed it and fired again, causing it to belch black smoke and dive away towards the sea. He did not see it crash but the 4th Staffel of JG3 lost Uffz. Gericke and Oberleutant Wipper at this time. Wipper force landed at New Lodge Farm, Hooe, sadly being recovered and given first aid, he died of his wounds.

610 Squadron returned home by 7:30pm and were released for the night. There was no further action that day.

Friday the 30th of August 1940 was another fair day in terms of the weather, but it was a day when Biggin Hill was almost knocked out of the battle.

At 10:30am about one hundred and twenty Heinkel 111's, Dornier 17's and their 109 escort were sighted over the Channel. Twenty minutes later Fighter Command controllers scrambled 79 and 610 Squadrons together with 43, 85, 111, 222, 253, 603 and 616 Squadrons.

Squadron Leader John Ellis led his ten Spitfires of 610 towards the coast where they made a head on attack against the Heinkel formation. Flying Officer Lamb claimed to have shot down a Heinkel and this was confirmed by both Sergeants Chandler and Beardsley.

Sergeant Ronald Hamlyn (Green Leader) was attacked by a formation of ME110's at 20,000 feet and he dived down to 10,000 feet and headed home to Biggin Hill. As he arrived at the airfield a major raid was dropping bombs all over the aerodrome at noon. He climbed back up to 20,000 feet and was attacked by a formation of five ME109E's from above. Hamlyn reported getting on the tail of the last aircraft and shooting him down. He claims it was near West Malling airfield and there was a fire in a nearby wood which he thought was the Messerschmitt 109. (I have been unable to locate this aircraft/crash for this date in Luftwaffe and British records).

Sergeant Beardlsey attacked a Heinkel 111 near Hawkinge and caused the starboard engine to smoke and the undercarriage to drop down. He attacked it again as it crossed the coast and out to sea. Beardsley attacked once more, and the bomber turned back for the coast between Dungeness and Folkestone. Beardsley dived on it a few times and the crew fired off four red verey lights (flares) possibly indicating that they were critically damaged and asking the British pilot to give them some quarter.

The Heinkel eventually ditched in the sea just off the coast near Dymchurch and the crew were rescued by a motorboat. The crew of the Heinkel from 10/KG1 consisting of Unteroffizier Burger, Gefreiter Hildebrand, Gefreiter Feierabend, Gefreiter Roggemann and Gefreiter Klappholz; were detained and taken to Dover.

Pilot Officer Pegge also shot down a Heinkel 111 from 1/KG1. In his combat report he reported attacking the lead bomber in a vic-formation which went straight down and into the sea, although later reports indicate that the aircraft of Oberfeldwebel Rauschert crashed at Roy Hill in Sussex at 11:25am. Flieger Zinoegger was killed, while Uffz. Stein and Feldwebel Ester were captured but injured. Sadly, Ester later died of his injuries.

Pilot Officer Eric Aldous claimed to have damaged a Heinkel 111 near Ashford and fired at a ME110 without any visible results.

Sergeant Chandler claimed a ME110 probable near Lympne. He had made a head on attack against fifteen Dornier's at 13,000 feet and he carried on into a formation of 110's 2,000 feet above them. He fired at one 110 and caused one of the engines to emit smoke before it dived away heading for France. This was possibly an aircraft from 3/ZG76 which returned to Calais-Marck on one engine with the two-man crew unharmed.

Sergeant Baker claimed a Dornier 17 damaged with an engine smoking, but only one Dornier 17 was lost that day. An aircraft of 9/KG2 crashed near Brugge, three of the crew were killed and one wounded. However, records do not cite the cause.

Meanwhile, 79 Squadron had joined the fray and Pilot Officer 'Teddy' Morris hit a Heinkel 111 from 5/KG1. He attacked head on but pressed home his attack too far, colliding with the bomber over Reigate. He broke his leg in the collision and his Hurricane fell to earth at Brockham. Somehow, he managed to get out of the fighter and pulled his ripcord. He came down without further injury before being taken to hospital. The Heinkel crashed at Swires Farm, Capel, Sussex. Oberfeldwebel Hornick, Feldwebel Stahlberg and Gefreiter Heimel were killed. Hauptmann Baess the Staffel Kapitan was severely wounded and Oberleutnant Foelisch was captured uninjured.

Pilot Officer 'Dimsie' Stones a very experienced pilot also attacked the bombers damaging two Dornier 17's. He then saw tracer fire passing him from the rear before the offending 109 passed him and was chased by a Spitfire.

Elsewhere, Pilot Officer Millington Mayhew returned to base with a damaged aircraft after being hit by a Messerschmitt 109E.

At about midday a high-level formation dropped its bombs on Biggin Hill. This time the bombing was heavy, and the landing area became pock-marked with deep craters and unexploded bombs. Ground crews placed red flags to mark the unexploded devices and the returning Pilots had to carefully land between them. Biggin Hill was so badly damaged that 79 Squadron were ordered to land at Hawkinge.

One hundred and fifty bombers and their escort had attacked Biggin Hill. Thankfully for the airfield, most of the bombs had missed the airfield and struck the villages of Biggin Hill and Keston causing some casualties.

The airfield's workshops, cookhouses and the NAAFI were all destroyed as were many vehicles. One hangar was destroyed, and two aircraft were burnt-out. The electricity, gas and telephone lines were all cut by bombs and a WAAF's trench shelter was hit and another had a near miss. As the bombing stopped the Spitfires of 610 Squadron started to return home.

Amazingly the WAAF trench shelter despite being destroyed had no fatalities, although many were injured. Sadly, a NAAFI girl and some WAAF's were killed on other parts of the airfield.

A huge amount of work managed to get the airfield back in operation and at about 3:00pm, ten Hurricanes of 79 Squadron left Hawkinge for Biggin Hill.

At 3:20pm 610 Squadron's 'A' Flight were scrambled and ordered to patrol over Biggin Hill at 18,000 feet. At 3:40pm a small formation of ME109E's appeared and Sergeant Chandler claimed to have shot one down. A gunner on the ground claimed to see the pilot bail out, but no aircraft loss appears to match this claim.

At 4:35pm 79 Squadron's 'A' Flight took off with five Hurricanes. As they took off, they spotted a formation of 109's above them but the leader did not order an attack. Pilot Officer Trevor Bryant-Fenn alone attacked and damaged a 109.

At 6:05pm six aircraft from 79 took off and were forming up as Biggin Hill was bombed once again. A formation of nine Junkers 88's flew across the airfield at less than 1,000 feet and dropped their bombs, as ME110's and 109's bounced 79 Squadron. The airfields defences and ground crews were caught unprepared and no siren had sounded as they attacked. Pilot Officer Paul Mayhew had his rudder shot away, but he managed to get down safely. Flight Lieutenant Haysom claimed to have got a probable 109 and Sergeant Henry Bolton claimed one too. Eventually the action fizzled out and the squadron returned safely and landed at 6:30pm. No ME109's appeared to have been lost in this action.

The air raid had rendered many of the airfields buildings too dangerous to use and others were destroyed. The armoury, guardroom, stores, barracks and the technical sites were hit hard. Another shelter was hit, and thirty-nine personnel were killed and another twenty-six wounded. It took all night to dig the wounded and deceased out.

Section Officer Felicity Hanbury was in a shelter during the raid and when the all clear was given, she exited to find chaos and destruction everywhere. A NAAFI girl was being laid out by airmen and covered with a blanket. In a state of shock, she lit a cigarette, oblivious to the smell of gas from the ruptured mains. A male shouted at her to put the fag out which she hastily did. This little piece of action would later be immortalised in the 1969 classic film 'Battle of Britain' when the actress Suzannah York repeated the 'error'.

The next day 610 Squadron were ordered north to RAF Acklington to join their old associates 32 Squadron. 72 Squadron were to replace them at Biggin Hill with their Spitfires.

Saturday the 31st of August started in many ways like the other days. 610 Squadron made their way to Acklington and the airfield awaited the arrival of 72 Squadron. 79 for a short time had the airfield to themselves.

The squadron were on dawn readiness, when at 7:55am the RDF stations identified three formations heading towards the south east. One was over the English Channel and heading for Dover and Dungeness, while the other two where over the Thames Estuary. Fighter Controllers scrambled two squadrons, but the first formation over the Thames was made up of fighters, so they were recalled. However, 253 Squadron became embroiled in a fierce dogfight losing three of their aircraft, while 1 Squadron RCAF managed to return unharmed. By 8:15am a large formation of bombers attacked North Weald and Hornchurch airfields in Essex.

At 8:40am 79 Squadron were ordered to take off and patrol over their base. They were then directed towards Dover and ended up in a dogfight with a formation of ME109E's and their Junkers 88 charges.

Flight Lieutenant Haysom claimed a 109 destroyed between Dover and Canterbury and Pilot Officer Millington claimed two more. Squadron Leader Heyworth claimed a JU88 probable, but none appear to have crashed in the UK that day. Pilot Officer Nelson-Edwards who had transferred from 610 Squadron was hit badly by a ME109 and managed to limp back towards Biggin Hill. He crash-landed at Limpsfield near Biggin at 9:30am. His aircraft N2345 was written off and he sustained a wound to his eye.

It appears, their antagonists may have been the Messerschmitt's of JG2. They made a number of victory claims at this time around Dover, but they only lost one aircraft from 2/JG2 which ditched in the Channel with the pilot being rescued.

2/JG77 was also involved and lost one pilot with Oberleutnant Eckehart Priebe being hit by a Hurricane. He baled-out wounded at 5,000 feet as his 109 crashed at Elham Park Wood near Folkestone at 9:30am. He was quickly captured and taken to hospital.

The squadron were heading back to Biggin Hill but were directed to land at 10:00am at RAF Croydon. This was because another raid was on its way towards Biggin Hill. At noon over one hundred bombers made up of Dornier's and Heinkel 111's was detected over Dungeness with a fighter escort.

At 12:30pm 79 Squadron was scrambled but could not get to the bombers due to their escorting fighter cover. In a brief fight, Pilot Officers Millington and Bryant-Fenn claimed a 109 each, while Pilot Officer Noble claimed a probable and a damaged 109.

JG77 were heavily engaged and lost aircraft to the other RAF squadrons with specific losses being attributed to 601 and 603 Squadron pilots. However, they also lost Uffz. Keck of 1/JG77 at 1:20pm at Boxley near Maidstone; while the ME109 of Feldwebel Gunther Kramer came down at Shoremead Fort near Gravesend at 1:20pm after a Hurricane attack. The pilot from 1/JG77 survived but was badly burnt having baled-out.

79 Squadron withdrew and were heading for home but had to land at Croydon again due to the bombing at Biggin Hill. However, Croydon had also been bombed and they had to land between craters on that airfield or at nearby Kenley.

At 1:00pm another formation of raiders dropped their loads on Biggin Hill and most of the previously undamaged buildings and hangars were hit and a number of ground personnel were killed and wounded. The Operations Room was now out of action as were the telephone lines once again. Biggin Hill as an airfield and sector base was close to complete destruction.

Just after lunch time, 72 Squadron's Spitfires arrived at Biggin Hill. They landed singly, picking their way through the bomb craters left from the recent raid. As they landed, they were quickly refueled and readied for action. Sixteen aircraft landed and as they arrived another pilot from the squadron who had travelled on ahead of the formation took over the aircraft. The squadron were lucky in having extra pilots so that the arriving pilots were allowed to settle in and rest before going on stand-by.

At around 4:30pm, six of 79 Squadron's Hurricanes took off to fly from Kenley to Biggin Hill. En route Sergeant Henry Bolton was attacked by ME109E's and tried to land his Hurricane serial number V7200, at Haililoo Farm at Warlingham but he was killed in doing so. It is unknown who the victor was.

Eventually 79 Squadron returned to Biggin Hill and at 5:45pm they sent seven aircraft to patrol over the airfield. In no time at all, 72 Squadron's Spitfires were also scrambled as the Luftwaffe arrived for another raid on Biggin.

As the two squadrons tried to gain height a formation of Dornier 17's and Junkers 88's swung towards Biggin Hill. The grass runways were plastered with more bombs and the few buildings that had not been damaged were struck causing further casualties. The South Camp hangar was badly damaged as was one of the triple bay hangars on the Northern Camp. Over the previous two days over fifty Biggin Hill personnel had been killed. Once again, all the telephone lines were cut including the emergency lines set up the day before. The Operations room was therefore 'cut off' from its HQ and squadrons. The Officers Mess and married quarters were also damaged, while four of 72 Squadron's Spitfires were destroyed on the ground and the station armoury was on fire. Fire engines and ambulances started to arrive from Bromley and the surrounding district as the raiders made off.

79 and 72 Squadrons having gained height attacked the raiders as they left the area. Pilot Officer Millington of 79 Squadron was giving chase to a Dornier which he damaged, when he was bounced by two Messerschmitt 109's. He managed to shake one off and attacked the other sending it down to make a forced landing on Romney Marsh. He then made the capital error of watching the pilot dragging himself from the wreckage, when the other 109 hit him. Cannon and machine gun shells racked the Hurricane and Millington was covered in hot oil as the engine was shattered. He was also hit in the left thigh and burnt, but he managed to make a forced landing at Hawkhurst. He was taken to Croydon hospital for treatment.

The ME109 he shot down was that of Oberleutnant Westerhoff of 6/JG3, a very experienced pilot who crashed on Lydd ranges near Dungeness at 6:30pm. Westerhoff was badly burned and captured.

Pilot Officer 'Teddy' Morris damaged a Dornier over Biggin Hill before he was damaged by a 109 and wounded in P3877. He made a forced landing at Biggin Hill airfield.

Pilot Officer 'Dimsie' Stones also claimed a Dornier destroyed and another probable, while Pilot Officer Tracey claimed one.

72 Squadrons Spitfires were ordered on to a patrol around 6pm and vectored towards Dungeness. They located a large formation of Dornier 17's over Rochester as they were climbing and attacked them.

Flight Sergeant Jack Steere in his combat report stated that the Spitfires were at 6,000 feet with the bombers at 11,000 feet. Steere who was Blue 3 made a frontal to quarter attack on one of thirty Dornier's and saw it 'wobble' as his rounds struck home. As he passed the formation, he moved away due to heavy return fire, but saw another formation of thirty Dornier's heading northwards. He carried out a similar attack on this formation but due to his rate of climb and firing his guns, he stalled and spun away. He therefore returned home claiming a Dornier damaged.

Flight Lieutenant Edward Graham and Sergeant Maurice Pocock also claimed to have damaged a Dornier each.

Elsewhere at 6:35pm, Flight Lieutenant Smith was shot down over Dungeness and bailed out with bad burns. His aircraft P9438 crashed at New Romney. It is possible he was shot down by a pilot of JG26 who had the whole Geshwader in the air at that time and place, but there were so many claims they cannot be linked with certainty.

Half an hour later and Flying Officer John Wilcox was also shot down and killed by an unknown aggressor. He had been in combat over Dungeness with Smith and crashed in

P9457 at Hungerford Field, Chickenden Farm, Staplehurst. Wilcox's body was recovered, and he was buried in All Saints churchyard in the town.

The squadron returned to Biggin Hill and that was the end of operations for the day. Many of the Sergeant Pilots headed off for a drink at the local pubs, while ground crews went to the Old Jail pub just outside the airfield boundary after servicing the aircraft. It is said that many of the ground crew would go through the boundary hedge for a pint.

It had been a hard day of fighting and sadly 72 Squadron had lost a pilot after only arriving at lunch time.

Chapter 6.

Towards a change of tactics

The 1st of September 1940 was a Sunday morning. It was cloudy and over fifty flag draped coffins awaited burial at the nearby cemetery. Group Captain Grice and the padre together with some relatives and friends were in attendance to bury Biggin Hill's dead.

At 7:45am 72 Squadron were ordered to move to Croydon as Biggin Hill was still too badly damaged for the operation of two squadrons. Anti-Aircraft Command had sent further 40mm Bofors guns to defend the airfield and found the base in a state of organised chaos. The airmen servicing, re-fueling, and re-arming the aircraft were a scruffy lot. Some hadn't shaved for a few days and had worn the same clothes for just as long, most of their barracks were in ruins and so too were their personal effects. Eventually some were sent off to Bromley to bathe and replacement uniforms and personal effects replaced.

It was just after 10am and there would be no peaceful funeral ceremony. Instead, the Observer Corps and the RDF chain had identified a large formation of Messerschmitt 109's on a 'Frei Jagd' (Free hunt). The Fighter Controllers wisely ignored this formation and concentrated their efforts on the second group that was forming up behind them. This contained sixty plus Dornier 17's, ME110's and an escort of 109's.

As the formation moved across Kent, it split up and hit the airfields at Detling, Eastchurch, Rochford and on to Biggin Hill. Ten fighter squadrons were scrambled, but at 10:45am 72 Squadron were ordered to scramble from Croydon and intercept bandits over Tunbridge Wells.

At 11:05am eight Hurricanes of 79 Squadron roared into the air from Biggin Hill as the funeral was underway. The air raid sirens sounded leaving the mourners to pause and look about them. As the Hurricanes left the airfield there was a drone of engines as the bombers arrived and delivered another blow to Biggin. Soon bombs began to fall and there was a pause in the service as the mourners took cover.

By this time, some fourteen fighter squadrons were airborne, and 54 Squadron joined 72 over Kent. They soon encountered a formation of over one hundred Dornier's and their ME109E escort between Gatwick, Rye and Beachy Head. In the following few minutes Flying Officer 'Pancho' Villa damaged a 109 sending it down with black smoke pouring from its engine. However, he had to spin away when three others attacked him. Pilot Officer Douglas

Winter claimed a HE113 fighter destroyed over Beachy Head, but the Heinkel was a test fighter which never entered production. Despite this, pilots had been briefed about them by intelligence and often mistook a ME109's for a HE113. This was surely the case with Winter.

Pilot Officer Basil Douthwaite claimed a 109 between Gatwick and Rye, but he was damaged in the action and made a forced landing with a dead engine at West Malling at 11:30am, he was not injured. Sergeant Malcolm Gray claimed a probable Dornier 17 two miles west of Rye in East Sussex.

However, Flying Officer Thompson baled-out wounded over Hythe after being attacked by the ME109's. His Spitfire crashed onto a bungalow at Stelling Minnis, a village between Canterbury and Folkestone.

Flying Officer Oswald Pigge was shot down and killed at 11:15am Pluckley, Kent; while Sergeant Maurice Pocock was wounded in the arm and leg by a 109 and also crash landed at West Malling airfield at 11:40am.

Flying Officer Desmond Sheen in X4109 was shot down when he was bounced by 109's over Ham Street at 11:52am. He managed to bail out uninjured; while Flight Lieutenant Edward Graham returned with a damaged oil system and Sergeant Norman Norfolk returned with a damaged tail unit.

72 Squadron had been badly hit. Elements of JG53 and JG54 were all in the area and made numerous claims for victories. 2/JG54 lost Oberleutnant Stangl when he came down at Bonnington near Ashford at 11:15am and was captured. A 3/JG53 aircraft came down near Rye and was attributed to an 85 Squadron pilot, and a number returned home with various degrees of damage.

At Biggin Hill the air raid had ended, and the funeral was allowed to continue. The eight Hurricanes of 79 Squadron were not involved in any action although they had seen aircraft and anti-aircraft fire over Gravesend. They landed at 12:10pm and were immediately refueled.

At 1:00pm 72 Squadron were ordered to take off from Croydon and patrol over Hawkinge at 14,000 feet. Flight Lieutenant Edward Graham led ten Spitfires down towards the coast.

At 1:30pm a large formation of over one hundred and fifty Dornier 17's, ME 110's and ME109E's started to head inland at Dungeness. 72 Squadron attacked the formation between the coast and Ashford, but were bounced by yellow nosed Messerschmitt 109's. Flight Sergeant Jack Steere claimed a 109 probably destroyed stating in his combat report, that after moving into line astern, he attacked a 109 and caused black smoke to come from its engine. The 109 stalled and fell away but Steer could not follow him due to the number of fighters around him. Another ME109E got onto Steere's tail and he shook this off. The 109 diving away towards Dover at 10,000 feet and Steere got onto the tail of another 109, but he had to break off as another attacked him. Jack Steere eventually broke off from the engagement and headed back to Croydon.

The raiders headed for Biggin Hill and dropped more bombs on to the airfield either destroying or damaging what few buildings were left to inhabit. Three WAAF teleprinter operators would be awarded the Military Medal for their brave exploits in dealing with the post-raid situation on the airfield. They dealt with several unexploded and delayed action bombs.

Pilot Officer Deacon-Elliott claimed a probable 109, while Flight Lieutenant Graham claimed to have damaged two and Flying Officer Villa another. Pilot Officer Thomas Elsdon claimed to have shot down two ME110's.

79 Squadron were scrambled from Biggin Hill at 2:00pm to re-enforce 72 Squadron and other units in the area. They engaged the bombers and their escorts between Maidstone and Biggin Hill.

Pilot Officer 'Dimsie' Stones attacked a Dornier 17 over Biggin Hill and damaged it. He attacked the rear most bomber from the stern and fired into the port wing and engine before breaking off. He claimed there were over a hundred 109's and 110's in the area, making life very difficult. Interestingly in his combat report he mentioned hearing a great deal of German talk over the R/T, meaning the radio bands were being mixed up.

Pilot Officer Paul Mayhew claimed a 110 destroyed at Brastead at about 2:00pm, but the escorts wounded Pilot Officer Bryant-Fenn who managed to land his Hurricane at Biggin Hill and was taken to hospital. Flight Lieutenant Haysom was shot down but made a forced landing at 2:45pm.

79's Pilot Officer Peters claimed a probable Dornier 17 and Pilot Officer Douglas Clift a probable 110. When the squadron returned to base Pilot Officer Brian Noble was found to be missing, he had been shot down and taken to hospital. His Hurricane L2062 came down at Court Road, Chelsfield near Orpington after being hit by a Messerschmitt 109 and he was taken to the local hospital. 79 Squadron returned to Biggin Hill at 3:00pm.

72 Squadron returned home with no casualties and landed before 79 at 2:30pm. Their antagonists appear to have been Adolf Galland's JG26. Four of their pilots including the aces Hauptmann Gerhard Schopfel and Oberleutnant Burschegens made claims for Spitfires at this time and location. 7/JG26 did lose Oberleutnant Josef Burschegens after he had shot down a machine but made a force-landed near Rye. He informed his RAF interrogators that he had been hit by stray rounds from the rear gunner of a 110, as he tried to attack a Spitfire which was attacking a circle of 110's. Whether this is true or not is open to speculation.

The evening was finally quiet for Biggin Hill and its squadrons. There was no further action for 72 and 79 Squadrons on the 1st of September 1940.

Biggin Hill's Operations Room was out of action and a temporary one was set up in a shop in Biggin Hill village on the Main Road. The shop still stands and many people who attend it today will be unaware of its valuable history. Later a full operations room was set up in Towerfield House, a Victorian mansion in Keston to the North West of the airfield. This is now a residential house with a flat's in it. How many of the residents today know of its valued 1940's past?

Monday the 2nd of September was a bright day with little or no cloud. At 7:30pm the RDF stations started to track two formations heading for Dungeness and the Thames Estuary. The formations were believed to consist of forty plus Dornier 17's, thirty plus Junkers 88's and over fifty ME109's covering each section.

At 7:30am 79 Squadron were ordered to take off from Biggin with just six Hurricanes, while 72 were scrambled from Croydon and vectored on to 110 degrees and Angels 15 (15,000 feet). Interestingly, the 72 Squadron formation consisted of only eight aircraft all piloted by Sergeants as the officers according to Bill Rolls in his biography (Spitfire Attack) had been away from their dispersal when the call came to scramble.

72 met a formation of Dornier 17's and ME110's between Maidstone and Chatham. The formation had over thirty bombers at 13,000 feet with the fighters up to 30,000 feet above them. Sergeant Bill Rolls in his combat report was Green 1. He saw a ME110 dive onto the tail of a Spitfire and he in turn got onto the 110's tail. He aimed at the port engine and fired causing it to catch fire and part of the wing to break away. The 110 went down on its back with the wing on fire. He then dived after a Dornier 17 and emptied all his ammunition into it causing the port engine to catch fire and the fuselage to blow to pieces. A ME109E got on his tail and he went into a spin to escape it. The Dornier crashed into a wood north east of Maidstone, with three parachutes coming down. Rolls headed home.

Although Rolls claims the Dornier crashed, only one was lost that day according to Luftwaffe records and that was at 4:00pm. Therefore, it is likely 'his' got home and the aircraft he saw crashing to earth was the 110 he had fired at. A 2/ZG26 ME110 flown by Feldwebel Schuetz and Gefr. Stuewe crashed at White Horse Wood, Birling near Maidstone at 8:10am. Sadly, Schuetz was killed but Stuewe was captured wounded.

Sergeant Jack Steere in his combat report states that the Spitfires moved into line astern behind him and attacked the formation. He attacked a 110 as it crossed his nose three miles south of Chatham and caused one engine to emit smoke. As Steere turned after him, he blacked out due to the effects of gravity; when he came to the ME110 had disappeared.

Sergeant John White claimed a Dornier 17 destroyed and Sergeant Gray a probable Dornier 17 near Maidstone.

The Sergeant pilots returned to Croydon and were on the ground by 8:45am, where according to Bill Rolls the irate officers were waiting for them! They were not pleased that the Sergeant Pilots had gone up without an officer, but this attitude soon changed.

While 79 Squadron remained on the ground at Biggin Hill for the rest of the day, while 72 Squadron were sent aloft at 12:10pm and told to fly to Dover at 15,000 feet. They were soon engaged with a number of Dornier 17's and their ME110 escort between Canterbury and Herne Bay.

Flight Sergeant Jack Steere claimed a 110 near Canterbury, stating in his combat report that they saw fifty ME110's over Herne Bay, but they started to form defensive circles as the Spitfires approached them. As he dived onto a circle, a 110 broke away and he followed it down firing at it. The 110 dived straight into the ground and exploded between Dover and Canterbury near Knowlton station. Steere returned to Hawkinge and refueled and re-armed. The aircraft he hit was that of Feldwebel Beil and Ogefr. Oehl from 6/ZG2 which crashed at Venson Farm, Eastry, a mile or so from Knowlton.

Flying Officer 'Pancho' Villa attacked four ME110's in their defensive circle climbing and diving while opening fire several times. He claimed to have shot one down, another probably destroyed and two damaged. Another 110 from 2/ZG2 force landed near St. Radigund's Abbey, West Hougham, Dover at 1:00pm. The gunner Gefr. Schockenhoff baled out uninjured, while the pilot Leutnant Schipper force landed the machine and set the aircraft alight. He too was unharmed and both men were soon captured.

ZG2 lost another aircraft, that of Uffz. Deuker and Uffz. Krapp which went missing, while another returned to Berck-sur-Mer and force landed due to combat damage.

Flight Lieutenant Graham, Sergeant Norfolk claimed to have damaged two 110's and Squadron Leader Collins a probable 110. Sergeant Douthwaite claimed a probable Dornier 17. However, it was not all one-way traffic, and Sergeant Norfolk after damaging a 110 was hit by one and force landed at Bekesbourne near Canterbury, writing off his Spitfire K9938 in the process.

At 3:55pm eight aircraft from 72 Squadron took off to patrol Dungeness. Interestingly the leader, Flight Lieutenant Graham was flying a 610 Squadron Spitfire which had been left behind when they had moved to Acklington. This machine was still carrying its 610 markings DW-S (X4241). The four machines soon tangled with 110's once again and claimed four to have been damaged, although the 610 Squadron machine was unlucky for Flight Lieutenant Graham who was shot down over Lympne. Luckily, Graham escaped injury. In addition, Wing Commander R. B. Lees who was flying with the squadron was wounded over Dungeness and crash landed his Spitfire at RAF Hawkinge.

At 5:10pm six aircraft of 72 Squadron took off from Croydon to patrol over their parent airfield of Biggin Hill. There were vectored by the controller towards Chatham, where at

6:00pm they engaged a number of Messerschmitt 109's. The 109's of LG2 made a number of claims for Spitfires around the Isle of Sheppey at this time, but all of the 72 Squadron machines returned home. Squadron Leader Collins flying another old 610 machine marked DW-N (R6806), was damaged over the Thames. He managed to land the aircraft, which was written off, even though he was wounded.

This brought to an end the action on the 2nd of September. The next day would bring some respite, even though it was a fair day with some cloud at 4-6,000 feet. Both sides needed to take stock of their losses and machines needed to be services and repaired.

The two Biggin Hill squadrons were up early and at dispersal on the morning of the 3rd. At 9:30am a large formation of fifty plus Dornier 17's, eight ME110's and forty plus ME109E's headed up the Thames Estuary. They went on to bomb the airfields at North Weald, Hornchurch and Debden in Essex.

72 Squadron remained on the ground all day, but 79 sent six aircraft up at 10:30am as they expected another raid on Biggin Hill and they patrolled overhead. When the raid moved towards the Essex airfields, 79 Squadron landed without making any contact at 11:15am.

At about 2:20pm another patrol was carried out by 79 Squadron and another at 3:25pm. One Spitfire was lost at 2:45pm over Marden when the pilot who is unidentified in records baled out and the aircraft crashed and burned out. The cause is unknown, and the pilot appears to have been uninjured. It may have been due to a technical fault.

There was no further action for the Biggin Hill squadrons that day and the pilots went off to relax while the ground crews repaired and serviced the aircraft once again.

On Wednesday the 4th September, 72 Squadron continued to operate from Croydon as repair work continued at Biggin Hill. The morning was misty, but it soon gave way to a fine clear day with good visibility.

At 8:30am enemy formations were seen over the Channel. The Luftwaffe intelligence was still faulty and at 9:30am bombers hit the secondary airfields at Eastchurch and Lympne once again, while the barrage balloons at Dover were shot-up by fighters.

At 9:20am 79 Squadron sent six aircraft aloft to patrol the airfield at 20,000 feet. After forty minutes they landed without incident.

At 12:30pm a hundred plus Heinkel's and Dornier's with an escort of two hundred ME110's and ME109E's headed in land from Folkestone and Dungeness. A total of fourteen fighter squadrons would soon be scrambled to deal with the huge formation.

At 12:55pm 72 Squadron scrambled nine Spitfires who were vectored towards the in-coming raid. Fifteen minutes later, six Hurricanes from 79 Squadron took off from Biggin Hill and were also vectored onto the incoming raiders.

72 Squadron soon encountered a formation of 110's in the area between Tunbridge Wells, Tenterden and Ashford, while 79 Squadron also met a unit of Messerschmitt 110's over Beachy Head.

The ME110's from ZG76 were attacked by 72 Squadron who had formed their sections into line astern. Flying Officer 'Pancho' Villa reported diving into attack them and they immediately formed a defensive circle once again. He fired at two 110's and had to keep diving to avoid other 110's in the circle. He then got on to the tail of another and hit it hard. The ME110 caught fire and dived away to the left. Villa fired at another 110 which was one of four which had broken off from the circle and were trying to escape to the coast. This one started to emit smoke, but he broke off and returned home as he was short of fuel.

Flying Officer Thomas Elsdon claimed two 110's destroyed, Pilot Officer Dennis Holland claimed one destroyed and one damaged. Desmond Sheen claimed a 110 probable while Sergeant Bill Rolls, also made claims in his combat report. He claimed two Junkers 86's destroyed between Ashford and Tunbridge Wells. This is odd as the JU86 was a rare high-level bomber and reconnaissance aircraft. It had twin engines and a twin tail, and in all probability, they were actually ME110's. One of them he claimed fell into a wood south east of Tunbridge Wells.

An examination of records finds this to have probably been that of Oberleutnant Piduhn and Gefr. Odene of 2/ZG76. They were killed when their Messerschmitt crashed at Cowden to the west of Tunbridge Wells at 1:23pm. (Pilots often got their distances and bearings wrong in their subsequent reports, as in the heat of battle the last thing on their mind was which side of Tunbridge Wells they were on!).

72 Squadron did sustain casualties themselves. Pilot Officer Elliott was hit and baled out at 1:20pm. His Spitfire crashed near Tenterden, while Pilot Officer Males was hit and set on fire before crashing to earth at Culvers Farm, Hartfield. He managed to bale out uninjured.

79 Squadron also fought the ME110's with Pilot Officer George Peters claiming one destroyed, and 'Dimsie' Stones one probable. The 110's had formed a defensive circle over Beachy Head at 15,000 feet, while Pilot Officer Thomas Parker claimed to have damaged two more.

In his combat report, 'Dimsie' Stones reported that as they formed a defensive circle, he approached them with Sergeant John Wright. He fired at one 110 and caused the port engine to catch fire and emit smoke. It fell away in a steep dive, but as they returned to base, Sergeant John Wright in P3676 was hit by a 110 and severely damaged and wounded at 1:40pm. He fought to control his Hurricane and crashed at Surbiton in Surrey. He was recovered and taken to hospital for emergency treatment, but sadly he died the next day. He was 24 years of age and was taken home to be buried in Dumbartonshire by his family.

The two squadrons returned home to Biggin and Croydon and there was no further action for them that day.

That afternoon, Group Captain Grice the station commander took to the sky above Biggin Hill in the Miles Magister. From 10,000 feet he surveyed his battered airfield. Although all the hangars and buildings were in various states of damage, one hangar looked intact from above even though internally it was burnt out. Upon landing he therefore decided to get the Royal Engineers to blow it up and prevent further loss of life. His thinking being that the Luftwaffe would not attack an airfield that looked out of action. His plan apparently worked, as there were no further large-scale day light attacks from the Luftwaffe during the battle and only minor raids followed.

Group Captain Grice was later called to answer for his actions and after giving his considered views, he was reprimanded by the board of enquiry for this unusual act.

The morning of the 5th of September was once again clear with good visibility. 72 Squadron were still detached to Croydon, while 79 Squadron remained at Biggin Hill.

At 10:00am an enemy formation started to make its way up the Thames Estuary. It split up and attacked the airfield at Eastchurch on the Isle of Sheppey and North Weald in Essex. Another raid hit Lympne near Folkestone. (Again, only North Weald housed fighter squadrons and the Luftwaffe intelligence was till faulty).

79 Squadron scrambled six Hurricanes of 'B' Flight from Biggin and attacked a small formation of Dornier 17's as they approached Biggin Hill. At 10:40am, Pilot Officer Tracey claimed a probable Dornier near Orpington. The Dornier's gunners and their escorting fighters did put up some resistance, and Flight Lieutenant Haysom landed forty minutes later with a shot-up port aileron. He immediately got into another aircraft and entered the fray once again. The pilot subsequently reported that there were forty Dornier's at 15,000 feet with about fifty to sixty fighters. All of 79 Squadron's aircraft landed by 11:10am without loss. The raid barely touching the airfield.

At 1:10pm eight Spitfires of 72 Squadron flew down to refuel and then patrol over RAF Hawkinge. They ran into a formation of Messerschmitt 109E's at 2:20pm and a dog fight ensued. The fighters had been escorting fifty plus Junkers 88 and Heinkel III bombers when they spotted the Spitfires. The battle was so hectic that Sergeant Bill Rolls remembered years later, being unable to get a bead on anyone as they were turning and twisting about so much.

Pilot Officer Holland claimed a Messerschmitt 109 destroyed and another one damaged, but the squadron lost three aircraft. Flying Officer Des Sheen was wounded and baled out of X4034, while Sergeant Malcolm Gray was missing when they returned home. Pilot Officer Douglas Winter was killed at Elham. He was too low when he baled out and was killed. Both Gray's and Winter's Spitfires crashed into woods at Elham, Kent.

Who the 109's belonged to is unknown, as I have been unable to positively identify the victors. No claims appear to exactly match these losses in terms of time on this day. However, JG2 made several claims south of Canterbury at 4:10pm (3:10pm local time?). Oberleutnant Otto Bertram claimed two Spitfires. At the same time Hauptmann Heinz Bretnutz of 6/JG53 claimed a Spitfire over Hawkinge which is about 3-5 miles south east of Elham at the same time.

In terms of losses that could match Pilot Officer Holland's claims, no JG2 aircraft losses match these claims.

The two RAF squadrons returned to their bases and at 3:00pm, 79 Squadron sent off another patrol, but they returned home without incident and were not called upon again this day.

Friday the 6th of September was misty at dawn, but this burned off to produce scattered clouds at 10,000 feet. At 8:50am 79 Squadron were ordered to send six Hurricanes up for airfield defence. A large formation of ME109E's and their Junkers 88 charges were believed to be on their way to bomb Biggin once again.

Pilot Officer George Nelson-Edwards was airborne as Red 2 and at 25,000 feet over nearby RAF Kenley. He saw a number of ME109's and JU88's 5,000 feet below the squadron. Picking out a JU88 on its own, Nelson-Edwards dived upon it firing a 5 second burst into the cockpit area before pulling out his dive. When he recovered from the dive the aircraft were nowhere to be seen and he returned to base to claim a probable JU88.

Squadron Leader Heyworth claimed a JU88 as damaged and Pilot Officer Bert Laycock claimed a probable ME109 near Redhill. Flight Lieutenant Rupert Clerke also claimed a probable 109 before they all returned to Biggin Hill without loss by 9:42am. The JU88's belonged to 6/KG76 who lost two aircraft on the raid, one crashing near Tonbridge and another into the sea off the Sussex coast.

At 10:00am another formation bombed Biggin Hill, causing minor damage to the dispersal areas and the landing ground, but most of the bombs thankfully landed on the far side of Westerham Road without causing much damage. The telephone system was down again for a short time, but compared to the August raids it seemed as if the Luftwaffe believed the airfield was out of action; and these smaller raids were just to ensure the RAF didn't get it back into action.

At 12:25pm, 72 Squadron who were still detached to Croydon, sent Flight Lieutenant Graham, Flying Officer Elliott and Sergeants Douthwaite and White on patrol. The four Spitfires ran into a unit of ME109E's and fought a brief but vicious dogfight. Pilot Officer Elliott claimed a ME109 destroyed near Marden in Kent; but he was shot down himself in N3070 and had to bale out. His Spitfire crashed at Wanshurst Green near Marden. 6/JG26 claimed three Spitfires at roughly this time over Littlestone some 20 miles to the south east of Marden. Oberleutnant Schneider claiming two of them in four minutes. It appears they were 72 Squadrons assailants, but they did not lose any 109's in reply. One of the other Spitfires was also damaged but returned to base with the unharmed pilot. The three remaining pilots were back on the ground by 1:35pm.

While 72 was airborne, 79 Squadron were up from 12:50pm. They were back on the ground without incident within an hour. Another patrol was flown at 5:50pm without incident and there was no further action for the two Biggin Hill units that day.

Saturday the 7th of September was a fine day with good visibility, but neither Biggin Hill squadron was active before 11:27am when six Hurricanes from 79 were ordered to take off and patrol over Biggin at 20,000 feet. After patrolling there was no sign of the Luftwaffe and they landed forty-five minutes later and had lunch.

At 4:30pm a large enemy formation was sighted, and seven 72 Squadron Spitfires were sent to patrol over the Thames Estuary. A few minutes later at 4:40pm, 'A' Flight of 79 Squadron (with six aircraft) took off to defend their airfield (Biggin Hill) against another approaching raid. Both formations would soon be in action.

72 Squadron attacked a formation of Heinkel 111 bombers east of Rochester and Flying Officer 'Pancho' Villa claimed one as probably destroyed. In his combat report he stated that he had attacked one from below in a quarter beam attack firing into the aircraft until he himself stalled and fell away. The Heinkel fell away in a dive, but he didn't see it crash. At 5,000 feet he saw Sergeant John White in R7022. White would also claim a probable Heinkel 111, but he was damaged by return fire and force landed on the 'K' site (a dummy airfield) near Eynsford east of Biggin Hill. Villa then returned to base to rearm and refuel as other raids were in-coming at the time.

Flying Officer Elsdon from 72 was hit hard by a 109 and sustained serious injuries to his knee and shoulder. Some-how, he managed to remain in control of his Spitfire (X4254) and crash landed back at Biggin Hill. He was taken to hospital and would be off operations for some time. The aircraft was however repairable.

It is possible the Heinkel 111 Flying officer Villa claimed was the one from 5/KG53 which came down at 5:30pm on the Isle of Grain. Two of the crew were wounded and another two were captured while the wireless operator Ogefr. Neumann was killed.

Within a few minutes of landing and refueling the 72 Squadron Spitfires were up again over their airfield. They were soon engaging a section of Dornier 17 bombers near Maidstone with Sergeant Norfolk claiming a Dornier 17 destroyed and five other pilots claiming several other Dornier's damaged.

Mean-while, six aircraft from 79 Squadron had been scrambled from Biggin Hill and attacked a formation of Dornier 17's with an escort of ME110's over the airfield. Squadron Leader

Heyworth led 'A' Flight into the formation and claimed a probable Dornier, as did Pilot Officer George Peters ten miles south east of the airfield.

Pilot Officer 'Dimsie' Stones bore into the formation aiming at one Dornier 17 in a frontal attack. He did not see any definitive damage but pulled round and found himself on the tail of a ME110. Taking careful aim, he was just about to fire when his Hurricane was raked from tail to cockpit by an unseen ME109.

Stones threw the Hurricane into a spiraling dive to shake off the 109, eventually flattening out at 2,000 feet. He had been wounded from flying splinters from the aircraft's structure. The Hurricane was badly damaged and virtually uncontrollable, with the fabric on the tail and fuselage torn to shreds, but it continued to fly.

Luckily, Stones saw an airfield ahead of him and gently put the Hurricane down on the grass with the wheels down. He taxied to a hangar and was removed from the cockpit and taken to the nearby Preston Hall hospital near Maidstone for treatment. Stones had been peppered with splinters in his leg which were removed under a local anesthetic. He had landed at the recently completed West Malling. The airfield was to become both a target and a refuge for fliers on both sides landing damaged aircraft during the battle.

It is possible that Stones was shot down by the German Ace Major Hannes Trautloft of JG54. He claimed a Hurricane over Maidstone at this time.

Both Squadrons were back on the ground by 6:30pm and there was no further activity that day. However, things were changing, and the Luftwaffe had bombed the East End docks in London. By evening, the residents of Biggin Hill could see the smoke rising from the docks a few miles to the north.

The next day (the 8th) 79 Squadron flew one last uneventful patrol before leaving for RAF Pembrey in South Wales. They were replaced by the Spitfires of 92 Squadron who made the reciprocal journey.

92 Squadron was a mixture of Volunteer Reserve Pilots and long service Commission pilots. They had a good reputation but could be a little 'unconventional' at times. Earlier in the war their Squadron Leader had been Roger Bushell who after being captured over Dunkirk would go on to become the officer in charge of escapes from the infamous Stalag Luft 111. He masterminded the Great Escape and was shot by the Gestapo in 1943.

With the movement of aircraft, the Biggin Hill squadrons were not involved in any combat on the 8th, but that would change the following day.

There was little flying due to early morning mist until late afternoon. At 4:30pm, 92 Squadron took off on their first combat flight from Biggin Hill. Squadron Leader Sanders led twelve Spitfires on a patrol near the airfield. As they started to patrol a large formation of

Heinkel 111 bombers and their ME109 escort arrived. 92 Squadron attacked the formation and harried it as it withdrew towards the coast near Rye in Sussex.

Squadron Leader Sanders claimed to have destroyed a Heinkel 111 near Biggin Hill and probably destroyed a 109. Flight Lieutenant Brian Kingcombe also claimed a probable Messerschmitt 109 in the area.

JG26 led by Hauptmann Gerhard Schopfel counter attacked the Spitfires. Pilot Officer Saunders in L1077 was hit and wounded with shrapnel in his leg, he crash-landed at Midley near Rye and was taken to RAMC Brookland for treatment.

Pilot Officer Watling was shot down and badly burnt near Biggin Hill. He managed to bale-out of P9372 and was taken to hospital. Pilot Officer Allan Wright's Spitfire was severely damaged but managed to return to Biggin Hill. Schopfel himself claimed three Spitfires, but he could not surpass his efforts of the 18th of August when he shot down four of 501 Squadron's Hurricanes over Canterbury. Leutnant Hermann Ripke also claimed a Spitfire at this time.

The Heinkel 111 that Sanders claimed may have been from 3/KG1 which crashed at Sundridge near Sevenoaks at about 6pm. The crew of Oberleutnant Kiunika were all captured with two of them being wounded.

At 5:40pm, 72 Squadron were scrambled and became engaged with a formation of Messerschmitt 110's to the south west of Croydon.

Pilot Officer Elliott claimed a ME110 destroyed at 5:50pm and this may have been the machine from 9/ZG76 piloted by Leutnant Eduard Ostermuncher and his gunner Gefr. Werner Zimmermann. They crashed at Woodmanstern, Surrey at 6:15pm a few miles south west of Croydon and west of Kenley. Both airmen died in the crash.

72 Squadron were back on the ground within half an hour and that ended their days participation. 92 however, sent three aircraft up at approximately 6:00pm, but there were no incidents, and the days flying was concluded.

Tuesday the 10th of September, 1940 was a cloudy day with occasional rain fall. At 10:30am 92 Squadron's Pilot Officer James Paterson went up alone on a weather test. He returned at midday without incident.

At 2:00pm Pilot Officer Roy Mottram flew another hour-long test and at 2:20pm, three Spitfires of 92 Squadron were sent to Hawkinge but no action was seen. The Luftwaffe appeared to have gone AWOL. The three Spitfires refueled at Hawkinge before flying a patrol out over the Channel towards Calais, but even this did not get a reaction from the Luftwaffe.

At 5:45pm Pilot Officer Trevor 'Wimpey' Wade and Sergeant Fokes took off from Biggin Hill and encountered a lone Dornier 17 bomber, believed to be from 9/KG76 near Biggin Hill at 6:05pm. In his later combat report Trevor Wade reported being ordered to take off and to patrol below the cloud layer over Biggin. At around 7,000 feet he and Ronald Fokes sighted the lone Dornier 17 at 10,000 feet. Wade made a stern attack and received fire from the rear gunner, but a burst from his eight Browning's stopped the fire and he believed he had killed the gunner. The Dornier dived into the cloud and Wade followed through the cloud to find the bomber again with its starboard engine smoking. Sergeant Fokes then attacked and the Dornier with its starboard engine now stopped, crashed into a clearing in a wood.

The aircraft is believed to have been that flown by Oberleutnant Walter Domenig, Uffz. Nurenberg, Uffz. Strahlendorf and Gefr. Greza. They came down at West Hoathly in West Sussex at 6:10pm, after making a lone armed reconnaissance to London. The crew ditched their bombs before coming down in the clearing. Walter Domenig and Uffz. Hans Strahldorf were killed and Uffz. Nurenberg seriously wounded and captured. Greza was captured uninjured. After their capture they reported being attacked by two Spitfires and hit by anti-aircraft fire from Gatwick airfield nearby. Wade and Fokes returned to Biggin Hill at 6:30pm to celebrate their victory. At the same time, the three aircraft from Hawkinge returned home to Biggin Hill.

Just before 6pm, 72 Squadron sent five of their Spitfires up to patrol. Three aircraft patrolled together, but Pilot Officers Villa and Ernie Males went separately. Villa later made a combat report claiming a shared Dornier with Pilot Officer Males. What is interesting is that his combat report is very similar to that of Wade's.

He reported being ordered to patrol Redhill just North of Gatwick airfield at 10,000 feet. The aircraft was just above the clouds and flying in a South Westerly course (away from Biggin Hill) towards Gatwick. He says he made an attack upon the Dornier and then further attacks before it went into the cloud and he lost sight of it with Pilot Officer Ernest Males also attacking it.

It appears that all four pilots may have attacked the same aircraft without seeing the other two. It appears the bomber crew also thought there were only two Spitfires when there were in fact four. However, each pilot appears to have been credited with a half victory each!!! While pilots may have over claimed on numerous occasions, even the authorities could over claim.

Wednesday the 11th September, started with a dawn mist and then variable cloud layers between 2,000 and 5,000 feet. This prevented a lot of morning aerial activity, but there were a few lone reconnaissance flights by the Luftwaffe.

At just after 3:00pm a formation of one hundred and fifty bombers with a similar number of 109 and 110 escorts headed across Kent. The Observer Corps spotted them at Foreness, Dover and Folkestone with smaller diversionary forces being seen crossing the coast.

At 3:30pm 72 Squadron who were still at Croydon, were scrambled to join thirteen other squadrons. Initially they were directed to patrol over Croydon before being moved forward towards Maidstone.

92 Squadron were also scrambled at 3:20pm and initially told to patrol Maidstone at 15,000 feet. Then they were vectored towards Dover and Folkestone by the fighter controllers.

Almost simultaneously the two squadrons were in action. 72 Squadron met a formation of Dornier 17's with a large escort of 110's and 109's east of Maidstone at 20,000 feet, at 3:50pm.

In his combat report, Sergeant Bill Rolls (Yellow 3) reported that the squadron made a beam attack on the bomber formation, but his section was by this time, making a stern attack. Rolls fired twice at a Dornier which shed pieces of its fuselage before diving away on its back and crashing near a wood and lake in the region of Cranbrook. Rolls started to climb again but ME109's were above him. He managed to fire at another Dornier which he damaged before he stalled and dropped away pursued by three Messerschmitt 109's. He managed to get away despite the 109's gun fire damaging his tail. He reported another Dornier shot down by Yellow 1 which crashed near his own claim at Cranbrook.

The other pilots also made various claims with Flight Lieutenant Edward Graham claiming a 109 damaged, Sergeant John Gilders a 110 destroyed and Pilot Officer Elliott and Sergeant Norfolk who claimed the other Dornier's destroyed at Cranbrook. Sergeant John White also claimed Dornier destroyed and another probable.

These claims are interesting as a retrospective search of Luftwaffe loss records shows that they did not lose any Dornier's over England on this day. They were operating over the area, but none were lost. They did however lose a number of ME110's around this time. One from 9/ZG26 (3U+LT) came down in a small wood called Barnes Cote at Harvel in Kent. It completely disintegrated and the two crewmen, consisting of Oberleutnant Joachim Junghans and Gefr. Paul Eckert were never found and are still missing, believed killed to this day. The site has been excavated by the Kent Battle of Britain Museum and various personal items, including Eckert's dog-tags found, which indicate that the two airmen's remains are probably still at this site in 2020 some eighty years later.

Pilot Officer Basil Douthwaite was wounded and force landed his Spitfire (R6710) at Gravesend airfield at 4:00pm before being taken to Gravesend hospital.

92 Squadron sighted a large formation of Heinkel 111's (KG1 and KG26) between Maidstone and Dungeness and attacked. The Messerschmitt 109 and 110 escort tried to intervene, but

seven pilots claimed to have destroyed Heinkel's with Flight Lieutenant Paterson claiming a 110 destroyed and Flying Officer John Drummond a 109 probably destroyed.

The pilots of 92 harried the bombers all the way down to the coast and Trevor 'Wimpey' Wade in his combat report states he saw a Heinkel with a Hurricane pulling away with smoke coming from it. He therefore attacked the Heinkel from astern and caused the starboard engine to stop. He then carried out two more attacks causing the engine to catch fire. The bomber made a forced landing in a field west north west of Lympne and the crew scrambled out dragging one 'body' out with them. The aircraft had a white letter 'A' on its fuselage. Wade satisfied with his 'work' landed at Lympne airfield to refuel and rearm, but as there was nothing available, he flew to Hawkinge and landed there.

Pilot Officer Desmond Williams also landed at Hawkinge to refuel before both pilots set out for Biggin Hill. Williams had claimed a Heinkel destroyed and in his combat report, stated that he saw another Spitfire attacking a Heinkel (Wade) and joined in. The Heinkel came down crashing through a hedge and the crew escaped with another injured man. This victory was shared with 'Wimpey' Wade.

It is difficult to ascribe individual losses to the claims as KG1 and KG26 lost a number of aircraft over England, with many others returning home badly damaged after fighter attacks. However, the fact Wade cites the white letter 'A' tends to indicate that he was responsible or partly responsible for shooting down the aircraft of Feldwebel Buttner, Hauptmann Kunstler (Staffel Kapitan), Feldwebel Schafer, Gefr. Schmidt and Uffz. Schang from 1/KG26. They had a visible white 'A' on their aircraft which came down at Gate Farm, Staplecross, East Sussex at 4:30pm. Sadly, Shafer and Schmidt were killed.

92 Squadron did however lose Pilot Officer Frederick Hargreaves. He was shot down in Spitfire K9793 at 4:15pm and is believed to have crashed into the sea off Dungeness. A number of Luftwaffe fighter pilots made claims around this time for a Spitfire in that area. However, by comparing records, it appears the most likely victor was Oberfeldwebel Georg Schott of 2/LG2 who claimed a Spitfire at 17:15 hours (CET) and therefore 4:15pm (BST) at Dungeness.

The remaining RAF aircraft all returned home, and it was thought there would be no more raids that day. However, at 5:45pm 92 Squadron launched another eight aircraft and were ordered to rendez-vous over Biggin Hill with 66 Squadron from Gravesend. Together they were vectored towards Ashford and Folkestone where they tangled with a formation of ME109E's believed to have been from Adolph Galland's JG26.

Squadron Leader Sanders and Pilot Officer Allan Wright both claimed probable 109's; but the squadron lost Pilot Officer Harry Edwards when he was shot down and killed crashing into a wood at Eve Gate Manor, Smeeth, Kent. At the time, he was posted missing but he was found a month later, on the 7th October by the local Home Guard. He was still in the cockpit of his Spitfire (P9464). He is buried in Hawkinge cemetery.

Flight Lieutenant James Paterson was also wounded by the 109's and crash-landed north east of Ashford. The victors appear to have been from the 7th and 8th Gruppen of JG26, with ace Oberleutnant Muncheberg claiming his 19th victory near Ashford, while Feldwebel Grzymalla claimed his sixth victory.

Pilot Officer 'Wimpy' Wade force landed his machine at Gravesend while the rest of the squadron returned home to Biggin Hill.

The 12th of September was a much quieter day, and 72 Squadron had no aerial movements at all. 92 Squadron made a number of flights for air tests, weather tests and patrols; but no enemy aircraft were encountered.

92 Squadron was happy to have Pilot Officer Tony Bartley arrive in an Avro Anson. He had been on leave when the squadron flew in from Pembrey and had not been informed of their move to Biggin. He returned to Pembrey after his leave to discover the squadron had gone without him and no one had thought of informing him! He subsequently caught a lift in an Anson and joined them at Biggin Hill.

In his autobiography 'Smoke trails in the sky', Tony Bartley graphically describes arriving at the badly damaged Biggin Hill, with filled in craters and damaged buildings. The Anson pilot who did not shut down the engines, gestured to him to get out quickly before he took off again and disappeared away from the wrecked aerodrome.

As Bartley spoke with his 92 Squadron colleagues a lone Junkers 88 flew across the airfield to a cacophony of Bofors gun shots before it too, disappeared from sight. This must have left quite an impression on the new arrival. Welcome to Biggin Hill!

The squadrons pilots rested and played with Brian Kingcombe's bulldog named 'Zeke'. He was a constant source of fun and regularly inebriated thanks to his penchant for beer. It is said that despite his alcoholic tendencies, he was a wise dog and would seek refuge in the air raid shelters during raids on the airfield.

Friday the 13th of September had a rainy start and a showery afternoon. One piece of good news was that 72 Squadron was being transferred back to Biggin Hill from Croydon. The raids against the airfields had lessened and repairs now allowed the two Spitfire squadrons to work side by side from Biggin once again.

There was however little flying on this day and apart from a few air tests, the aircraft stayed on the ground at Biggin Hill.

Unbeknown to many pilots, Hitler had ordered that the Luftwaffe start to hit Britain's cities and in particular, London.

The RAF had bombed Berlin on the 25th of August and the Luftwaffe accidentally hit London leading to five more RAF raids on Berlin in answer to the Luftwaffe raids. Hitler demanded on the 6th of September that London and other cities be hit. RAF Fighter Command and airfields like Biggin Hill were off the proverbial hook. The reduction in attacks on the airfields allowed squadrons like 72 to return to their mother base and for supply and control systems to be strengthened once again. This has been seen by many historians as a classic error by Hitler and Fighter Command grew in strength.

Chapter 7.

Towards Battle of Britain Day.

Saturday the 14th of September was a cloudy day with evening showers. Biggin Hill's two Spitfire squadrons remained on the ground until late morning.

At 11:40am 72 Squadron were scrambled, and five aircraft were ordered to patrol over Biggin Hill at 15,000 feet. In his autobiography, 'Spitfire attack' 72 Squadron's Bill Rolls recalls being airborne in the morning and tangling with ME109's and bombers as they headed back for France, but the Operations Record Book does not record this.

At 11:15am Pilot Officer 'Pancho' Villa and Sergeant White who had been two of the five to take off, shared in the destruction of a Heinkel 111 in the Halisham – Eastbourne area. It is believed that this was an aircraft from Stab KG55 which crashed into the sea just off the south coast. The crew of Leutnant's Parey and Schlink, Obergefr. Petersen, Gefr. Wanger and Uffz. Geiger were all picked up by a small boat and detained.

'Pacnho' Villa in his combat report states that they were ordered by controllers to take off and patrol over Biggin at 10:55am. Villa spotted a lone Heinkel 111 at 14,000 feet heading south. He opened-up his throttle and called for Blue two to keep up with him. Over Hailsham, he opened fire making a quarter attack which ended in a stern attack. The port engine started to emit white smoke and the flaps and undercarriage dropped down. Sergeant White also made attacks upon the wounded bomber which started to drop down. The aircraft was at 1,000 feet a few miles off Eastbourne when they left it. Observers however saw it crash into the sea.

There was a lull in operations until 3:15pm when large formations of Heinkel's, Dornier's and Junkers 88's with a large fighter escort started to gather over the English Channel. Just before 6:00pm when 92 Squadron were scrambled and vectored to patrol over Canterbury at 20,000 feet. Almost immediately, 72 Squadron was also scrambled and directed to patrol the Ashford area. A large formation of bombers and fighters was in bound from France and together with other fighter squadrons, the controllers were placing their squadrons like chess pieces on a board.

72 Squadron met a force of over fifty Messerschmitt 109E's near Canterbury. Sergeant Bill Rolls claimed a 109 which came down near Canterbury, while Pilot Officer Ernest Males also claimed one destroyed some five miles West of Lympne; and Pilot Officer John Lloyd

claimed another destroyed south of Ashford. However, Sergeant Howard Bell-Walker (K9960) was shot down and had to bale out over Ashford at 6:30pm. He was not injured.

Lloyd's 109 was possibly the one flown by Uffz. Blazejewski of 6/LG2. He baled out and the aircraft crashed at Thanet Wood, New Street Farm, Great Chart near Ashford at 6:35pm. No other ME109's where lost in the area at this time and it is likely the others returned home. It is not known who shot Bell-Walker down, but Uffz. Blazejewski when interrogated, claimed to have shot down a Spitfire before he himself was brought down.

72 Squadron returned to Biggin Hill where Howard Bell-Walker would later join them.

92 Squadron soon became embroiled in combat with the 109's over Canterbury at 6:30pm. Pilot Officer Tony Bartley damaged a 109 and claimed to have damaged a Dornier 17 as well. Flight Lieutenant Brian Kingcombe claimed to have damaged two ME109's and Flying Officer Allan Wright damaged another one.

Sergeant Robert McGowan was shot down by a 109 and crashed at Sole Street House, Faversham at 7:00pm. He was wounded but managed to bale out and was taken to Faversham hospital for treatment.

Sergeant 'Jacky' Mann was wounded over Canterbury in the same action, but he managed to return home and land his aircraft at Biggin Hill before he too was taken off to hospital; in his case to Orpington hospital.

It is once again difficult to identify specific losses and victories. There were various 109 Gruppen in the area and there are no 109 losses that can be matched up with the RAF pilots claims. 92 Squadron returned to Biggin Hill by 7:45pm, but Pilot Officer Patinson for an unspecified reason landed at RAF West Malling. He would fly back to Biggin Hill the next morning and it was either due to the poor evening light or some battle damage that needed repairs.

The next day was a Sunday. Most Sunday mornings would be quiet, but this was the 15th of September 1940, a day we now remember as Battle of Britain Day. The day would be one of massed air attacks upon London with the recovering RAF airfields dispatching large numbers of Spitfires and Hurricanes to repel the Luftwaffe.

The day started with low level mist and heavy cloud at 2,000 to 4,000 feet; but this started to thin out by afternoon allowing for good flying conditions. Despite the conditions, 92 Squadron were up early and at dispersal before dawn. The pilots slept in armchairs and deck chairs at dispersal with the stove sending out a comforting warmth in the pre-dawn cold.

At 9:30am RDF identified two large formations over Calais and Cap Griz Nez. The two formations were estimated to have nearly three hundred aircraft in each of them. Four Spitfires from 92 Squadron were ordered to take off and patrol over Gravesend at 25,000 feet, while another two patrolled over Biggin Hill at 10,000 feet. No enemy aircraft were sighted, and they all landed back at Biggin Hill.

At 10:40am as an enemy formation started to head towards Dungeness, 72 Squadron took off at intervals in flights and were ordered to head towards Canterbury to patrol the area. Within minutes, 92 Squadron were also scrambled and vectored to Canterbury where they were to patrol at 25,000 feet.

At 11:05am the Dornier 17's off 1/KG76 and 3/KG76 as well as KG3 moved inland with an escort of 109's provided by the various Geschwaders. The two Biggin Hill Spitfire squadrons were scrambled and together they were vectored towards Maidstone and then onto Canterbury at 20,000 feet. Brian Kingcombe led 92 with Red two being Tony Bartley.

The Biggin Hill controller call-sign 'Sapper', called Kingcome and 92 Squadron, call-sign 'Gannic' directing them onto vector 120 and Angel 22 (22,000 feet). The controller then warned of 'Snappers above' (enemy fighters). The two squadrons searched the sky above them as they climbed waiting for the inevitable black dots which would sprout wings.

Deep in the operations room at RAF Uxbridge, Prime Minister Winston Churchill watched the markers indicating the RAF squadrons and the enemy formations, as they were moved around the table map by the WAAF plotters. It was clear something big was building.

In the next twenty minutes, Fighter Command scrambled 229 and 303 Squadrons from Northolt, and vectored them to cover the airfield at Biggin Hill. 253 and 501 Squadrons were vectored from RAF Kenley to Maidstone; while the Hurricanes of 17 and 73 Squadrons were sent to Chelmsford. 603 sent their Spitfires to Dover while 257 and 504 headed to Dover.

With the main forces of No. 11 Group scrambled, the call was made to No's. 10 and 12 Groups to send their squadrons into the fray in the south east. 12 Group sent Douglas Bader's 'Big wing' from RAF Duxford with three squadrons of Hurricanes (242, 302, 310) and two squadrons of Spitfires (19 and 611) to cover RAF Hornchurch and the eastern approach to London at 20,000 feet.

Dornier's of KG76 and their escort from 2/LG2 were heading towards them when 72 Squadron engaged the Messerschmitt 109's. In seconds, the two formations were engaged and 'Pancho' Villa claimed two ME109's and a Dornier 17 destroyed, while Sergeant Bill Rolls claimed a 109 as damaged. In his combat report, Flight Lieutenant Villa stated that he was leading the squadron radio code named 'Tennis', when they were patrolling over Canterbury with 92 Squadron. They sighted the bombers some 4,000 feet below them and their escort a thousand feet above the bombers, but still 3,000 feet below the Spitfires. Villa ordered 72 into line astern and dived down on to the enemy fighters from out of the sun. He opened fire at one ME109 which caught fire and suddenly exploded. Five other 109's then attacked him and he made a tight turn to starboard, managing to out-turn the less maneuverable 109's. He ended up on the tail of one of the five and opened fire. The

Messerschmitt burst into flames and Villa spun away to get out of danger. He headed back to base but was informed that there were bandits over the airfield at Biggin Hill at 14,000 feet. These turned out to be Dornier 17's and he selected a machine on the outside of the formation. The Dornier emitted some smoke and another five or six RAF fighters arrived and attacked it. The Dornier was seen by Villa to crash into a wood and exploded on contact with the ground.

The high number of claims and losses on the 15th of September make any direct links virtually impossible. The pace of the aerial battle was frantic and there is no doubt that many combats were not even officially reported this day.

Elsewhere, 92 Squadron also engaged the same formation and made several claims. Pilot Officer Hill claimed a probable 109 over Maidstone, Flight Sergeant Charles Sydney claimed a probable 109 over Canterbury, but he was damaged by a 20mm cannon shell. He made it home safely and unharmed.

Pilot Officer Holland damaged a ME109 over Canterbury as did Pilot Officer Tony Bartley who also claimed a Dornier 17 damaged. Bartley had opened fire and saw the Dornier jettison its bomb load in a bid to escape him, when he saw tracer fire whizzing past his cockpit and heard the thud of cannon shells hitting his machine. He dived away and after another Dornier 17, but he was now out of ammunition. Four yellow nosed Messerschmitt's then attacked Bartley and hit his ailerons. He managed to get away in a power dive, just missing a squadron of Hurricanes below him as he dived through them. He managed to get home to Biggin Hill but was soaked with sweat. Sergeant Ronald Fokes also claimed to have damaged a Dornier.

The two squadrons returned to Biggin Hill to refuel and re-arm and had a visit from Air Chief Marshal Sir Hugh Dowding. He could not have picked a worse day! 92 Squadron busied themselves as the intelligence officer Tom Weise tried to get their combat reports from them and they grabbed some lunch.

By 1:00pm further large formations of enemy aircraft were gathering over the French coast. As the markers indicating the noon raiders slowly moved over the table map towards France, the WAAF plotters started to add new markers detailing the forming raids. This time the main formation was made up of Dornier 17 and Heinkel 111 bombers of KG2, KG53 and KG76, together with smaller sections from KG1, KG4 and KG26 making a total of nearly two hundred bombers. They were escorted by numerous Geschwaders of 109's and 110's totaling another three hundred plus fighters. The formations once formatted started to make their way across the English Channel.

Flying Officer Alan Wright of 92 Squadron was given a special task. He flew down to Hawkinge from Biggin Hill and sat in his cockpit as his Spitfire was refueled. His job was a new one that Fighter Command was starting to use. He would be directed to take off and act as a pair of airborne eyes for the Fighter Controllers, reporting the size of the enemy formation. At 1:45pm he was given the order to take off and report back to the controllers.

As he climbed to 26,000 feet midway across the English Channel, Wright spotted a number of 'specks' and reported their position. He then saw a formation of six Messerschmitt 109's climbing towards him. Deciding not to wait, he dived towards the 109's and opened fire getting on to the tail of one which he damaged. However, he could not get another 'bead' on the 109 and it managed to escape him. He lost control and blacked out in the dive coming to at 7,000 feet with his Spitfire on its back. He regained consciousness and headed for home to claim the 109 as damaged.

At 2:10pm 72 Squadron were ordered to patrol over Biggin Hill and sent up eight Spitfires led by 'Pancho' Villa. They joined Gravesend's 66 Squadron, while 92 Squadron put up nine machines and were ordered to patrol at 20,000 feet with 41 Squadron over RAF Hornchurch, just across the River Thames in Essex.

As the large formations headed across Kent, 72, 92 and various other fighter squadrons encountered the enemy. 72 Squadron hit a formation of Heinkel 111 bombers between Maidstone and Dartford at around 2:30pm. The ME109's of JG26 tried to intervene, but Sergeant White claimed one north east of Maidstone, Pilot Officer Holland claimed one in the Dartford area, as did Flight Lieutenant Villa and Sergeant White who shared it. Sergeant Norman Norfolk claimed a probable Heinkel III near Maidstone and Pilot Officer John Lloyd a damaged Heinkel over Dartford.

In his combat report 'Pancho' Villa reported that he was leading the squadron when they attacked a formation of Heinkel's in the Dartford area. He attacked a Heinkel from astern and fired a short burst from a range of 200 yards down to 30 yards, aiming at the starboard engine of the bomber. The engine started to smoke and the under carriage dropped down. Villa then used the rest of his ammunition on the port engine which stopped. The badly damaged bomber spewed oil from its engines which covered the Spitfire's windscreen. It is unclear what happened to this bomber, 1/KG26 had one come down after a fighter attack at Foulness in Essex at 3:00pm; while Stab KG53 had one come down near Woolwich Arsenal a few miles west of Dartford at 2:50pm. 3/KG53 also lost one which crashed at Orsett, Essex at 2:55pm.

72 Squadron had no casualties and returned to Biggin Hill in small groups and singularly between 2:50pm and 3:00pm. These times appear to be quite quick after the combats, but they were only a couple of minutes flying time from the area of action.

92 Squadron simultaneously hit the Heinkel's as well as a formation of Dornier 17's between Ashford, Maidstone and Rochester. Pilot Officer Hill claimed an amazing four Heinkel's destroyed. They were apparently all confirmed although the Luftwaffe only appear to have lost seven during the entire day.

Pilot Officer Williams claimed a Heinkel destroyed between Rochester and Maidstone and then two Dornier 17's damaged off Dungeness. Tony Bartley claimed two probable Dornier 17's in the Rochester to Maidstone area; and Pilot Officer Mottram claimed a Heinkel destroyed and a Dornier damaged. Sergeant Fokes claimed a damaged Dornier 17, while Squadron Leader Sanders claimed a Dornier 17 shot down over Maidstone. In summary, the squadron claimed in the space of a few minutes, six Heinkel's and two Dornier's destroyed, another two probably destroyed and five more damaged. What is interesting is that although it is admittedly difficult to attribute victories to crashed aircraft, I could not link any to the combat claims of 92 Squadron. There are many other crashed aircraft linked to many other squadrons in the record books, but not for 92 on this occasion. As I have said before in this book and others, pilots feel the strain and stress of combat. They often fire at the same machine as other pilots and they all claim it as their own. Stress causes an enhanced feeling of elation which can cause a pilot to believe a damaged machine is in fact destroyed and so on.

Trevor 'Wimpey' Wade claimed a probable Messerschmitt 109 in the Maidstone area around 3:00pm. In his combat report he says he was Red 2 and followed his leader into the attack on the Heinkel formation. He then saw a formation of 109's above them and broke off to attack them. Wade opened fire with a short burst from 150 yards head on and the 109 he aimed at broke away with smoke pouring from it. He then had to leave this one and get away as the other 109's attacked him. JG3 lost a couple of ME109's around this time to the north and east of Maidstone, but again nothing can be proven.

Pilot Officer Tony Bartley who claimed two probable Dornier 17's was hit by return fire and damaged over Ashford. He managed to get home without injury.

Pilot Officer 'Bob' Holland was hit by a Messerschmitt 109E to the west of Ashford and baled out of R6606 safely. However, he was injured upon landing and taken to East Grinstead hospital. 2/JG26's Oberleutnant Losigkeit claimed a Spitfire about the time the unit came into contact with 92 Squadron and it was probably this pilot who shot down Holland.

92 Squadron eventually broke off the engagement and was soon back on the ground at Biggin Hill, arriving at about the same time as 72 was landing.

72 Squadron remained on the ground for the rest of the day, but between 5:10pm and 5:40pm, sections of 92 Squadron took off to join 66 Squadron over at Gravesend. The reason is unclear, but they all returned safely to Biggin Hill by 7:00pm.

The two squadrons were soon released for the night and went off to the local pubs for a break. That afternoon 141 Squadron or rather 'B' Flight returned to Biggin Hill in their Boulton-Paul Defiant's from Turnhouse in Scotland. They were now a dedicated night-fighter unit with a brief to protect London from the night raiders. At 1:00am the next morning a single 250lb bomb was dropped on the airfield causing slight damage to the landing ground and the aircraft responsible escaped.

Later that night, between midnight and 1:16am, one of the Defiant's from 141 Squadron finally got some revenge for their hammering in July. Pilot Officer Waddington and his gunner Sergeant Cumbers caught a Heinkel 111 trapped in searchlights and fired hundreds of rounds into it. The Heinkel fell away and they would claim it as destroyed and confirmed by the authorities. Within minutes they encountered another Heinkel and claimed this one as a probable victory.

An examination of Luftwaffe loss records finds no Heinkel's as being lost that night. However, both the first and third Gruppe's of KG54 had Junkers 88's up that night. Leutnant Richter, Uffz. Breuker, Uffz. Hirschfeld and Unteroffizier Schubert were posted missing that night over Southern England, while the first group had a machine return to Melun-Villaroche badly damaged with two wounded crewmen. It is likely these are the two aircraft that fell fowl of Waddington and Cumbers that night.

The next day the 16th was quiet, which is not surprising considering the effort both sides put into the battle. (The 15th of September would soon be recognized as Battle of Britain Day). That morning at 9:00am there was a formation of nearly two hundred and fifty enemy aircraft which crossed the south coast, but they turned around and headed home. This was possibly due to the deteriorating weather with cloud being over-taken by rain and drizzle in the early afternoon.

Before the large formation headed across the English Channel, 92 Squadron were on patrol above their base after 7:00am. Nothing untoward was encountered and they landed by 9:15am.

At 9:40am four Spitfires headed down to Hawkinge followed at 10:55am, by the rest of 92 Squadron. The whole squadron patrolled over Hawkinge at 8,000 feet, but again no enemy activity was encountered.

At 11:00am Pilot Officer Hill returned in R6616 and side slipped upon landing causing the under-carriage to collapse. Hill was unharmed but his pride probably took a dent or two. The aircraft was recovered from the grass runway and repaired.

72 Squadron went up once, but they too have no contact with the Luftwaffe. With no enemy activity and the poor weather, there were a few air tests in the evening; but the squadrons were released allowing the ground crews to repair and service the battle-weary aircraft.

The 17th of September was also poor with drizzle and a gusty wind all day. The morning got off with a bang when four 250lb bombs were dropped on the south east corner of the airfield at 8:05am. There was slight damage to the landing ground, but the raid was more of a nuisance than a threat.

72 Squadron made a few local flights but nothing operational. 92 mean-while, had a few air tests and in the afternoon at 3:10pm they patrolled over Biggin Hill at 15,000 feet. A further patrol was flown that evening, but there was no enemy activity to deal with.

That night at 11:45pm Sergeants Laurence and Chard of 141 Squadron caught another Junkers 88 of 1/KG54 and sent it crashing to the earth in Maidstone for another Defiant victory. The crew and the pilot Leutnant Ganzlmayr were all killed.

It was soon decided that the simultaneous use of Biggin Hill for both day and night fighters, was impracticable. Therefore, a decision was taken at headquarters for 141 Squadron to be moved to Gatwick.

Thursday the 18th of September was cloudy, but there would be more action for the Biggin squadrons. The Luftwaffe was still smarting from its losses on the 15th and started to deploy smaller formations of bombers with massed formations of fighters.

At 9:15am 72 Squadron sent up eleven Spitfires to patrol over Gravesend. They had been airborne for over an hour when they were bounced by a formation of Messerschmitt 109's over the town and the swirling combat gradually moved eastwards towards Dover.

In his autobiography 'Spitfire attack', Sergeant Bill Rolls recalls meeting the 109's at 25,000 feet. He managed to get his sights on one and was about to open fire when there was a 'puff of white smoke' from the Spitfire's instrument panel and a smell of cordite. He was partly blinded by the smoke in the cockpit and felt the aircraft shudder and go into a spin. He pulled the canopy open and cleared the smoke from the cockpit. He thought about baling out but decided to stay and try and pull out of the spin. Checking there was not a 109 on his tail, he kicked the rudder bar and corrected the spin. He checked his instruments and decided that he could make Biggin Hill. Flying back at low level and keeping a look-out for other 109's, he managed to land safely but his Mae west was covered in oil spots. Upon inspection he found a large hole in his port wing near the gun ammunition can and another hole into the side of the cockpit. Rolls says the ground crew performed miracles and had it ready for action in no time at all.

Sergeant Norman Norfolk who had been in Rolls' section was also hit hard in X4337 and had to land at Hawkinge at 10:30am; while Sergeant Bell-Walker was badly wounded over Gravesend by a 109 in his aircraft R6704. Bell-Walker force-landed the Spitfire and was taken to hospital for treatment, while the Spitfire was recovered and repaired.

Pilot Officer Lloyd was seriously wounded, and force landed at Martin Mill, near Dover at 10:30am. He was quickly rescued and taken to the underground hospital at Dover Castle.

The remaining aircraft returned to Biggin Hill making no claims against the aggressive ME109's.

Which unit the ME109's belonged to is unclear, but JG53 and JG54 made several claims in the Ashford area around this time.

At the same time as 72 Squadron were sent up (9:15am), 92 Squadron were also scrambled. They were also ordered to patrol over Gravesend at 20,000 feet, but they were soon vectored by controllers onto an in-coming raid of Dornier 17's and their escorting 109's over Folkestone at 9:45am.

As the Spitfires headed for the bombers they were attacked from above and out of the sun, almost head-on by the 109's. 'Wimpey' Wade made a claim for a damaged 109 and in his combat report, states that as Yellow 2 with 92 Squadron, the 109's attacked almost head-on and broke up the squadron. Wade dived down a couple of thousand feet before climbing to 27,000 feet when he ensured no 109's where on his tail.

He then sighted four 109's below him between Dover and Folkestone heading away from London. He wheeled around and attacked the third 109 in the finger four formation, firing long bursts from astern from 250 yards down to 100 yards. He broke away and attacked another but ran out of ammunition. The first 109 dived vertically for the sea off Folkestone, but he did not see it crash. He landed at Hawkinge to refuel and rearm before heading home to Biggin Hill.

Other members of 92 Squadron managed to get through to the Dornier 17's and Pilot Officer Tony Bartley hit one which he claimed to have shot down. However, he forgot to check behind him and a 109 hit him with a cannon shell exploding behind his seat armour, while a bullet scraped his head and hit the gun sight in front him. The Spitfires oil and glycol tanks were punctured causing smoke to pour from the machine. In his autobiography, 'Smoke trails in the sky', Bartley recalls being about to bale out when he saw the 109 preparing to finish him off, so he held off. He then turned the mortally damaged fighter towards the 109 and opened fire. The Messerschmitt pilot backed off immediately and headed off for France.

Bartley lacking altitude by this time, made a forced landing at Appledore. He was catapulted from the cockpit and luckily landed in a nearby haystack. He was unbelievably uninjured and taken by the locals to a pub and given numerous pints before the army collected him. Bartley states in the book that the command post officer told him the Dornier had crashed with no survivors. However, a check of the official records shows that no Dornier 17's crashed that day.

Pilot Officer Roy Mottram in N3193 was also hit by a ME109 over Hollingbourne near Maidstone. He crashed and the aircraft burnt out, with Mottram suffering slight burns. He was taken back to Biggin Hill but went on to Orpington Hospital for treatment.

Once again it is difficult to identify the 109's involved. The official claims list only mentions the three already mentioned by JG53 and JG54. It is possible records were lost or never completed, but what is certain is that the two squadrons had been hit hard by the Geschwader force.

Most of the 92 Squadron survivors were back on the ground by 10:30am, although they came back in ones and twos to rearm and refuel. At 11:30am two 92 Squadron machines were ordered to patrol above Biggin Hill at 25,000 feet, but they landed at 12:30pm without incident. At 12:20pm two sections of 92 Squadron were ordered to patrol over West Malling airfield, but yet again, there was no sign of the Luftwaffe.

72 Squadrons spent the entire day on the ground, but 92 Squadron was scrambled at 3:55pm and ordered to patrol over Tenterden at 20,000 feet. By 5:00pm they were vectored onto a large raid of over three hundred Junkers 88's, Heinkel 111's and 109's coming in from the coast. Their target was London.

Flight Lieutenant Brian Kingcombe claimed a Junkers 88 with two other unknown pilots in the Tenterden area and Pilot Officer Hill also claimed one destroyed. Kingcombe turned his attention to the Heinkel's and claimed one as probably destroyed and another as damaged. The RAF fighters followed the bomber trail as it headed north west towards London, but Flight Lieutenant Paterson had to crash land K9991 at RAF Debden in Essex at 5:40pm. He was not harmed and returned to Biggin Hill by road. Pilot Officer Hill landed at the Shorts Factory airfield at Rochester to refuel before he too returned to Biggin Hill.

Nine Junkers 88's came down during this raid across Kent and Essex. Some belonged to KG54, but most came from KG77. The numbers of claims and the fact that many of the bombers were attacked by large numbers of fighters prevents any definitive accreditation to individual pilots.

This brought an end to the day's aerial activity. The two squadrons had lost five aircraft, but thankfully the pilots were alive, although three were wounded. They had claimed three destroyed, one probably destroyed and three damaged. It had not been a very successful day for 72 and 92, but things would get better.

The 19th of September was a quieter day with low, heavy thick cloud and rain in the morning. This gave way to a showery afternoon before the rain returned in the evening. 72 Squadron undertook no operational flying on this day.

At 12:45pm Flying Officer Wright of 92 Squadron claimed a Junkers 88 probable near Biggin Hill, but it appears to have got back to its base. Pilot Officer Hill also claimed a probable 109; but the Luftwaffe recorded no Messerschmitt 109 losses on this date.

Friday the 20th started off with rain and developed into showers, but this did not stop flying. At 9:05am, 92 Squadron's Sergeant Ayling flew an hour-long weather check flight. He was followed at 10:40am by Pilot Officer Tony Bartley who flew to Hamble in Hampshire and back again.

At just before 10:45am 72 Squadron were ordered to patrol over Maidstone. They were followed just before 11:00am by 92 Squadron who were directed to take off and patrol over Gravesend at 5,000 feet.

No long after take-off, 72 Squadron were attacked by fifty plus ME109's between Maidstone and Canterbury. Pilot Officer Denis Holland in X4410 was hit and went down. He was very seriously wounded in the attack, but somehow managed to bale out of his stricken Spitfire; before it crashed to earth at Stiff Street near Sittingbourne. He was found as soon as he landed and taken to hospital, but he sadly died of his wounds the next day.

The combat continued and Bill Rolls claimed to have destroyed a 109 between Canterbury and Ashford. In his combat report he states that they were directed to intercept enemy fighters and were climbing to attack one formation, when the 'tail end Charlie' reported another formation diving on them from above. As they broke formation, Rolls found himself alone near Ashford. He then spotted what he thought was a lone Hurricane or Spitfire diving and climbing. As he got closer, he identified it as a ME109 with a yellow nose and tail fin. Rolls dived from out of the sun and as the 109 climbed again, he opened fire with a three second burst. The ME109 did a stall turn and a large piece of the fuselage fell away. He followed it down and gave it another four second burst before it started to emit smoke. A further burst resulted in more debris and it dived into the ground near Wye between a wood and a lake.

Pilot Officer 'Pancho' Villa also claimed a 109 as damaged in the same action, but the rest of the squadron returned to Biggin Hill and made no further flights that day.

92 Squadron were also engaged with Squadron Leader Sanders claiming a ME109 shot down between Dover and Dungeness at around 11:50am. However, he was hit and damaged with fuel leaking into the cockpit. He managed to get home in one piece before his machine burst into a flaming torch.

Pilot Officer Wade claimed a 109 as damaged, stating in his combat report that at 27,000 feet they were attacked by ME109's. He managed to get onto the tail of one and fired a short burst into it. It dived down to 4,000 feet with Wade in pursuit before it climbed up to 5,000 feet while making various evasive maneuvers to try and thrown Wade off. He continued to fire odd bursts and reported bullets visibly entering the 109's wings, but with little noticeable effect. The Messerschmitt eventually entered a cloud layer some fifteen miles from France and disappeared from sight.

The 109's from various Geschwaders did hit 92 hard who lost Pilot Officer Hill (in X4417) and Sergeant Eyles (N3248). Both pilots appear to have fallen victim to Major Werner Molders of Stab JG51. He claimed two Spitfires over Dungeness at this time. Hill and Eyles were in the same section and the instant 'hit' of the two Spitfires in close succession bears all the hall marks of this top ace. Sadly, both Hill and Eyles were killed. Hill crashed at West Hougham and Peter Eyles crashed into the Channel and has his body had never been recovered.

The Messerschmitt 109's came from a number of Geschwader, including JG51, JG27 and JG53. The pilots from these units made various claims at that time, but 5/JG53 and 7/JG53 had 109's return and make force landings in France with damage. The only machine that was lost was one from 9/JG27 which came down at 11:50am at Ospringe, near Faversham. Its pilot Unteroffizier Clauser was killed in the crash. It is unclear whether this was the one claimed by Sergeant Rolls, Squadron Leader Sanders or another unit's pilot.

'Wimpey' Wade's combat report comments about his .303 ammunition having little effect on the 109 he claimed as damaged, is an excellent example of how the .303 bullet had little punch; especially when compared to the 109's cannon shells. By 1941 the Spitfires and Hurricanes would be armed with the Hispano 20mm cannon giving them a much harder punch.

That afternoon and evening, the 92 Squadron pilots flew a number of short localised patrols and air tests around Biggin Hill, but there was no further enemy action for them.

That night at about 11:00pm a single bomber flew across the airfield and dropped a large number of incendiaries, but they caused no damage and were soon extinguished by ground crews.

On the 21st of September, the cloud covering continued but started to reduce in the afternoon. 72 Squadron's Squadron Leader Tony Collins was posted to Station Head Quarters as he was 'non-effective sick' (the actual reasons are unclear).

That morning a strange incident took place which caused 92 Squadron to lose their Squadron Leader. 'Judy' Sanders who had returned with damage the day before had oil on his uniform tunic sleeve. He was 'advised' to use some fuel from the bowser to remove the oil, but a careless cigarette caused his sleeve to catch fire at dispersal. He was quickly extinguished but not before his arm was badly burnt and he was sent off to hospital leaving Flight Lieutenant Brian Kingcombe to lead the squadron.

Apart from some air tests and local flights, both squadrons operationally remained on the ground. However, at 5:05pm Flying Officer Tony Bartley and 'Wimpey' Wade took off as a pair to patrol over Beachy Head at 10,000 feet. They returned at 5:35pm and ten minutes later the squadron was scrambled with eleven Spitfires heading for Maidstone at 15,000 feet. At 6:00pm 72 Squadron were scrambled and followed 92 towards Maidstone.

A large force of over one hundred and fifty bombers with a large 109 escort were heading for London.

The two Biggin Hill squadrons had little effect on the large formation, but Sergeant Sherrington of 92 Squadron (in N3032) force landed at Manston after combat at 6:45pm. He was unharmed. Some sources state he landed at Hildenborough, but the squadron Operations Record Book states it was at RAF Manston.

Tony Bartley in his autobiography reported being hit hard by a ME109 although he does not give an exact date. However, he says it was a couple of days after his landing in the haystack, so it appears to have been on this date. He managed to find a layer of cloud and headed back to Biggin Hill, but his engine was losing power. He thought about baling out, but as he broke through the cloud layer, he was only 800 feet above the ground and over a built-up area at Sevenoaks. He gently landed and while sweating profusely headed back to dispersal. Later, it was found that his control cables were damaged and one final movement of the control column, could have caused it to snap and undoubtedly would have ended in his death.

The 22nd of September was yet another day of rain and drizzle. Squadron Leader Charles Lister arrived to replace 'Judy' Sanders as CO of 92 Squadron. Lister did have operational experience and had flown with 41 Squadron during the battle before he was shot down and slightly wounded on the 14th of September. Now he had 92 Squadron.

The weather was poor, and the Luftwaffe decided to stay at home. Apart from a pairing from 92 Squadron who patrolled over Beachy Head, there was no other operational flying from Biggin Hill on this day.

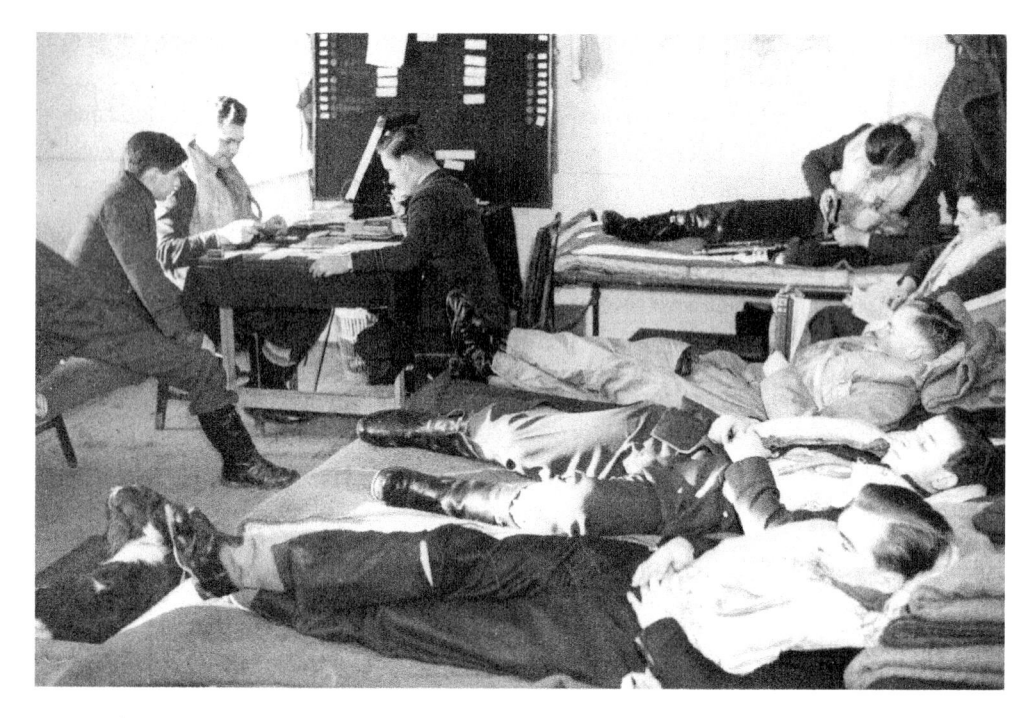

74 Squadron at Dispersal (courtesy of WW2images.com).

Johnny Freeborn and Henryk Szezesny at the card table.

(Above) 610 Squadron at Hawkinge in July 1940 (courtesy of WW2images.com)

(Below) 4th of September 1940: Luftwaffe fighter leaders meeting, left to right: Hauptmann Wilhelm Balthasar (3/JG 3); Hauptmann Walter Oesau (3/JG 51), Leutnant Oberst Adolf Galland (JG 26 "Schlageter"); General Ernst Udet; Leutnant Obsert Werner Mölders (JG51); Hauptmann Rolf Pingel (1/JG 26); and Hauptmann Grasser (2/ZG 2). (Image courtesy of WW2images.com).

32 Squadron at Hawkinge July 1940, taken while the film unit was at the airfield. (IWM)

Left to right: Flying Officer Rupert Smythe, Flying Officer PM Gardner, Pilot Officer JE Proctor, Flight Lieutenant Peter Brothers, Pilot Officer Keith Gillman, Flying Officers Dougie Grice and Alan Eckford.

Spitfire of 66 Squadron (believed to have been at Gravesend during the Battle) (IWM)

92 Squadron in late 1940 (courtesy of WW2images.com).

Left to right FO Garland (Eng. Officer), FO Weiss (Intel), Roy Mottram, Titch Havercroft, Brian Kingcombe, Johnny Kent, Sherringham, Cecil Henry Saunders, Rob Holland, Allen Wright, Hugh Bowen-Morris & John Lund.

'Sailor' Malan the legendary and charismatic commander of 74 Squadron in 1940. (Courtesy of WW2images.com).

Chapter 8

A battle of attrition.

With the high number of bombers being lost, the Luftwaffe started to employ more and more fighter sweeps or deploying 109's with single bombs slung under their fuselage. The aim was to make the RAF to enter into a war of attrition. The Luftwaffe now realized that the RAF had a significant command and control system and avoided fighter verses fighter combat were ever possible. They therefore sent over small units of bombers with out of proportion fighter escorts or fighter bombers who could dump their bombs and fight the Spitfires and Hurricanes. In addition, the JU87 Stukas and twin engine ME110's, were relegated to secondary tasks due to their high losses.

On Monday the 23rd of September, some cloud remained but the visibility was much better at about twelve miles. At 8:40am the RDF chain detected large numbers of aircraft in massed formations crossing the English Channel. Many of those crossing the Channel were Messerschmitt 109's with the Observer Corps estimating their numbers at over two hundred.

In response Fighter Controllers scrambled both 92 and 72 Squadrons and ordered them to patrol over Gravesend at 20,000 feet just after 9:05am. Six other RAF squadrons were scrambled and vectored onto the approaching formations.

As the British fighter squadrons engaged the enemy, a running combat continued for about twenty minutes stretching from Gravesend, down past the Isle of Grain and Canterbury to Folkestone. Adolph Galland's JG26 were the main unit facing 92 Squadron and Flight Lieutenant Brian Kingcombe knocked down a 109 from 8/JG26 which crashed at Biddenden, Kent at 10:00am. The pilot was Unteroffizier Gerhard Grzymalla an ace with seven victories to his name. He was flying home with his comrades at 22,000 feet when they were hit from above by 92 Squadron. Gerhard Grzymalla baled-out uninjured and was soon captured.

8/JG26 also lost Feldwebel Arnold Kupper who was slightly wounded after being attacked by Pilot Officer Drummond of 92 Squadron over the Isle of Grain. He had been the wingman to Hauptmann Gerhard Schopfel (Galland's deputy) when they encountered several British fighters. Kupper became separated from Schopfel and had his radiator damaged, causing him to make a forced landing near Grain Fort, Isle of Grain at 9:55am. He was immediately captured by the fort's garrison. Unlike Grzymalla he had just one previous victory claim to his name.

However, 92 Squadron had Pilot Officer John Patinson slightly wounded over Gravesend when he was attacked by a 109. He tried to land at West Malling airfield but came down short and crashed before he was taken to Preston Hall hospital near Maidstone.

Several JG26 pilots claimed a Spitfire at this time including Oberleutnant Mickey Sprick of 8/JG26 and Gefr. Schenk of 9/JG26. 92 Squadron eventually broke off the combat and returned to Biggin by 10:30am.

72 Squadron were also engaged at the same time and against the same formation which extended for many miles. They tangled with JG2 over the eastern end of Kent and down towards Folkestone. Flight Lieutenant Ivor Cosby and Sergeant Norman Glew destroyed a ME109 off Folkestone at 10:00am. This was Unteroffizier Dilthey of 4/JG2 who ditched just off the end of Folkestone pier. He was rescued and detained with some minor injuries.

Sergeant John White also claimed a 109 probably destroyed, but it is hard to identify the aircraft concerned. JG3 lost two fighters around this time and location and another returned home with damage.

Pilot Officer Brown of 72 Squadron was shot down by a 109 over Gravesend on his way home to Biggin Hill. The aircraft (X4063) came down in a crash landing near Sittingbourne and Brown escaped injury. The likely victor was Hauptmann Wilhelm Balthasar of Stab JG3, their leading ace. He claimed a Spitfire at this time South of Chatham. This was his 25th victory.

That afternoon, 72 Squadron flew an hour-long patrol over Maidstone without incident, while 92 Squadron flew one over Swanley a few miles from Biggin Hill. 92 Squadron was then sent up on two more occasions in the late afternoon on patrols, but on each occasion, they were recalled after just a few minutes flying time. They finally flew another hour-long patrol at 5:30pm over RAF Kenley at 5,000 feet, but the Luftwaffe were not seen, and they returned home to Biggin. This drew to a close the action on the 23rd of September.

The 24th started off just like the preceding few days. At 7:15am, 92 Squadron sent a three-man section to patrol over Hawkinge at 8,000 feet. Nothing untoward happened and they soon returned home.

At 8:10am Squadron Leader Robert Lister and six other 92 Squadron aircraft were scrambled and ordered to patrol over Swanley. Within ten minutes of them taking off, 72 Squadron were scrambled and ordered to join up with 92 Squadron. A large formation over about five hundred Junkers 88's, Dornier 17's and their ME109 escort were heading for London. The two squadrons were moved forward by the fighter controllers and joined a third squadron.

This took time and they encountered a smaller formation of just nine Junkers 88's, but these were escorted by over one hundred ME109's as they moved from Maidstone towards the River Thames near Dartford and Gravesend.

The three fighter squadrons engaged the formation trying desperately to get through to the JU88's. 72 Squadron made a number of claims and Flight Sergeant Jack Steere claimed a 109 probably destroyed.

In his combat report, Steere states that he was weaving at the rear of the squadron formation when they were directed to 20,000 feet over Maidstone. They met a formation of bombers and fighters in the midst of the Thames Estuary and Steere latched on to the final Messerschmitt 109 in a line of four. He opened fire hitting the 109 which started to emit smoke and pulled away from the others apparently out of control. Steere could not stay to watch and he was attacked by two more 109's, hence his claim for only a probable 109. The two 109's hit Steere's Spitfire which was damaged, but he managed to get safely back to Biggin Hill.

The rest of 72 Squadron attacked a following larger bomber formation which was made up of Dornier's and JU88's. Sergeant Lee claimed to have damaged a Dornier and another unnamed pilot claimed one to be damaged. Another unnamed pilot claimed a 109 probable and another damaged.

92 Squadron encountered the Junkers 88's and the 109's head-on over Maidstone. Brian Kingcombe was leading the squadron with the new CO Squadron Leader Lister on his wing. After breaking formation Lister found himself alone and being circled by nine Messerschmitt 109's. Despite various manoeuvres, he was eventually hit by a cannon shell in the bottom of the cockpit and wounded in both legs. He went into a spin, which he pulled out of and managed to get back to Biggin Hill. However, he only had one flap working which caused him to lose control and enter into a skidding diving-turn which fortunately took the Spitfire into the valley at the end of the runway. He managed to re-gain control and made a high-speed landing without flaps stopping just ten yards short of a wood at the far end of the airfield. He was taken to Farnborough hospital and 92 Squadron had lost another CO.

Flight Lieutenant Brian Kingcombe damaged a JU88 while also claiming a ME109 as probably destroyed. Sergeant Fokes claimed one as a probable and Pilot Officer Drummond damaged JU88 and claimed a 109 damaged and another probably destroyed.

Sadly, Pilot Officer John Bryson a tall ex-Canadian Mounted Policeman was hit by a 109. He managed to fly to RAF North Weald in Essex where he landed. When they ground crew got to him, they pulled back the canopy to find the poor pilot covered in blood. One leg had been blown off just below the knee and as soon as he landed, he died of his injuries and loss of blood. To have flown to the airfield in excruciating pain and landed his Spitfire was a very brave act and spoke volumes for the ex-Mountie.

In his autobiography, Tony Bartley remembers the funeral of this popular pilot. The pilots were so drunk that one who marched to the graveside to give a salute, fell in on top of the coffin. Whether he was put on a charge is unknown.

Sergeant Ellis (X4356) crash landed on Higham Marshes (between Gravesend and Chatham) near the Thames at 9:30am. He had been hit in the starboard mainplane and the glycol tank. He was unharmed and returned to base later that morning.

Despite the claims, the Luftwaffe did not lose any Messerschmitt 109's on the 24th of September. In addition, all the Dornier 17's and Junkers 88's returned home, although many were damaged and made emergency landings in France.

72 Squadron made no further patrols on the 24th, while 92 Squadron made another two patrols without making contact with the Luftwaffe. The next day 72 Squadron was rested, while 92 Squadron made several patrols with Brian Kingcombe as the acting commanding officer. However, there was no contact with the Luftwaffe.

The 26th of September saw the arrival at Biggin Hill of one of the most famous Battle of Britain pilots. Sergeant Donald Kingaby arrived on 92 Squadron from 266. He became known as a ME109 specialist due to the number of victories he would stack up against the Messerschmitt fighters.

Although the 72 Squadron Operations Record Book (ORB) shows no operational flights on the 26th of September, Sergeant Malcolm Gray claimed a Dornier 17 shot down east of May Island at 8:48am. However, no Dornier's were lost on this day and May Island is in the Firth of Forth! It is likely this report had the wrong date.

92 Squadron put up several flights, but at 3:50pm Green section comprising of Flight Lieutenant Allan Wright, Pilot Officer Lewis and Sergeant Trevor Oldfield took off to patrol over Tenterden at 10,000 feet. They reported sighting a lone Dornier 17 which kept dropping in and out of the clouds to escape them. Allan Wright claimed the Dornier 17 destroyed (remember none were lost that day according to official records), while it appears Lewis may have been damaged by return fire as he had to land at a Maidstone airfield (West Malling or Detling probably). It is possible, that they actually attacked a Messerschmitt 110 as they were operating over Sussex and Hampshire at this time, but none came down in Kent.

Friday the 27th of September 1940 was a cloudy day, but the evening was clearer. The day was a brutal one for the Biggin Hill squadrons who would lose the lives of five pilots in combat.

At 6:30am 92 Squadron sent Sergeant Ellis up on a quick weather test flight. At 7:10am and 7:25am two pairs of aircraft were sent up by the controller, but no contacts were made.

At 8:00am the RDF and then the Observer Corps spotted about sixty Dornier 17's and Junkers 88 bombers with an escort of about one hundred and twenty fighters heading over the coast and into Kent. Fighter command scrambled several squadrons, including 72 and 92 at 8:20am and 8:45am. The two squadrons linked up over Swanley, before being vectored towards the raiders.

The Biggin Hill units soon made contact with the enemy and a running fight took place between Sevenoaks and the coast at Dungeness. The massed escort of Messerschmitt 109's took their toll of the Spitfires and Hurricanes as they desperately tried to get at the bombers.

72 Squadron made a number of claims going head on against the bombers. Sergeant Bill Rolls reported seeing a 72 Squadron flight commander's machine get hit and another one 'go to pieces' after the 109's reacted over Sevenoaks. Rolls said he could not fire at anything as there was always half a dozen ME109's firing at you. Pilot Officer Males the youngest pilot in the squadron was shot down by 109's and fell with his aircraft into Shadwell Dock, at Stepney in East London. Flying Officer Davies-Cooke in N3068 baled out but fell dead near Hayes railway station, a few miles from Biggin Hill. His Spitfire came down on 70 and 72 Queensway in West Wickham, Kent.

72 Squadron made a number of claims, with Flying Officer Douthwaite claiming a probable Dornier at Sevenoaks and Sergeant Glent a Dornier south of Dungeness. Flight Sergeant John Gilders claimed a JU88 and a 109 destroyed at Dungeness, while Pilot Officer James O'Meara claimed a probable Dornier 17 and a damaged Dornier 215 (actually a Do.17) between Sevenoaks and Redhill. Sergeant Robert Staples claimed a probable JU88 four miles north of Sevenoaks and Flying Officer Norman Robson claimed a Dornier with an unknown pilot south east of Biggin Hill. Sergeants White and Norfolk claimed to have shot down Dornier's near Sevenoaks.

Sergeant Glew chased a Dornier to the coast and forced it down to just fifty feet. He then ran out of ammunition and dived one more time towards the Dornier, but this time its pilot panicked and crashed into the sea.

As Glew circled above the floating wreck, the crew were seen scrambling out of the aircraft before it sank. Glew then gallantly spotted a fishing trawler and led it to the airmen for their rescue. It appears this may have actually been a Messerschmitt 110 of 2/ZG76 and not a Dornier. One came down in the sea off Hastings and the pilot Oberleutnant von Eichborn was rescued by a fishing boat. Eichborn was quite badly burned and his gunner Unteroffizier Bartmus died of his injuries.

Sergeant White was hit by a ME109 and made a forced landing upon his return to Biggin Hill, but he was not injured.

92 Squadron lost Flight Lieutenant James Paterson a 20 year old New Zealander, who was shot down by a ME109 at 9:20am and crashed in flames at Sparepenny Lane, Farningham, Kent. Paterson was still not fully sighted from the last time he had to bale-out and was injured. Whether this led to his death is unclear, but he did not need to fly with his injuries unhealed. The other pilots reported seeing him fighting against the flames and struggling to get out of the cockpit as he dived away. He is buried in the Biggin Hill War Graves plot at the Star Lane cemetery in St. Mary Cray.

Flight Sergeant Charles Sydney was shot down and killed landing at Walton on Thames in Surrey. He crashed at Station Avenue having attacked four enemy aircraft. He too was buried at St. Mary Cray cemetery in a joint funeral with James Paterson.

'Wimpey' Wade claimed a Dornier 17 destroyed near Lewes in East Sussex and Pilot Officer Mansel-Lewis claimed another, however he returned to base with a large part of his tail missing.

Wade made a forced landing on Lewes racecourse and over-turned P9544 in the process. He was lucky to escape without injury. Some-how he managed to persuade the local police commander to give him a ride in a fast police car back to Biggin Hill. In his combat report Wade stated that over Sevenoaks he attacked the Dornier 17 bomber formations leader but on breaking away he blacked out. When he came to, he found two ME109's in front of him and fired a burst at one of them. They both dived down from 20,000 to 12,000 feet and headed for the coast. Wade attempted to follow the 109's, when he saw a formation of Dornier 17's near Brighton. He therefore broke off the 109 chase and approached the bombers. They soon formed a defensive circle (the standard tactic of ME110's not Dornier's); and he joined the circle firing at the last machine which broke away. Wade was damaged by return fire and had to break off, leading to his forced landing on the racecourse.

Flight Lieutenant Brian Kingcombe claimed a probable and a damaged Dornier 17 in the same area and Flying Officer Drummond claimed a Messerschmitt 110 destroyed over Sevenoaks. In his combat report he says he hit it from behind and caused the starboard engine to smoke, before several Hurricanes attacked it and it came down in a ploughed field just south of Westerham in Kent. This was the ME110 of Oberleutnant Otto Weckeiser and his gunner Gefr. Horst Bruggow who was wounded. They were attacked by a numerous fighter's and both engines were hit and put out of action. They made a forced landing at Stockets Manor, Oxted where both men were captured.

It is very hard to decipher who shot down who on the morning of the 27th of September. No Dornier's, whether DO17 or DO215's where lost that morning and it appears the enemy was made up of Messerschmitt 110's and their ME109 escort. In fact, that morning approximately twenty ME110's of Erpr.Gr.210, LG1 and ZG26 were lost or damaged along the south coast of England. The Junkers 88's belonged to KG77 who lost four machines that morning.

It is also impossible to identify who shot down the four pilots of 72 and 92 Squadrons. Various 109 pilots from JG27 and JG54 claimed Spitfires at this time and in the area. The ME109 claimed destroyed by 72 Squadron's Flight Sergeant Gilders may have been that of Gefr. John of 5/JG27. He baled-out and was captured at 9:45am after combat, with his machine crashing at Mays Farm near Lewes, Sussex.

In no time at all, the two squadrons were soon back at Biggin Hill, refueling and re-arming, as well as being repaired. However, they would not be on the ground for very long.

At 11:40am both squadrons were scrambled again and ordered to patrol over Biggin before being sent towards Maidstone. Another formation of just twenty-five bombers with over two hundred fighters had crossed the Channel. (The new Luftwaffe tactic of small bomber formations and larger formations of fighters was now in full swing. They were also starting to bomb at night – the start of the Blitz).

The two Biggin Hill squadrons had little contact with the enemy, but Sergeant Trevor Oldfield of 92 Squadron claimed a ME109 destroyed in the Canterbury area at 12:15pm. This may have been the 109 of Oberleutnant Schon of 8/JG54, he was hit and was trying to land in a field when he hit a fence and crashed; somersaulting over a road at Boughton to the east of Faversham at 12:05pm. Sadly he was killed in the crash.

72 Squadron claimed to have damaged three more ME109E's near Dungeness at 12:30pm but there were no losses to the two Biggin squadrons who returned home.

By 3:00pm both squadrons were ordered to scramble once again. They were both directed to patrol near Biggin Hill, as just fifteen Heinkel 111's and Junkers 88's with an escort of about one hundred and fifty fighters crossed into Kent.

72 Squadron fought a battle against Heinkel 111's between Croydon and Brighton between 3:35pm and 3:40pm. 'Pancho' Villa was leading his section and attacked the bombers and their 109 escort. As 72 positioned themselves to attack, they were bounced by a Hurricane squadron who thankfully did not open fire. Six Heinkel's had become detached from the main formation, so Villa led the squadron into the attack at 17,000 feet. Firing three bursts at a Heinkel, the starboard engine caught fire and various pieces of metal fell away. Villa broke off to avoid hitting another Heinkel and suddenly felt 'a bullet' hit the armour plating on the back of his seat. Villa turned his machine around and made several further attacks upon the Heinkel. He fired until he ran out of ammunition, then watched it crash into the sea about six miles off the coast, between New Haven and Brighton. He was then attacked by a ME109, but he managed to avoid it and watched it heading off for France. In his combat report, he says that when he landed the Spitfire had nine bullet holes and his parachute had stopped one of them. Although Villa claimed this to have been a Heinkel,

none were lost, and it appears to have been a Junkers 88 of 5/KG77 which crashed into the sea off Hastings at 4:00pm. Oberleutnant Ziel, Feldwebel Niederer and Unteroffizier Isensee were killed. Gefr. Teichtmayer was wounded but rescued by the local lifeboat and taken ashore for treatment.

Flight Sergeant Jack Steere reported a damaged 109 over Brighton. He followed the formation of Heinkel's towards Brighton where they were attacked by Spitfires and Hurricanes before the 109's intervened. He therefore opened fire on a 109 which broke away 'smoking violently'. Steere could not fire again as two other 109's attacked him, and he had to avoid them. He therefore broke off the engagement and headed home.

Sergeant Lee also claimed a Heinkel 111 destroyed but this cannot be confirmed (and none were in fact lost).

Mean-while, 92 Squadron were over north west Kent with 66 Squadron and attacked a formation of Junkers 88's of KG77, claiming a number destroyed as the ME109 escort from JG26 tried to defend them.

Sergeant Don Kingaby who would become known as a 109 specialist, did not claim a JU88, but he hit and damaged a 109. In his report he says he was at 15,000 feet when they encountered the JU88's over Biggin Hill. He fired at the bombers but was attacked by the 109's. Kingaby dived away to avoid them and five of them followed him downwards. One of the 109's over shot and presented itself as a target, so he fired hitting the starboard wing. The other 109's made it too hot for him and he made an aileron turn and dived again to avoid them. When he levelled out the ME109's had gone so he returned home. He was not hit once by the group of Messerschmitt's.

The ME109 he hit appears to have been that of Unteroffizier Horst Perez who was severely injured and made a forced landing at East Dean near Eastbourne as he was too weak to get across the English Channel. The aircraft was salvaged at the time and put-on public display, before being preserved and later restored. It is now on display at the Imperial War Museum at Duxford in a diorama depicting its forced landing in Sussex that day in 1940. When restored and the paintwork was peeled off, the Gruppen Commanders chevron markings were found under its number '14' indicating that it had previously been the commander's own aircraft.

Brian Kingcombe claimed two JU88's damaged and a share of one destroyed in a wood near Redhill and Sevenoaks. This may have been the machine of Oberleutnant Seif and his crew from 6/KG77 which crashed at Sevenoaks at 3:30pm. Seif and two of his crew were killed, while Feldwebel Zinsmeister was captured but injured.

Flight Lieutenant Allan Wright also claimed a Junkers 88 destroyed near Sevenoaks as did Sergeant Ellis and Flying Officer Thomas Sherrington. Tony Bartley claimed one near Redhill, and this may have been that of Stab2/KG77 which crashed near Penshurst. Oberleutnant Leitze and two crew members were killed, while one was captured.

'Wimpey' Wade claimed to have chased a Heinkel 111 until it crashed through a hedge near Lympne, but this is likely to have been another JU88.

Flying Officer John Drummond claimed a JU88 near Sevenoaks and in his combat report he says the squadron attacked twelve of them at 12,000 feet over Seveonaks. He carried out a beam attack on the outer aircraft of the rear section. The bomber broke away and he attacked it once more and black smoke came from the port engine. Another Spitfire also attacked it and it caught fire. Two crewmen baled-out and it turned over and dived into a wood. He described the location as being about a mile from High Halden railway station near Tenterden and at the edge of a small lake. This is believed to have been the aircraft from 3/KG77 which crashed at Hononton Park, Horsmondern, Kent at 3:30pm. Three of the crew were killed and one wounded and captured.

Flight Lieutenant Brian Kingcombe claimed a JU88 and another two damaged, while Flying Officer Geoffrey Wellum shared one south of Rochester with three other unknown pilots. Sergeant Bowen-Lewis shared one with a 66 Squadron pilot near Sherness. This may have been the aircraft of Unteroffizier Ruhlandt and his crew from 3/KG77 which came down on Graveney Marshes near Faversham. The crew of four were all captured and unharmed.

The Junkers 88's over Sevenoaks and Biggin Hill appear to have been poorly defended on this evidence, but Sergeant Trevor Oldfield of 92 Squadron was shot down over Dartford. He crashed in his aircraft R6622 at Hesketh Park near the edge of the current Dartford Cricket Club pitch and was killed. He is believed to have been hit by the escorting 109's but this cannot be confirmed. The local 'legend' is that Oldfield stayed with his aircraft to avoid the surrounding houses. A memorial to the pilot stands next to the cricket pitch at Hesketh Park and the Dartford Borough Council chamber has a painting depicting his aircraft over the area on that fateful day.

Sergeant Bowen-Morris was damaged by return fire from the bombers, but he landed at Biggin Hill without injury.

Although 72 and 92 lost one Spitfire, 41 Squadron lost one over East Malling, 66 Squadron lost one, 222 lost one as did 229 Squadron. 249 Squadron lost two Hurricanes. Various others were damaged. The various escorting ME109 Geschwaders made numerous claims around this time and location, so it is difficult to attribute them to individual pilots.

The two squadrons were back on the ground at Biggin Hill by 4:30pm and there was no further action that day for them. It had been a very hard day for the Biggin Hill units. They had lost five pilots and several other machines were damaged or destroyed. They had however, destroyed or damaged a number of enemy machines.

Saturday the 28th of September was not surprisingly much quieter. The Luftwaffe had made a major effort the day before to entice the RAF into combat. RAF Fighter Command had responded in kind and the losses on both sides were heavy. The 28th would therefore be a day of reflection and recovery.

72 Squadron were tasked with escorting a small formation of Bristol Blenheim bombers to France that morning to attack invasion barges and supply routes according to Sergeant Bill Rolls. This is not recorded in the squadron Operations Record Book, but they did not meet the Luftwaffe and they returned home safely.

After a fairly quiet morning, at 1:15pm 72 Squadron took off and patrolled over Sevenoaks. They were then moved forward and tangled with 109's around the Canterbury area. Flying Officer 'Pancho' Villa claimed a ME109 destroyed north of Hastings, but the only 109's lost that day were from JG26 and neither of these matches the claim.

The 29th of September was a rainy day with some drizzle. 72 Squadron appear to have remained on the ground according to their ORB, but there are official reports that James O'Meara shot down a Junkers 88 and damaged another, but the location is unclear.

The 92 Squadron Operations Record Book says the two squadrons patrolled with 66 Squadron over Biggin Hill at 25,000 feet for an hour, but it does not mention any contact with the enemy. The battle was by this stage so tiring and frenetic that it is not implausible that entries were missed and that there was indeed contacts and victory claims made.

At 5:45pm Pilot Officers Williams and Sherrington took off and patrolled over Biggin at 8,000 feet before widening their patrol. Williams claims to have attacked and damaged a Dornier 17 between Canterbury and Maidstone, but this cannot be confirmed.

Another pair from 92 flew a patrol, but they were on the ground by 6:30pm and the days flying was concluded as far as Biggin Hill was concerned.

The early autumnal weather hit Biggin Hill on the morning of the 30th with a thick dawn fog. It remained on the ground and was slow to disperse although some patrols were flown over Mayfield in Sussex. At 9:00am a large formation of Messerschmitt 109's crossed the coast near Dungeness and flew towards Biggin Hill, but the Biggin Hill squadrons were kept away from them.

At 10:20am 92 Squadron took off and made a patrol in squadron strength as another large formation of 109's came in over the coast. Once again 92 were kept away from by the Fighter Controllers. There was no point engaging them and wasting lives and aircraft when there were no bombers.

At 12:55pm the squadron was scrambled once again and ordered to patrol over Biggin Hill airfield. The RDF and Observer Corps had identified one hundred and fifty enemy aircraft building up over the Channel. This time it included about forty Dornier 17's. The enemy formation started to make their way towards the coast and 92 Squadron were moved to meet them as they approached at 1:45pm.

92 moved forward and intercepted them as they crossed the coastline near Folkestone and Pilot Officer Desmond Williams claimed a probable Dornier near Hawkinge. In his combat report he stated that he was Green 1, and the squadron was at 20,000 feet when they were attacked by ME109's. The squadron was split up as a result of the attack, and he dived down to 15,000 feet to circle around Hawkinge. He then saw a formation of twenty Dornier's and about thirty 109's being attacked by four or five Hurricanes and Spitfires. Williams joined in and carried out a quarter and stern attack on the bombers. One of them dropped out of the formation trailing smoke from its engines as it headed back out over the Channel. He tried to attack it again but the 109's intervened and he had to break off, losing sight of the Dornier. The bomber may have made it home as KG3 had two crash land on their return to France.

Pilot Officer Alan Wright claimed a probable 109 near Redhill and Sergeant Fokes another probable 109 near Beachy Head. Sergeant Parker damaged one at Maidstone which may have been that flown by Gefr. Erich Mummert of 4/JG52. He was with a formation of six 109's escorting bombers when they were attacked by Spitfires. They formed a six aircraft defensive circle, an unusual tactic for 109's; but as the last aircraft in an incomplete circle, he had a Spitfire attack him from behind. He claimed to have shaken off the Spitfire and was attacked mistakenly by a 109 which hit his radiator. With an over-heating engine, he was forced to make an emergency landing and tried to land at RAF Detling at 2:00pm; but ended up on the boundary and was captured. Was he hit by a 109 or did the initial Spitfire cause the damage?

Various other Messerschmitt 109's of JG52 and JG54 failed to return from this action and they littered a corridor between South London and Beachy Head.

92 Squadron all returned home to Biggin Hill without loss.

At 4:20pm 92 Squadron was scrambled again and ordered to patrol over the airfield below the cloud cover which was below 5,000 feet.

A Formation of eighteen Heinkel 111's, escorted by over a hundred 109's was heading for London, so 92 Squadron were vectored to meet them near Lewes and Shoreham in Sussex. The squadron climbed rapidly and met the escorting ME109's over Brighton at 27,000 feet.

In his combat report, Flying Officer Desmond Drummond says about fifty Messerschmitt 109's were above them but there were bombers at 10,000 feet below the squadron. The RAF fighters formed into line astern and dived into the bombers while the 109's peeled off after the Spitfires. Drummond was attacked by a number of 109's and managed to fire bursts at one which started to emit white smoke from its exhausts. It headed for Beachy Head, but he could not follow it due to the presence of the other 109's.

Sergeant Don Kingaby the '109 specialist' attacked another and claimed it as damaged near Lewes. In his combat report he stated that he attacked two of them causing one to emit black smoke, but he was attacked and had to break off so he could only claim it as damaged.

Pilot Officer Allan Wright was attacked in X4069 and wounded, he managed to make a forced landing at Shoreham in Sussex and was taken to the local hospital with cannon splinters in his thigh. He may have been shot down by either Oberleutnant Gerhard Homuth or Leutnant Heinz Schmidt of 3/JG27. They both claimed a Spitfire near Eastbourne at this time.

The squadron returned home and were released. The hospitalising of Allan Wright meant that Bob Holland took over the command of 'B' Flight, but other pilots were having their own problems on the ground. Tony Bartley had a septic wisdom tooth and was way-laid by the dentist until it could be removed, and the infection stopped.

92 Squadron had fought well and in the following few days Brian Kingcombe and Tony Bartley would both receive the Distinguished Flying Cross.

The new Luftwaffe tactics were not really working, and they were losing many fighters, while the main bomber force now attacked at night, using the darkness to shield them from RAF fighters. The RAF were still losing fighters and pilots, but it seemed that the battle was turning against the Luftwaffe.

October would become even more of a fighter verses fighter scrap, with more 109's carrying bombs in a bid to entice the RAF into combat.

Chapter 9.

The month of fighter battles.

The first few days of October were quiet. Both 72 and 92 Squadrons flew patrols on the 1st but the enemy were absent. The Luftwaffe started to withdraw their bombers for the night blitz, but they continued to harass the RAF fighters with massed fighter sweeps across Kent and Sussex. The airfield hardly received any attention from the bombers, as they dropped their bombs onto London and its docklands. The capital presented itself to the observers at Biggin Hill, night after night as a burning skyline with groping search light beams and the crump of bombs and what few anti-aircraft guns that were available.

On the 2nd of October, Squadron Leader Alan MacLachan arrived to take command of 92 Squadron. He arrived from Number 7 OTU at Hawarden in Cheshire where he had undertaken a refresher course of Spitfires. An experienced pilot he had been at HQ No. 11 Group Fighter Command and had served with 600 Squadron. He was 29 years of age and a steadying hand.

At 9:00am 72 Squadron flew a patrol without incident. At 9:25am 92 Squadron took off and linked up with 603 Squadron to fly a patrol at 20,000 feet from Biggin Hill and down to the South Coast. They spotted one or two ME109's at 30,000 feet but no actual contact was made.

At 11:45am 72 Squadron flew another patrol and despite not encountering the Luftwaffe, their squadron Operational Record Book cites Pilot Officers Herbert Case and Norman Sutton as crashing. The other official records do not mention this, and it must have been a minor crash or collision as both pilots were flying over the next few days. However, Case's Spitfire X4245 was flying over the next few days, while Sutton's X4488 was not seen on operational flying again that month.

In the early afternoon, 72 Squadron took off to patrol and were joined after an hour by 92 Squadron over Sevenoaks at 20,000 feet. The Luftwaffe failed to attend the party!

The 3rd of October had terrible weather with rain and fog 'socking in' the airfield. As a result, neither Biggin Hill squadron got off the ground and they had a much-needed day of rest and servicing.

The poor weather continued into the 4th of October with a gusty wind making flying difficult and rain and thick cloud at times. 92 Squadron sent off small patrols and an unknown pilot claimed a probable Dornier 17 near Deal at 9:40am. The pilot is unknown because the official records record it as unknown and the Operational Record Book does not name the pilots involved.

92 Squadron took part in further small-scale section patrols without incident until 2:30pm when Blue 1 and Blue 2 were patrolling over the airfield. Pilot Officer Desmond Williams (Blue 1) later reported in his combat report, that they were sent after a lone Junkers 88 which ventured across the airfield. As they climbed after the JU88, they lost it but soon saw it again being attacked by three Hurricanes (from 213 Squadron). The two Spitfires joined in the attack and the Junkers dived into the heavy cloud to escape them. After searching the sky, they saw the Junkers again, or another one; but this again disappeared into the cloud layer. Williams says he then saw the bomber and fired about eight seconds worth of ammunition at it and could see the flashes as his 'de Wilde' ammunition hit him. The bomber was lost again in the cloud and re-appeared again to be given another burst. Williams and a Hurricane shadowed the twin-engine aircraft as it passed in and out of the cloud, but eventually Williams broke off the engagement and headed home. He reported that the aircraft had no markings, and control stated it was actually a Bristol Blenheim that had been bombing the Brooklands factory. This is interesting, it is more likely the JU88 had a black wash camouflage applied for night-time operations which the bomber force was now undertaking.

The Junkers 88 was claimed as damaged and was possibly from KG54 and KG76 who had Junkers 88's damaged on operations that day over the south east of England.

72 and 92 Squadron's flew further patrols on this day, but there was no contact with the Luftwaffe and nothing further to report.

Saturday the 5th of October had better weather with a mainly clear morning and some occasional afternoon showers. At 9:35am 72 Squadron were ordered to take off and patrol over Maidstone at 15,000 feet. Unfortunately, ten minutes after take-off Sergeant Robert Staples in X4544 collided mid-air with Pilot Officer Norman Sutton in K9989. While Robert Staples managed to return to Biggin Hill and landed his damaged Spitfire, Pilot Officer Norman Sutton was killed when his aircraft crashed to earth and burnt out. Norman Sutton was taken home by his family and buried in St. Helens cemetery (Lancashire now Merseyside).

The rest of the squadron was soon engaged with a number of Messerschmitt 109E's over the English Channel and Flight Sergeant Jack Steere's Spitfire was hit and damaged at 10:20am. He kept his machine aloft and returned to land at Biggin Hill. The 72 Squadron pilots did not make any claims of their own and returned home.

There are no German claims that appear to correspond with the damage to Jack Steere's machine and it is likely that neither side made any claims. This was probably because on this day, most of the day-time action was by bomb carrying 109's who were dropping them on coastal targets and sought where-ever possible, to avoid fighter verses fighter combat.

72 Squadron flew several further patrols on the 5th of October, but the Luftwaffe were becoming a much more elusive foe.

92 Squadron had taken off at 10:20am with a full complement of twelve Spitfires. They flew a patrol initially with 72 Squadron but were detached and moved on to patrol between 11:00am and 11:30am, along a line between Maidstone and Dungeness.

Flying Officer John Drummond had taken off ten minutes after the main squadron and tried to catch up with them. In his later combat report, he states that he was alone at 22,000 feet over Dungeness, when he saw a flight of twelve Messerschmitt 109's. He dived after them and carried out a beam attack on the two 109's to the rear of the formation. As he was approaching them, they turned away and dived for the coast. Drummond followed them and fired at the rear most machine which started to smoke before hitting the sea.

As he chased after another one, he saw a Henschel 126 spotter plane low over the sea. He immediately attacked it and after a few bursts of fire it landed clumsily on the sea with its fixed undercarriage and wings digging into the waves. As he circled it, a Heinkel 111 and a Dornier 17 flew by, but he was out of ammunition and turned for home to claim his two victories.

Elsewhere the squadron was in action against some ME110's and Pilot Officer John Lund claimed a probable over Maidstone. 92 Squadron eventually managed to get home without incurring any losses.

The Henschel 126 was from 4(H) A.Gr.31 and was on a reconnaissance flight. It came down off Calais with Leutnant von Kladen reported as missing and the unnamed observer, a Feldwebel being killed. The Messerschmitt 109E was either that from 9/JG3 who had a machine shot down over the Channel with the pilot being rescued, or from 2/JG77 who similarly had a 109 shot down over the Channel and the pilot rescued by the ever-efficient German air sea rescue services.

Epro Gruppe 210 lost two Messerschmitt 110's to the east of Maidstone at around 11:30am. One crashed at Millbank Place in Ashford and the crew of Feldwebel Duensnig and Feldwebel Keppisch were killed; while another was never seen again and the crew of Oberleutnant Weimmann and Unteroffizier Huebener are missing to this day. It is possible one of these was Lund's probable, but we cannot say for certain.

92 Squadron returned to base and flew another late afternoon patrol, but there were no further incidents. With the evening darkness closing in, they were released for the night and the ground crews got to work of repairing damage and servicing the aircraft.

Sunday the 6th of October was a cloudy day with some rain. As a result, 72 Squadron only flew two section patrols in the morning without incident. 92 Squadron also put up two Spitfires in the late morning for a section patrol, but again there were no incidents to report.

Despite the poor weather and the low cloud which varied between one hundred and six hundred feet in altitude, a single low flying bomber managed to sneak in and drop a stick of bombs across the airfield. This severely damaged a 72 Squadron Spitfire (K9940) and three barrack blocks as well as causing some injuries. The anti-aircraft defences claimed to have damaged the intruder who made off into the low cloud layer.

The 7th of October was a better day with early cloud but a fair afternoon. There were a number of raids reported across the south east of England and some penetrated in land to London where the docks were bombed, and some warehouses destroyed.

At 8:00am 92 Squadron put up Red and Blue sections to patrol over Tenterden and Ashford at an altitude of 15,000 feet. No enemy aircraft were encountered, and they had landed by 9am.

At 10:05am 92 squadron were up again, patrolling over Maidstone at 20,000 feet for over an hour without incident. 72 Squadron flew similar section sized patrols in the morning, but at 1:40pm both squadrons flew a joint patrol over Maidstone at 25,000 feet. They returned by 2:35pm and there was no further action that day. The standing patrols were tiring for the pilots, while increasing their stress levels, it also increased the wear and tear upon the aircraft and the need for servicing by the groundcrews.

Tuesday the 8th of October found a crisp but fair morning and day. The Luftwaffe made a number of raids over the south east of England with formations crossing the Kent coastline and heading for London.

92 Squadron were scrambled at 8:15am and ordered to patrol over their base at 15,000 feet as the first raiders approached. They appear to have tangled with some Messerschmitt 109's, but the reports do not give details of pilots or any claims; but official combat records report two 92 Squadron pilots as claiming a Messerschmitt 109 destroyed and another as a probable victory over East London at 9:15am. 4/JG52 lost a Messerschmitt 109E at 9:30am which crashed at Little Grange Farm, Woodham Mortimer in Essex. The pilot Feldwebel Paul Boche was attacked at 22,000 feet by Spitfires and was hit in the radiator causing the Daimler-Benz 601 engine to over-heat. He hit a haystack while making a forced landing on the farm and was wounded. Unable to make any escape bid, he was quickly captured by the local home guard. No other RAF pilots made claims around this time, so this is he likely to have been one of the two ME109's claimed by the 92 Squadron pilots.

92 Squadron returned to Biggin Hill at 9:40am. It was about this time that 92 lost another commanding officer when Squadron Leader MacLaclan, who was flying as wing man to Brian Kingcombe, was hit and wounded. Once again Kingcombe assumed temporary command of the unit.

At 9:55am 72 Squadron took off on a patrol. They were followed about thirty minutes later by the refueled and rearmed 92 Squadron. The two squadrons joined up and made a joint patrol. At 10:00am, 72 Squadron's Sergeant Norman Glew forced landed K9847 at Halstead near Biggin Hill when his engine failed. He was unharmed and soon returned to the airfield. It appears his engine may have just failed, or he may have been damaged in combat as the remaining pilots were soon engaged with ME109's. Two aircraft returned with some combat damage, but no claims were made by the pilots of 72 Squadron. It is believed their antagonists were from JG52 and Feldwebel Bielmer of 5/JG52 claimed a Spitfire around this time.

That afternoon 92 Squadron flew single and paired aircraft patrols without incident. The smaller section and single aircraft patrols were indicative of the lessening of Luftwaffe activity and what appears to have been a growing sense of ease for the RAF. 72 Squadron did not fly again on that day.

The 9th of October was quite unsuitable for flying with rain in the morning and a gusty wind. However, at 11:00am raiders started to head across the Kent coastline. At 11:45am both of Biggin Hill's squadrons were scrambled and vectored by the fighter controller towards Dungeness at 30,000 feet.

As they approached the coastline, the two Biggin Hill squadrons fought with Messerschmitt 109's and Sergeant Erith was hit in Spitfire X4597. The aircraft caught fire and Erith was badly burnt while taking to his parachute over Ashford at 12:50pm. He landed and was immediately transported to Willesborough Hospital with major burns. Sadly, he died of his injuries just eight days later, on the 17th of October. It is believed he was shot down by Oberleutnant Hans Ekkehard Bob of 7/JG54 who claimed his fifteen victory around that time and location. Despite the large dog fight, no further claims or losses were recorded, and the squadrons returned to their airfield at Biggin.

At 1:50pm 92 Squadron flew another patrol and although some pilots spotted enemy aircraft in the distance, no actual combat was undertaken. At 2:45pm 72 Squadron flew a patrol without incident returning to base at 4:15pm. As the autumnal sun started to go down the squadrons were released for the day.

Thursday the 10th of October 1940 would be a black day for 92 Squadron. The Luftwaffe put a large number of aircraft into the air, but very few actually ventured over Kent.

At 7:10am nine Spitfires of 92 Squadron took off and headed out on a patrol over their regular patrol area of Maidstone at 15,000 feet. The squadron was vectored on to a lone Dornier 17 to the east of Brighton and they set off in pursuit.

The single bomber should have been an easy victory for nine Spitfires, but it put up a very spirited fight and Flying Officer John Drummond and Pilot Officer Desmond Williams collided as they attacked it and crashed at 8:15am near Tangmere. Both pilots were killed with Drummond's aircraft crashing at Portslade. Desmond Williams was still alive when he came down near a church and the local priest gave him the last rites before he died in the priest's arms. John Drummond was wounded in arm and leg, before baling out too low for his parachute to deploy correctly.

Desmond Williams was just 20 years old and is buried in the London Road cemetery in Salisbury. John Drummond was 21 years old and is buried in the Thornton Garden of Rest, near Litherland north of Liverpool. Williams had crashed at Fallowfield Crescent, Hove.

The bombers rear gunner also damaged the Spitfire of Sergeant Ellis who had to make a forced landing at Poynings Station at 8:35am He was thankfully unharmed. Ellis and Pilot Officer Mansell-Lewis later claimed the bomber as a probable victory, claiming to have killed or injured the rear gunner before it escaped into the cloud and headed home to France. To make matters worse the propagandist Lord Haw-Haw mentioned the losses in his nightly broadcast, goading the fighter pilots that a single bomber had shot down three Spitfires before escaping.

The bomber is believed to have been a 1/KG2 Dornier 17 which returned to base with damage following combat with RAF fighters. Leutnant Dilcher was killed and the other three crew were unharmed.

At 10:05am the seven remaining Spitfires from 92 Squadron met up with 66 Squadron and flew a short patrol over Biggin Hill airfield without incident. That afternoon 92 Squadron were released from stand-by, while at 1:50pm 72 Squadron flew a patrol without any contact with the Luftwaffe.

Friday the 11th of October was a fine day with a few scattered clouds at 3,000 feet. At 7:30am 72 Squadron took off for a patrol over a convoy in the English Channel off Deal. As they were patrolling, they were bounced by a formation of Messerschmitt 109E's and Pilot Officer Peter Pool was hit and wounded. As his crippled Spitfire (K9870) started to lose height, he baled-out and upon landing he was taken to hospital. His aircraft crashed near Sittingbourne. The victory was either that of Hauptmann Heinz Bretnutz or Oberleutnant Gerhard Michalski of Stab II/JG53 who both claimed to have shot down Spitfires at this time and in this area. 72 squadron returned home without any other losses and without making any claims themselves.

Flight Sergeant Jack Steere took off at 7:40am to carry out an engine test. While airborne he spotted a lone Dornier 17 at 30,000 feet and after a short chase and climb, he managed to catch up with it. At the mouth of the Thames Estuary, he opened fire and carried out four attacks causing an undercarriage leg to fall away and the other one to hang down limply. The starboard engine stopped with the bomber in trouble. Steere later claimed that the Dornier tried to ram his Spitfire before it dived vertically and was last seen at 3,000 feet, about ten to fifteen miles off the North Foreland heading for France. No Dornier 17's where reported lost in this area and it is likely that it did manage to get home.

Elsewhere at 10:30am Sergeant Glew collided with an obstacle while taxying at Biggin Hill and damaged R6777. The rest of the squadron took off on a patrol without incident, although there are reports that Flight Sergeant Jack Steere shot down a Messerschmitt 109E near Sittingbourne at 10:55am.

At 10:40am 92 Squadron took off and met up with 66 Squadron from Gravesend over Biggin Hill. They were vectored by control on to a patrol line from Maidstone to Dover and on to Dungeness, but they returned to base without sighting the Luftwaffe. They again took off at 2:05pm to patrol with 66 Squadron, but 66 were already engaged with the enemy and they did noy link-up.

At 3:40pm five Spitfires of 92 Squadron's 'A' Flight took off to patrol over Maidstone, but as they climbed away from Biggin Hill they spotted a formation of Messerschmitt 109's over the Thames. They quickly engaged the 109's and Flight Lieutenant Brian Kingcombe claimed to have shot one down at 4:30pm. It is believed this was from 5/JG27 who had Unteroffizier Wiemann wounded and rescued from the sea by the German air sea rescue services. The other pilots appeared to have had non-effective combats an no other claims were made by the squadron.

92 Squadron were back on the ground at Biggin by 4:50pm and the twilight prevented any further flying that day. One welcome piece of news was the transfer and promotion of Flying Officer John 'Pancho' Villa from 72 squadron to 92 Squadron on the other side of the airfield! He was an experienced fighter pilot who would be missed by 72 Squadron, but a find addition to 92 as a flight commander.

The 12th of October 1940 was another settled day once the morning fog had dispersed. Despite the low-lying cloud, 92 Squadron put up two Spitfires just before 8:00am for a patrol and at 8:55am they sent up seven Spitfires for a patrol.

72 Squadron put up a formation of seven aircraft at 8:50am and another two at 9:55am for a patrol, but there was allegedly no sign of the Luftwaffe and they all returned home without incident. However, despite the reported lack of enemy activity, Pilot Officer Herbert Case crashed and was killed for an unknown reason at Capel le Ferne near Folkestone at 9:20am. (This is the site of the cliff top Battle of Britain memorial today).

For many years, the cause of his death was unknown, although according to records on the bbm.org.uk website, Case's mother received a letter from an army officer's wife. This said he had been shot down by enemy fighters. Case was buried near his family home at St. Nicholas's churchyard, Withycombe in Somerset.

Major Werner Molders of JG51 claimed two Hurricanes around this time at Lympne and Canterbury and one of these may have been Case's Spitfire - a case of misidentification. Hauptmann Walter Oesau of Stab JG51 also claimed a Spitfire in the area around this time for his 36th victory and this may have been the actual correct claim. Either way, it would appear Case was shot down without the rest of his unit even knowing it.

Although the Operational Record Book does not record his participation, the former 92 Squadron Pilot, Squadron Leader Robert Stanford Tuck was visiting Biggin Hill from 257 Squadron. He followed his ex-colleagues aloft in his Hurricane and claimed a Messerschmitt 109E near Dover at 10:15am. This was Leutnant Bernard Malischewski of Stab 3/JG54. He crashed at Small Hythe near Tenterden, Kent and was detained by the Home Guard and a Kent Police officer. Malischewski who was a Knights Cross holder, told his interrogators that he had not been shot down and that his engine had failed. Examination of his aircraft by the Intelligence officers found no sign of bullet holes in his machine and it had not over-heated. The aircraft was so well-preserved that it was recovered and sent on a fund-raising tour, allowing members of the public to examine it for money. Whether the engine had over-heated is not recorded and is something of a mystery to this day.

72 Squadron remained on the ground for the rest of the day, but at 3:50pm, 92 sent up the whole squadron to link up with 66 Squadron and patrol over Maidstone at Angels 20 (20,000 feet). The two squadrons soon tangled with a formation over Messerschmitt 109's between Rochester and Margate at 4:40pm. The 109's were from JG52 who were engaged on a sweep across Kent escorting bomb carrying 'Jabo' Messerschmitt 109's. The 109's had tried to drop their bombs on Biggin Hill airfield with little effect, before heading for home and encountering 92 and 66 Squadrons on their way to the coast.

Pilot Officer Trevor 'Wimpey' Wade claimed a probable victory and two more as damaged, while Sergeant Donald Kingaby claimed one destroyed and another probable. Flight Lieutenant Brian Kingcombe claimed one destroyed near Margate.

JG52 lost four 109's between 3:30pm and 4:30pm. The machine of Feldwebel Siegfried Voss (3/JG52) came down at West Brabourne, some fifteen miles south west of Margate and this may have been Kingcombe's victim, while Kingaby may have accounted for Feldwebel Willi Reichenbach of 4/JG52. He was killed when he crashed into the sea off Sheerness. Another candidate who crashed at 4:30pm, was Oberleutnant Karl Sauer of 2/JG52 who was wounded and baled-out at Hollingbourne near Maidstone.

Oberleutnant Karl Sauer claimed that his aircraft was slower than the others in his formation and was clearly making excuses for his demise.

It is interesting to note the 'excuses' from these Luftwaffe pilots. The Luftwaffe was under extreme pressure and their losses over the summer months had been high. Whether they were showing signs of combat stress is debatable, but Kanalkrankheit or Channel sickness was a well-known 'condition' among Luftwaffe fighter pilots in 1940. This it is said was due to the fear of coming down in the cold sea.

However, 92 Squadron lost the impressively named Pilot Officer Aberconway 'John' Patinson in X4591. Patinson (sometimes spelt Pattinson) was on his first combat sortie when he was shot down and killed over Hawkinge at 4:40pm. The aircraft came down and burnt up at Bartholomew's Wood, Postling. The body of the 21 years old was recovered and he was buried at Parkstone cemetery, Poole.

It is hard to identify a victor as Leutnant Franz Essl of 1/JG52 and Oberleutnant Helmet Bennemann of 2/JG52 both claimed Spitfires at this time and area.

On the 13th of October, 72 Squadron moved north to RAF Leconfield in Humberside for a well-earned rest. They had just seven effective pilots still on strength. Before they left, the mornings fog cleared, and Flight Lieutenant Robson and Pilot Officer Elliott flew a patrol at 9:55am without incident. Flight Lieutenant 'Pancho' Villa led nine aircraft on a final patrol at 11:30am before they returned, refueled, and left Biggin for Leconfield. Villa then 'hopped' across the airfield to join his new colleagues at 92 Squadron.

At 12:40pm ten Spitfires of 92 Squadron took off to patrol at 30,000 feet over the airfield. The squadron saw four Messerschmitt 109E's and were preparing to attack them, when another 109 attacked the rear of their formation. Flight Lieutenant Brian Kingcombe managed to shake it off and chased it all the way to Kennington near Ashford where he shot it down. The pilot Gefr. Hubert Rungen of 7/JG3 reported later that he was part of an escort to 109 'Jabo' bomb carriers when they were attacked by ten Spitfires. He was hit in the radiator and was heading for the coast, chased by the Spitfires when he made a forced landing at Roberts Dane, Hastingleigh near Kennington at 2:10pm. Like the earlier losses the day before, this almost intact Messerschmitt went on fund raising tours of the United Kingdom. The public were not only allowed to view the enemy aircraft close-up, but on occasion allowed to inspect the cockpit in return for cash for Spitfires.

The morning of the 14th started with the usual autumnal fog and drizzle once again. 92 Squadron were to be joined today by 74 Squadron led by the famous Squadron Leader, Adolph 'Sailor' Malan. They flew in at 1:20pm from Coltishall in Norfolk where they had been resting after having already claimed many victories while flying from RAF Hornchurch during the battle. After a quick rest, a bite to eat and refueling, Malan led the squadron on a patrol at 4:30pm returning without encountering the enemy. Most of 74 Squadrons pilots knew the area well having already taken part in many aerial battles over Kent.

74 Squadron were run by a strict disciplinarian in Malan and his two flight commanders Mungo-Park and Stephen. They were everything that 92 Squadron were not, but they were both ruthless squadrons in the skies.

92 Squadron only sent up two patrols by two sections of two Spitfires. However, Pilot Officers Robert Holland and John Lund claimed to have sighted and attacked a Junkers 88 between Maidstone and Ashford which they damaged at 12:30pm. No record can be found to substantiate this from the perspective of the Luftwaffe, although this does not mean it did not happen.

The 15th of October 1940 was a drizzly and showery day, but there was still good enough visibility for flying.

At 8:45am 92 Squadron took off to patrol with Gravesend's 66 Squadron over Biggin Hill at 30,000 feet. (66 were a regular link squadron for the Biggin Hill units as they came under the control of the Biggin Hill Sector).

Over South East London the two squadrons came into contact with over fifty Messerschmitt 109's who had been dropping bombs on the railway lines at Waterloo and Vauxhall stations. As the 'Jabo' 109's tried to return home a running battle ensued, and Donald Kingaby claimed another 109 destroyed off Dover at about 9:30am. A Messerschmitt 109E flown by Oberfeldwebel Willi Bauer force landed on the beach below the high-water mark next to Princes' Gold Course, Sandwich at 9:17am. Bauer who was unsure what to do, just sat for nearly an hour next to his aircraft before he was detained!

Sergeant Ronald Fokes mean-while claimed a now rare sight over the South East of England – a Heinkel 111 off Dover at 9:30am. An aircraft from 1/KG26 did get home with damage and three wounded crewmen that morning following a fighter attack, and this was likely to have been the same machine.

92 Squadron did lose Sergeant Kenneth Parker in R6838. He was apparently shot down at 10:00am and was killed when he crashed onto the mud flats at Hoo Marina, All Hallows on the Grain Peninsula. It has not been able to link any Luftwaffe claims with his loss. Parker's body was washed up many miles away in Holland where he was buried in the military plot of Terschelling Island off the Dutch coast.

92 Squadron eventually returned to Biggin Hill and refueled and re-armed.

At 11:20am they were ordered to send nine aircraft up to patrol over Sevenoaks at 30,000 feet. They were then vectored to head westwards at 27,000 feet and intercepted fifty Messerschmitt 109's at 20,000 feet near Maidstone.

The fact the RAF fighters were now under-taking patrols at higher altitudes was placing them in better tactical positions. As a result, for once they were often above the enemy formations and able to attack from above and out of the sun.

Sergeant Ronald Fokes followed up his Heinkel claim, by claiming to have destroyed a 109 over Ashford at 1:00pm. This was possibly the Messerschmitt 109E of Oberleutnant Gunter Deicke of 8/JG27 who crashed north east of Ashford at Trimworth Manor and was captured. Pilot Officer Holland claimed a probable 109 and this may have been that of Feldwebel Gotthardt Freis of 6/JG27. He was seen to ditch in the channel off Cap Griz Nez but was reported missing and sadly never found.

Flight Lieutenant Brian Kingcombe was hit by a ME109 and wounded. He was badly wounded in the right leg causing his flying boot to fill with blood as he tried to control the Spitfire. He later reported in his book, that the aircraft was hit, and it sounded like a bucket full of pebbles being thrown against the aircraft. With the controls unresponsive, he decided he should bale out as he was frightened the loss of blood from his leg might cause him to pass out and crash to his death. He therefore went quickly through how to bale-out in his mind and decided to either roll the aircraft over or push the stick forward suddenly when the canopy was open. He went for the latter option and no sooner had he gone through the motions, he was falling like a rag doll through the air with his arms and legs flailing around.

He pulled the rip-chord and the parachute opened with the customary 'jerk'. He then came down to land as he gathered his senses. He then remembered as he landed, that he was wearing a captured Luftwaffe kapok life jacket. These had become especially prized by RAF pilots with a number using them instead of the RAF yellow/tan version. He quickly removed this when he landed as a group of farmers with pitch forks headed towards him. Exposing his RAF tunic had the desired effect, and he was quickly taken to the Royal Navy Hospital at Chatham for treatment.

Brian Kingcombe was to receive what he later recalled as horrific treatment in the Naval hospital. The doctor rather than x-ray the leg to locate the bullet, chose to probe it and in the process cut an artery. As Kingcombe started to bleed to death, the doctor sliced open the leg to locate and stitch up the two halves of the artery he had detached. As soon as he could, Kingcombe left the hospital and headed to Orpington hospital for more considerate treatment!

Uffz. Gerhard Scheidt of 1/JG26 claimed a Spitfire at this time and rough location, and he may have been the man who shot down Kingcombe. (Scheidt as a Feldwebel on the 5th of November would be shot down and captured in Kent. Once again, a pilot declared to his interrogators that his engine had failed and he had not been shot down, although this may have been the case as no bullet holes were located in what remained of his 109).

92 Squadron also had Pilot Officer John Lund shot down over the Thames at 11:50am. He baled out of R6642 and was fished out of the sea off Bee Ness Jetty by the crew of HMS Nysan without injury.

JG26 made a number of claims around this time including those by their commander Major Adolph Galland and Gustav 'Micki' Sprick of 8/JG26.

The rest of 92 squadron returned to Biggin Hill and remained on the ground for the remainder of the day.

On Wednesday the 16th of October, the weather was very poor with thick cloud and showers. The visibility at times was down to just 600 yards which meant that flying was too dangerous, but 74 Squadron did put up three Spitfires around 9:00am. They did not make contact with the Luftwaffe and returned home in the gloom.

92 Squadron did not send any Spitfires aloft that day. In the afternoon there was some activity from the Luftwaffe over London with sporadic raiders, but Biggin Hill's squadrons remained firmly on the ground.

On the 17th of October, the day started with early morning mist which cleared to produce a fine day. At 9:05am, 92 Squadron sent thirteen Spitfires to patrol over Maidstone at 30,000 feet. Fifteen minutes later at 9:20am, 74 Squadron were led up on a patrol by 'Sailor' Malan. They both returned home at 10:20am and 10:45am respectively without incident.

At 11:40am 92 Squadron scrambled a flight of four Spitfires after a small raid, but no contact was made, and they returned home. (Again, this was probably a small unit of 'Jabo' Messerschmitt 109's on a nuisance raid).

At 3:05pm 74 Squadron was sent up with Sailor Malan in the lead. They soon encountered about sixty Messerschmitt 109's after Malan had spotted anti-aircraft fire towards the Thames Estuary. Maneuvering his unit carefully, they engaged the formation between Gravesend and Maidstone. The 109 formation, consisting once again of 'Jabo' fighter bombers and an escort of standard ME109E'.

In his subsequent combat report, Pilot Officer Bryan Draper reported that he fired at a ME109 with sixty degrees deflection as it crossed his sights, at a distance of some 200 yards. The three second burst resulted in a stream of black and white smoke spewing from its engine and it appeared to be in difficulty. Draper however could not follow the 109 due to the number of Messerschmitt's above him, but he claimed it as a probable victory.

Draper then saw another seven M109's in line astern and he positioned himself behind and slightly above the rear most fighter. Taking careful aim, he shot this one down in flames before going after another which was actually a Hurricane. When he realized his error, he broke off the combat, before sighting another twelve 109's to the south. He prepared to attack this unit, but they turned to face him. He fired off a quick burst which caused the leading two 109's to break and he dived away, spiraling down to avoid the other 109s. Draper eventually returned to Biggin Hill, where he claimed a victory as well as the probable. His victim was Oberleutnant Walter Rupp of 3/JG53 who force landed on Manston airfield at 3:45pm where he was duly detained by the army unit based to protect the site.

'Sailor' Malan claimed a 109 probable near Ashford when he saw two yellow nosed 109's crossing his nose. Malan targeted the right-hand machine and opened fire with a quarter deflection from 200 yards, hitting the fighter's elevators and probably its control wires as it suddenly bunted downwards rather than making the usual 109 defensive split-s maneuver.

Malan could not follow due to the Spitfire's float carburetor which choked off the fuel supply in a negative-g dive. The 109 continued to dive away trailing smoke and Malan tried to catch it but blacked out for a few seconds due to the g-stresses. He chased it down to 9,000 feet when it disappeared into the cloud layer. When Malan landed, he discovered that only his starboard four guns had fired. A strict disciplinarian, one can only imagine what happened to his armourer!

Pilot Officer St. John claimed a 109 destroyed in the Ramsgate area. Flying Officer William Nelson claimed a 109 destroyed between Gravesend and Maidstone, but 74 Squadron lost Flying Officer Alan Ricalton who was shot down (in P7360) by a ME109 and killed over Maidstone at 3:40pm. His aircraft crashed near Hollingbourne and he was buried at Sittingbourne cemetery. He was 26 years of age.

The likely victors and losses were from JG53. They lost Hauptmann Mayer the Gruppe Kommandeur (Stab 1/JG53) who crashed into the Channel, while another 109 from 8/JG53 came down in the Channel and the pilot was rescued by the German air sea rescue service.

74 Squadron had returned to Biggin Hill by 4:00pm and there was no further action that day.

Friday the 18th of October was a day of fog and autumnal drizzle. There was some flying, but the Luftwaffe only sent odd aircraft over in nuisance raids; the raiders hiding in the thick clouds which made interception very difficult.

The 19th was a very similar day with poor visibility and the Luftwaffe made further small-scale nuisance raids on London.

At 2:25pm 92 Squadron made a squadron strength patrol over Maidstone. There are no details of any combat, but they lost Sergeant Leslie Alton in R6922 who crashed at Tuesnoad Farm, Smarden in Kent. The cause of his death to this day is unknown, but oxygen supply failure is suspected.

Alton who was from Nuneaton was an accomplished sportsman having captained his Grammar School's cricket, football and hockey teams. He was just 20 years old. The RAF tried to recover the wreak which had smashed into the ground, they managed to recover Alton who was buried in his hometown. However, further recovery of the wreck was abandoned when a paraffin storm lamp was knocked over setting the aircraft's remaining fuel alight.

74 Squadron also made a squadron strength patrol, but once again they returned home without incident.

Although the Luftwaffe was 'missing', this allowed the RAF squadrons to regain their strength while giving pilots practice time and rest. The newer younger inexperienced pilots desperately needed more airtime and tactical flying experience.

Sunday the 20th of October would be a very busy day for the Biggin Hill squadrons with claims and losses for both 74 and 92. The day was fair with a slight haze allowing much better flying conditions with visibility of between two to four miles.

During the course of the day the Luftwaffe sent over six formations of fighters with the usual mix of bomb carrying 109's to London. The bombs were dropped sporadically and were again more of a nuisance than a general threat. As a result, the RAF fighter squadrons rose to meet them in combat making various claims.

At 11:20am, 92 Squadron flew a patrol over Maidstone at 30,000 feet, linking up with 222 Squadron. They were soon vectored onto a Messerschmitt 110 of 7F/LG2 which was on a photo reconnaissance mission over the Thames Estuary. The Spitfires gave chase and the 110 headed towards the east of Tunbridge Wells, when it was attacked by Sergeant Don Kingaby, Flight Lieutenant 'Pancho' Villa, Flying Officer Roy Mottram and a 222 Squadron pilot. They collectively sent it down to a forced landing at Bockingfold near Horsmonden at 12:50pm. The pilot Oberleutnant Lemmerich was captured, but the gunner Unteroffizier Ebeling was killed possibly by the Spitfires guns.

Flight Lieutenant 'Pancho' Villa's Spitfire was damaged by return fire from Unteroffizier Ebeling, but he managed to get home to Biggin Hill, as did another 92 Squadron Spitfire which was also damaged by return fire.

During the course of the morning 74 Squadron put up various sections on patrols. At 10:15am and again at 2:15pm they put up the squadron in strength to make further patrols. Not long after take-off at 2:30pm, the squadron together with various other RAF units, tangled with Messerschmitt 109's from LG3, JG52 and JG77.

In a vicious combat Sergeant Thomas Kirk flying P7370 damaged a ME109E but was badly wounded over Coxheath near Maidstone. He baled out with gunshot wounds and after landing he was taken to Preston Hall Hospital on the other side of Maidstone. Sadly, he died there some months later from his wounds. He was 22 years old and buried by his family in the churchyard of St. Oswald's in East Harsley, North Yorkshire.

Sergeant Clive Hilkin baled-out of P7426 and was wounded over South London by a 109. He baled-out as his Spitfire crashed at Cowden. He was admitted to Orpington hospital for treatment.

Pilot Officer Bryan Draper (Yellow 2) reported intercepting thirty plus ME109's near the Thames and singled one out as it turned northwards over the river. He fired two long bursts at it and damaged it before he was hit by another 109 and he had to make a forced landing near Tonbridge. His aircraft had a dead engine due to a damaged oil cooler. Before he went down, Draper reported seeing the aircraft he shot at, crashing in the Kidbrooke or Woolwich area. It is believed Draper's victim was Oberfeldwebel Albert Friedemann from 6/JG52. His Messerschmitt exploded over Woolwich and he baled-out too low and was killed. The official records give the time as 1:45pm, but Bryan Draper was airborne after that time and he gives the time as 2:45pm. Was this a clerical error in the records?

Pilot Officer H.M. Stephen claimed another ME109 destroyed and another probable between Sevenoaks and Dungeness. One of these may have been the 3/JG77 machine of Feldwebel Wilhelm which crashed at Waldron near Uckfield at 2:38pm. The pilot was captured unharmed.

Flying Officer (acting Flight Lieutenant) John Mungo-Park destroyed a ME109E near Maidstone and this was the machine of Unteroffizier Franz Mairl which crashed at Chapel Farm near Lenham to the east of Maidstone. Franz Mairl was killed after baling out. He had successfully exited the 109, but his parachute caught fire and he fell to his death as the silk burned away.

74 squadron returned to Biggin Hill and remained on the ground as the dark evening drew in before they were released from duty.

Chapter 10.

The end of the battle.

On Monday the 21st of October, the weather returned to the drizzle and cloud of previous days. At 7:35am 92 Squadron put up Yellow section to patrol over Maidstone, but there was no contact with the enemy and they returned home.

In the mid-afternoon, 74 Squadron put up two flights on two separate patrols, but they also returned home without incident. It was becoming more apparent that the Luftwaffe was losing their enthusiasm for massed raids on the South East of England and the threat of a likely invasion was receding.

At 5:44pm in the twilight, Red one and two of 92 Squadron were scrambled after a single bandit, but no interception was made and once again they returned home, this time to a difficult landing as darkness enveloped the airfield. Thankfully, they managed to land thanks to a runway marked out with goose neck paraffin lamps.

Tuesday the 22nd of October started off fair but with high pressure, fog returned after dusk. Despite this the window of good weather allowed a number of operational flights during the day and at 7:00am, 74 Squadron's Pilot Officer Bryan Draper took off on a weather sortie and returned unharmed. Half an hour later, Pilot Officers Stephen and Spurdle took off for a short two-man patrol. They flew along the coast and had another uneventful sortie before returning home.

At 10:00am, 92 Squadron took off for a ninety-minute patrol over Maidstone at 30,000 feet. Despite the clear weather and good visibility, the Luftwaffe failed to show up. A few single Messerschmitt 109E's tried to sneak in and drop their bombs on the coastal ports, while the long-range guns near Calais also hit the Kent coast a few times; but it was difficult to intercept these lone raiders.

At about 10:20-10:25am, 74 Squadron also took off and were directed to link up with 92 Squadron on their ninety-minute patrol. Flying was in some respects becoming tedious for the tired and weary pilots. The poor weather was becoming just as dangerous as the Luftwaffe who seemed more reluctant to fight. The Luftwaffe very rarely sent Heinkel's and Dornier's over in the day-light and they were used in the night-time Blitz raids on British cities and towns. This left the ME109's to continue making the hit and run raids. Any thought of the battles of attrition from the summer were now being forgotten.

At 12:32pm 92 Squadron sent up three Spitfires to investigate a reported enemy aircraft over Biggin Hill, but no contact was made, and they returned to earth.

After lunch, at 1:40pm, nine Spitfires from 74 Squadron took off and were ordered to patrol near the airfield. Fifteen minutes later, 92 Squadron took off to patrol once again over Maidstone where the two squadrons eventually linked up.

A number of single Messerschmitt 109's where moving across the Kent and the Sussex borders and the fighter controllers moved the two squadrons and several others around accordingly like aerial chess pieces.

'Sailor' Malan was leading 74 Squadron and they flew at 30,000 feet were their contrails could easily be seen by the single ME109 fighter-bombers. This it was hoped would make the 109's retreat to France without causing any damage.

92 Squadron reported sighting some of the enemy fighters, but Malan and 74 could not see them. 92 appear to have then engaged some of the lone fighters, but no claims or losses were made, and it is likely the raiders dived into the cloud and made good their escape.

At just after 2:00pm Malan spotted six ME109's flying south east at 26,000 feet. He gave the order to attack but managed to lose four of his own unit as they winged over to go after the 109's.

Malan singled out the leader in a fast dive, opening fire at 200 yards and hitting the 109 which started to emit black smoke. A second burst of gunfire added to the damage, but Malan's windscreen frosted over, and he had to break off. The Messerschmitt levelled off at 8,000 feet and Malan watched it as his windscreen slowly de-iced with the 'warmer' air temperature. The ME109 headed out to sea off Hastings leaving a trail of thick smoke before it hit the sea. The pilot Leutnant Karl Mueller of 3/JG51 managed to get out and was captured by a boat crew who pulled him from the cold sea.

Flight Lieutenant John Mungo-Park also claimed a 109 in the same action near Hastings. However, post war assessments appear to show that Mungo-Park had also fired at Lt. Mueller and this was probably a shared victory.

An hour later the squadron lost Flying Officer Peter St. John aged 23 in P7431. He was shot down by a ME109 and killed at South Nutfield in Surrey. In the same action, Pilot Officer Robert Spurdle was also hit and baled-out unharmed at Hadlow Place in Tonbridge. The offending 109's, have not been identified. Peter St. John was 23 years old and is buried in Amersham cemetery in Buckinghamshire.

The two squadrons returned to Biggin Hill and there was no further flying that day or the next, due to the fog and drizzle. This allowed the pilots to rest and the aircraft to get an urgent servicing.

Thursday the 24th of October was a mixed day weather wise, with a cloudy morning, rain at noon and a fair afternoon and evening.

At 9:25am, 92 Squadron put up nine aircraft to patrol over Maidstone at 13,000 feet. There was a 10/10ths cloud layer below them at 5,000 feet which hindered operations. However, 74 Squadron soon joined them on patrol over mid-Kent.

During the patrol Sergeant Don Kingaby attacked a single Dornier 17 to the east of Deal at 10:20am and claimed to have shot it down; but it appears it was an aircraft from KG2 which crashed on its return to base in France. No other contact was made, and the two units returned home.

In his later combat report, Don Kingaby stated that having taken off with red section as their 'weaver', he spotted an aircraft above the cloud layer at 6,000 feet. He went down to investigate and after flying a parallel course in the sun he made a beam attack and hit the port engine which started to smoke. His gun fire then entered the cockpit area and the aircraft dived away to the port side vertically. Kingaby believed the pilot was either killed or wounded. The cloud layer was at 5,000 feet and the Dornier disappeared through it with Kingaby carefully following it down. When Don Kingaby broke through the cloud layer there was no sign of the Dornier, but he saw a 'green area' on the sea and assumed this was the crash site, about five miles to the east of Deal. It would appear therefore, that the Dornier was the aircraft from KG2 which managed to get home.

Further patrols were flown that afternoon by Biggin Hill aircraft, but yet again, there was no contact with the enemy; the autumnal weather continuing to cause major disruption to the airmen of both sides.

Friday the 25th of October was cloudy with some showery rain, but the visibility was good enough to allow for operations by both sides to resume. A short early morning weather reconnaissance flight was made by 74 Squadron's at 6:45am which reported the improving weather and the likelihood of operations.

At 8:30 and 8:35am 74 Squadron took off in two flights for a patrol. However, the weather must have deteriorated again as Pilot Officer Stephen landed at Starrington airfield, while Flying Officer Nelson landed at RAF Hornchurch and 'Sailor' Malan and three others landed at Gravesend. The remainder of the squadron managed to land back at Biggin Hill.

An hour later at 11:05am, the six absent pilots collected at Gravesend and after having their fuel tanks 'topped up' they flew back to Biggin Hill, landing after the short five-minute flight.

The day was notable for 92 Squadron with the arrival of Squadron Leader Johnny Kent from 303 (Polish) Squadron at Northolt. Kent was a no-nonsense Canadian who had molded the Poles into one of the most effective fighting units during the Battle of Britain. He arrived with 92 Squadron having lost a number of commanding officers over the past few weeks for one reason or another.

What the CO-less squadron lacked in discipline, they made up for in fighting ability. Now Kent would instill both into this premier fighter squadron. In the days after his arrival there were more than a few 'run-ins' with his new pilots; but he eventually knocked them into shape and the talented pilots added discipline to their skills to make them even more formidable.

At 9:30am, 92 Squadron took off and linked up with Gravesend's 66 Squadron for a morning patrol. The patrol was uneventful, and they returned without loss or incident. They did not have the problems that 74 Squadron had with the weather which must have improved where they were operating.

At 1:00pm having been refueled, 92 Squadron was ordered to take off and patrol over Rochford and Southend at 30,000 feet. Within half an hour they were vectored back over Kent, towards an incoming raid heading for Maidstone. The Luftwaffe had put numerous smaller formations of fighter bombers over Kent, with large fighter escorts; and 92 were heading towards one of these.

At about 1:30pm they met the formation between Maidstone and Sevenoaks. The formation they met belonged to their old foes from Abbeville – Adolph Galland's JG26. Pilot Officer Sherrington shot down a Messerschmitt 109 believed to have been Leutnant Hermann Ripke of 8/JG26. His aircraft came down at Riverhill House to the south of Sevenoaks. He had baled-out but his parachute failed, and he sadly fell to his death some miles away from the wreck of his aircraft.

Flight Lieutenant John 'Pancho' Villa, who was now an integral part of 92 Squadron, shot down another ME109 to the south west of Maidstone, severely damaging its rudder. Feldwebel Josef Gartner of 8/JG26 found his machine totally unresponsive and in an involuntary dive, so he baled-out with slight wounds and was captured when he landed. His ME109 crashed on New Barn farm at Yalding in Kent. Josef Gartner was a very experienced pilot with a Knights Cross, having flown over France and the Battle of Britain, with several victories to his name.

Sergeant Don Kingaby claimed another Messerschmitt 109 as damaged over the English Channel after he chased it all the way to France. He did not realise he was over France until he broke through the overcast. The ME109 which was emitting glycol had disappeared so Kingaby beat a hasty retreat back to Kent claiming the 109 as damaged. RAF pilots were still under strict orders not to chase enemy aircraft back over France.

Two of JG26's ME109's returned home with damage around this time and one of these may have been Don Kingaby's 109.

Pilot Officer John Mansell-Lewis in X4480 made a forced landing at Penshurst airfield after this combat at 1:30pm over Marden. He was unharmed, having been hit by the 7/JG26 commander Oberleutnant Joachim Munchenburg, a top pilot and ace who would go on to lead the unit's Gruppe over Malta and North Africa, before being killed in 1943 with 135 victories to his name.

92 Squadron returned home at 1:45pm but they were ordered up again at 3:25pm and directed to meet with 222 Squadron over Hornchurch at 15,000 feet. However, no contact was made with the Luftwaffe and they returned home at 4:45pm as the daylight faded.

This brought an end to the stations flying for the day and the pilots went off to the nearby pubs and the ground crews went to work on the Spitfires.

The 26th of October was another cloudy and showery day with reasonable visibility and clouds at 3,000 feet. At 7:20am two 92 Squadron pilots took off and were directed by fighter control towards a bandit, but no contact was made.

At 8:55am Malan led his flight on a short patrol without incident before returning to Biggin to refuel. Just after 10:05am both 92 and 74 Squadrons took off for a joint patrol with 66 Squadron from Gravesend. The three squadrons now basically formed the Biggin Hill wing, a sign of things to come in 1941; and patrolled over Biggin at 15,000 feet before climbing to 30,000 over Maidstone. The 'wing' was soon vectored towards an incoming raid and attacked the twenty-thirty aircraft from JG53 and JG52 which led to a massed dogfight back towards Dover.

Sergeant Ronald Fokes of 92 Squadron, shot down a ME109 which he reported to have come down at Pembury near Tunbridge Wells. The aircraft of Uffz. Karl Geiswinkler (of 6/JG53) who was killed, crashed at Chalket Farm near Tunbridge Wells at 10:30am.

Flying Officer Hammond claimed a Messerschmitt 109 destroyed off Dover and this is believed to have been either an aircraft from 4/JG53 whose pilot was rescued by the German rescue service; or it could have been Oberfeldwebel Oskar Strack of 1/JG52 who was lost in the Channel.

Pilot Officer Trevor 'Wimpey' Wade claimed a Messerschmitt 109E as damaged, as did Pilot Officer Cecil Saunders off Dungeness; while Flying Officer Roy Mottram also claimed a probable 109 destroyed.

Flight Lieutenant Holland according to the squadron Operations Record Book claimed a ME109 destroyed, but this is not reflected in the official combat reports or figures; and it is likely he was only reporting seeing one of the other pilot's victories.

A number of other patrols were flown that afternoon by the squadrons, but there was no further combat.

The 27th of October continued in the same vein with a misty start, but with some operations by both sides during the course of the day.

At 7:50am Squadron Leader 'Sailor' Malan was leading his squadron on a patrol when they encountered a large number of Messerschmitt 109's around Maidstone. JG27, JG52, JG53 and JG54 had sent formations across Kent with a number of bomb-carrying 109's. JG52 were 74 Squadron's main protagonists and both sides incurred losses in a swirling dogfight over the Maidstone area.

Flying Officer William Nelson shot down a Messerschmitt 109E as did Pilot Officer Stephen. Pilot Officer Peter Chesters shot one down which force landed at Penshurst aerodrome. This was the aircraft of Feldwebel Lotham Schieverhofer of 3/JG52. His machine was hit at about 23,000 feet and the engine was damaged. He dived into the cloud and managed to pull out just above the ground before making a forced landing on the old airfield. Despite numerous bullet holes in the air frame, he managed to escape personal injury and was happy to go into captivity in one piece. He was however surprised when Peter Chesters landed his Spitfire next to his wreck and assisted in his detention! In his combat report Chesters stated, "The enemy aircraft which I attacked was diving down to the clouds and I followed him. He saw me and tried to get on my tail, I managed to turn inside him and put a burst into his engine causing it to stop. I jockeyed him earthwards, and he landed on Penshurst Aerodrome with his wheels in the 'up' position. I fired two three second bursts at 150 yards. As I did not know my position and was short of petrol, I landed on the same aerodrome. This engagement took place at 3,000ft".

What is missing from his account is the alleged conclusion to this incident. Johnny Freeborn would later state that after landing beside the ME109, Peter Chesters had dragged the unfortunate German pilot from the cockpit. The German spat in Chesters face and a punch up started with the two swearing at one another in German (Chesters having studied German which he spoke fluently). The fight was eventually broken up by a Kent police officer, an Air Raid Warden and a soldier. This must have been the strangest punch up the police officer had ever attended! Clearly Chesters chose not to report this in his official account.

Peter Chesters managed to liberate the pilot's Iron Cross from his flying jacket, but he was forced to return it by the policeman who chose to uphold the law even if that included theft from the Luftwaffe. Demanding a trophy for his victory, Chesters took the first aid kit from the 109 which he kept in his own Spitfire.

Flight Lieutenant Mungo-Park also claimed to have damaged a 109 to the south of Maidstone.

Another of the victims of 74 Squadron appears to have been Oberleutnant Ulrich Steinhilper of 3/JG52. He was hit in the radiator by a Spitfire and had to bale-out. His Messerschmitt

109E coming down at Upstreet in Kent. Steinhilper was slightly wounded and captured when he landed and was given medical treatment. Examination of reports tend to point to his victor being Sergeant Skinner from 74 Squadron. In later years, Steinhilper would appear on many television documentaries about the Battle of Britain. He always maintained that his capture in 1940 probably saved his life, although he would later make up to six escape attempts from the POW camps in Canada.

The third victory may have been Oberleutnant Anton Pointer of 8/JG27. He was shot down at this time and baled-out at 6,000 feet, coming down near Hooks Wood at Lenham to the east of Maidstone. Pointer was a Knights Cross holder and a very experienced pilot. (The Luftwaffe were by this stage losing many of their experienced pilots who despite surviving were falling into British hands and captivity).

Pilot Officer John Scott a pre-war Volunteer Reserve pilot was hit and went down and was killed at Dundas Farm, Elmsted, Kent at 9:00am (in Spitfire P7526). Scott had only been with the squadron four days and was still a relative novice in terms of combat experience. The combat must have been hard as 'Sailor' Malan was also hit and damaged. He managed to get back to Biggin Hill but made a forced landing without injury.

Flying Officer Nelson despite his own victory was also hit by debris from the Messerschmitt he had dispatched and managed to return home to Biggin. With fuel running out and short of ammunition, Flying Officer Roger Boulding and Sergeant Wilf Skinner landed at RAF Kenley, while Sergeant John Glendinning landed at Gravesend. The remainder of the squadron returned home to Biggin Hill safely, with the stragglers following them home over the next hour or two.

At 9:20am, 92 Squadron had been ordered to patrol with 603 Squadron at 5,000 feet over Rochford in Essex. They soon spotted a small formation and Pilot Officer Thomas Sherringham claimed to have damaged a Dornier 17. Two Dornier's from KG3 returned with some damage following fighter attacks and one of these must have been due to Sherringham.

At 1:35pm both 74 and 92 Squadrons were scrambled and directed to patrol over Biggin Hill at 15,000 feet. They returned seventy minutes later without encountering the enemy, but Sergeant Don Kingaby had force landed at Effingham near Leatherhead in Surrey for an unknown reason. It is believed to have been due to a technical failure. He was uninjured and returned to base that afternoon by road.

At 4:35pm 92 Squadron having returned and refueled, where ordered up and met with 66 Squadron. With deteriorating weather and darkness descending, seven of 92 Squadrons Spitfires had to land at Gravesend with 66 Squadron. One landed at Shoreham and only three managed to return to Biggin that evening.

74 Squadron put up six aircraft for a patrol at 4:45pm and they returned at 6:05pm. 'Sailor' Malan, with Johnny Freeborn and Pilot Officer Peter Chesters took off at 5:10pm, but with the deteriorating conditions they landed at RAF Kenley at 6:15pm. This left a number of Biggin Hill's aircraft scattered across a number of airfields for the night.

The next day (the 28th) was a misty wet day with no flying in the morning. Once the weather started to improve, those pilots who had landed at other airfields returned home to Biggin Hill. In the afternoon, several patrols were flown in squadron and section strength, but the Luftwaffe remained safely on the ground in France and there was no combat.

Tuesday the 29th of October was a fair day which allowed several formations of the Luftwaffe to cross the English Channel.

At 7:25am 74 Squadron conducted a patrol without incident and returned home. At 10:30am they put up another eight Spitfires for a patrol and Sergeant Harry Soars in P7385 made a forced landing when he returned at 11:25am. The reasons for this are unknown.

At 7:30am 92 Squadron were to send nine Spitfires up for a patrol, but Sergeant Don Kingaby and Sergeant Bowen-Morris collided during the taxying to take off, meaning that only seven aircraft went up on the patrol. Neither pilot was injured (apart from their pride) and both aircraft were repairable. Whether they were put on a charge by disciplinarian Squadron Leader Kent is unclear. The Spitfire as has been well-documented, had a long nose and needed to be swung left and right when taxying so that the pilot could see ahead. Failure to do so could lead to such accidents.

The remaining seven Spitfires met up with 74 Squadron for an uneventful patrol although as already mentioned, Sergeant Harold Soars had already force landed upon his return to Biggin Hill, making the airfield more dangerous than the Kentish sky!

At 4:30pm Flight Lieutenant Mungo-Park led eight Spitfires of 74 Squadron up on a patrol. They were joined by eleven machines from 92 Squadron and the whole of 222 Squadron. Together they patrolled over RAF Hornchurch at 15,000 feet when they were vectored towards an incoming raid of Messerschmitt 109's and 110's between Maidstone and Gatwick. The twin engine 110's where becoming a rare sight over South East England and this was a chance for more victories against the less than agile fighter.

74 Squadron tangled with the Messerschmitt 109E's in an area encompassed by East Grinstead, Kenley and Tunbridge Wells, while 92 dealt with the ME110's in the same area and down towards the coast at Rye in Sussex.

The 109's were from JG51 and Flying Officer William Nelson shot down Leutnant Turnow of 4/JG51 who crashed and was killed at Dodds Farm, Langton near Tunbridge Wells at 5:20pm. Flight Lieutenant Mungo-Park claimed two more ME109's destroyed near East Grinstead but these cannot be identified in subsequent reports.

New Zealander Pilot Officer Robert Spurdle claimed another as a probable as did Sergeant Neil Morrison; while fellow New Zealander Pilot Officer Edward Churches claimed a probable Heinkel 111 at Tunbridge Wells although no losses or actions appear to match the bomber at this time. JG26 and a number of Heinkel's were operating near the RAF airfields at North Weald and Hornchurch at the same time and it may have been a straggler.

3/JG51 also lost a ME109 flown by Feldwebel Bubenhofer. He baled-out and was captured following the combat, his aircraft crashing to earth at Gate Inn, near Elham in East Kent. This was probably an aircraft claimed by the 74 squadron pilots, while Stab 1/JG51 also reported Oberleutnant Terry missing over England at this time. 74 Squadron returned home without loss.

92 Squadron claimed a Messerschmitt 110 off Rye and two probable 110's near Gatwick, while Pilot Officer Sherringham claimed one damaged near Kenley.

Flight Lieutenant 'Pancho' Villa and Pilot Officer Saunders claimed to have brought down the 110 mention above, some fifteen miles off the coast at Rye, but no known losses match this. Two aircraft did return home damaged from 3/ZG76 at Denain (with a crewman killed) and from 2/Erpro Gr. 210 at St. Ingelevert (crewman also killed). Like 74 Squadron, 92 returned home to Biggin Hill without loss or reported damage.

The bombing continued over London at night, but Biggin Hill was now relatively unmolested and the airfield was almost back to normal.

The 30th of October was damp with evening rain. There was some patrolling by both of Biggin Hill's two squadrons, often with other units, but there was no combat and no losses were incurred. This continued into the 31st with another wet start to the day leading to no flying. By late afternoon, the weather had started to improve, and two weather test flights were made by 74 Squadron. Despite this, the Luftwaffe remained firmly on the ground.

This effectively brought an end to the Battle of Britain as we now know it. The threat of invasion continued into 1941, but the pilots knew the Luftwaffe had been beaten, at least until the better weather in Springtime.

Despite this, the pilots remained on stand-by and patrolled along the Channel coast. The poorer weather and the shorter days at least allowed them more rest and new aircraft and pilots arrived from the OTU's and aircraft factories.

Pilots would lay in their beds listening to the drone of the Heinkel's, Junkers and Dornier's as they made their way to bomb London. The remains of the massed day-light formations from the summer raids were now effectively hidden by the dark nights.

Sadly, the Biggin Hill losses continued. On the 1st of November, the JU87's returned to the fray over a Channel convoy with a heavy escort of ME109's. 74 Squadron's Pilot Officer Nelson was shot down and killed in combat with the ME109's over Stanford in Kent, possibly by JG/26's Commander Adolf Galland. Sergeant Soars was also wounded and damaged before he was forced to make a forced landing at Biggin Hill.

In the spring-time fighter sweeps would be made over the continent, but as we now know, Britain's fight for survival had been won and Biggin Hill had played a massive part in that effort.

Post-script

Biggin Hill had stood at the forefront of the defence of the nation and its capital London.

The pilots of the Biggin Squadrons had caused considerable damage to the enemy throughout the summer, but they had sustained significant losses themselves.

In time, both 74 and 92 Squadron, together with other units, would take the total number of victories for Biggin Hill's squadrons to 600. They continued day after day, week after week hitting the Luftwaffe hard and this continued into 1941 and beyond when they started to mount sweeps over occupied France and Belgium.

The score board would rise to 1,000 enemy aircraft destroyed by Biggin Hill squadrons in later months, and sadly many more pilots would lose their lives.

Biggin Hill is synonymous with the Battle of Britain and the defence of the country in the summer of 1940 and there is no doubt, that they were the first and best line of defence for London during the battle. They were the 'Strongest link' in that defence.

Appendix A

32 Squadron profiles

This appendix and the following profiles give brief outlines of each pilot serving with the relevant squadron at Biggin Hill between 15th July 1940 and 31st October 1940. If there are any omissions, they are in error and the author will be happy to correct anything.

Sergeant Dennis Ashton

Sergeant Dennis Ashton had been a member of the RAF Volunteer Reserve as a pilot under training when the war started. He was called-up and sent to the Fleet Air Arm for carrier training and was offered a full-time transfer to the FAA. He declined and joined Aldergrove. He was re-called to the FAA in May 1940 and trained to fly Sea Gladiators. He then transferred to fly Hurricanes and after training joined 32 at Biggin Hill in early July 1940. However, after two weeks he was sent to join a group of pilots who would fly Hurricanes of the aircraft Carrier HMS Argus onto Malta. There he shot down an Italian CR42 before himself being shot down and killed on 26th November 1940.

Sergeant Donald James Aslin

Donald James Aslin was aged 24 when he was called-up from the reserve for pilot training in 1939. After training at 7 OUT he joined 32 on the 29th July 1940. He damaged a Dornier 17 on the 22nd August before transferring to 257 Squadron at Martlesham Heath on the 22nd, September 1940. The next day he was shot down over the Thames and suffered major burns. He was taken to East Grinstead and treated by Archie McIndoe the pioneer plastic surgeon. He was commissioned in 1941 but was released from the RAF in 1946.

Pilot Officer Anthony Barton DFC*

Anthony Barton was trained at the Royal Navy College at Dartmouth and passed out in 1935. He had obtained a civilian pilots licence in 1934. He transferred to Fleet Air Arm with the rank of Lieutenant in 1937, serving on carriers flying Skua and Shark aircraft.

On the 5th July 1940 he transferred to the RAF with the rank of Pilot Officer and started training on Hurricanes. On the 5th August 1940 he joined 32 at Biggin Hill. On the 11th he claimed a 109 but the next day was shot down himself. He was unharmed but on the 14th of August, he had a forced landing after combat with 109's. He made further claims, but on the 10th September joined 253 Squadron. However, on the 20th September he was shot down and wounded. He returned to operational flying in Feb. 1941 and moved to Malta in 1942 were he had success.

He was awarded a DFC in early 1942 and a bar in July. He then became an instructor at Llanbedr with the rank of Squadron Leader. Sadly, he was involved in a collision with a student's Spitfire on the runway and both men died in April 1943.

Sergeant Edward Bayley

Edward Bayley was from Eastbourne and joined the RAF after gaining a civilian flying licence. He joined the RAFVR in 1937 and when the war started was called-up and posted to 32 Squadron in September 1939. He scored two victories with 32 before transferring to 249 Squadron at North Weald. On the 10th October 1940 he was killed when his Hurricane crashed on Cooling Marsh, Kent. It is believed he died through anoxia (oxygen starvation) and blacked out. He is buried in Bromley, Kent.

Flight Lieutenant Peter Brothers DSO DFC*

Peter Brothers was born in Lancashire in 1913. He learned to fly at school when he was 16 and joined the RAF in 1936. He joined 32 at Biggin Hill in October 1936 and became a flight commander in 1938.

He was very successful with 32 during the battle and was posted on the 257 Squadron in early September 1940. He was awarded a DFC and became an instructor in 1941.

In June 1941 he helped form and command 457 (RAAF) with Australian pilots and was again successful before moving to command 602 at Redhill.

In October 1942 he became a Wing Commander and commanded the Tangmere Wing. He became an instructor and held a Staff role before returning to operations and earning a bar to his DFC and a DSO.

His continued his distinguished RAF until 1947 when he joined the Colonial Service. He later became Chair of the Battle of Britain Fighter Association and died in December 2008 aged 91.

Sub Lieutenant Geoffrey G. Bulmer

Geoffrey Bulmer trained as a fighter pilot with the FAA, but due to the shortage of RAF fighter pilots in 1940, he converted to Hurricanes at 7OTU Hawarden and transferred to 32 at Biggin Hill in June 1940.

On the 20th July 1940 he was shot down by Oberleutnant 'Pips' Priller off Dover. He bailed out but was never seen again and is believed to have drowned. He was 20 years old. A new housing development at Biggin Hill has a road named in his memory.

Squadron Leader Mike Crossley DSO DFC

Mike Crossley was educated at Eton and joined the RAF in 1935. He had held a licence to fly for a few years having worked at the Elstree film studios as a director.

He joined 32 on the 24th August 1936 and was an acting Flight Lieutenant by the start of the war. During the Battle of France and the Dunkirk retreat, he shot down six enemy aircraft and was awarded a DFC.

During the Battle of Britain, he led 32 as a Squadron leader and continued to score but was shot down twice himself. He was unharmed and continued to fly. He was awarded a DSO before going to the United States to test aircraft for the British. In 1943 he contracted tuberculosis and he was retired from operational flying.

In 1946 he left the RAF and moved to farm in South Africa. He died there in 1987 aged 75.

Pilot Officer Victor Daw DFC AFC

Victor Daw was born in 1918 and joined the RAF in 1938. After training he joined 32 at Biggin Hill in early 1940 and went with them to France. He scored and shared in six victories being awarded a DFC in June 1940.

On the 25th July 1940 he was shot down and made a forced landing near Dover. Slightly injured he was admitted into hospital. He flew later in 1941 and 1942 and was awarded an AFC in 1945. He stayed in the RAF post war and was an instructor at the Fighter Leaders School. In March 1953 he was killed during a practice sortie while flying a Meteor Mk8. Daw and his aircraft were never found, it is believed they crashed into the Wash.

Pilot Officer Count Rudolphe De Hemricourt De Grunne (Belgium)

Rudolphe De Hemricourt De Grunne was born in Brussels in 1911, he joined the Belgian army and qualified as a civilian pilot.

In 1936 he served as a soldier in the Nationalist forces in the Spanish Civil War. He was wounded in the arm and while in hospital joined the Nationalist Air Force. He flew a variety of aircraft including Italian made CR42 fighters and he claimed the Messerschmitt 109E. This knowledge it is said, benefitted him and his squadron colleagues in 1940. He claimed 14 victories in the war, but this cannot be verified.

In 1939 with the Spanish war over he returned to Belgium and was mobilised and learned to fly Hawker Hurricanes. With the fall of Belgium and France he went to England and commissioned into the RAF. He joined 32 and made a couple of claims before being shot down and badly burned at Ruckinge. He was admitted to hospital and was released in early 1941. He went to Portugal to recover and some have claimed he was involved in espionage, but this cannot be confirmed.

He returned to RAF flying in April 1941 with 609 Squadron. He was shot down on the 21st May 1941 and bailed out over the Goodwin Sands. He was never found. The following month he was awarded the Belgian Croix de Guerre.

Pilot Officer Alan Eckford DFC

Alan Eckford was from Thame in Oxfordshire. After studying engineering at Loughborough he joined the RAF on a shirt service commission in 1938. He joined 32 at Biggin Hill just before the war started and shot down a ME109 on the 19th May 1940.

On the 3rd June he joined 242 Squadron and went with them to France. Only a couple of weeks later they were withdrawn to England and Eckford re-joined 32 Squadron. He was involved with 32 through-out the Battle of Britain making several claims before transferring to 253 Squadron at RAF Kenley. He continued to score and was awarded a DFC in December 1940.

He became an instructor before returning to ops and seeing action over Dieppe in 1942 where he again scored victories and damaged aircraft. He moved to North Africa and commanded 242 Squadron before being released from the service in 1946 as a Squadron Leader. He died in Norfolk in December 1990 aged 71.

Pilot Officer John 'Polly' Flinders

John Flinders born in Chesterfield he joined the RAF on a short-term commission in January 1936. He flew with 74 Squadron and obtained his civil navigators licence with a view to a civilian role with Imperial Airways. However, the war changed things and he remained with 74 Squadron.

He moved to 32 Squadron in April 1940 and was their training officer. He scored victories over France and during the Battle of Britain. He had been shot down during the Dunkirk withdrawal by flak and crash landed in France. He managed to get via a boat at Calais which at the time was still in Allied hands.

He became an instructor in 1941 and later a test pilot. He was attached to the RCAF and returned to the UK being released as a Squadron Leader in 1945. From 1948 to 1953 he was a reservist but in 1978 retired to Canada where he died in 1998 aged 81.

Pilot Officer Peter Gardner DFC

Peter Gardener from Grimsby joined the RAF on a short service commission in 1937. After pilot training he was sent to 32 at Biggin Hill and on to 3 Squadron in France in May 1940. He made several claims before returning to 32 at Biggin Hill with whom he served in the Battle of Britain. He also made claims during this period. He was awarded a DFC in August 1940 and served with 54 Squadron as a flight commander in 1941. He was shot down over France and captured spending the war in the infamous Stalag Luft III.

He returned to the RAF as a Squadron leader when the war ended and retired in 1948. He moved to the Bahamas in 1956 and opened a restaurant which was frequented by the rich and famous. He died in May 1984.

Sergeant Raymond Gent

Ray Gent was from Sussex and joined 32 on the 27th July 1940 with Sergeants Whitehouse and Tony Pickering. Squadron leader John Worrall was unhappy with their training having not converted onto Hurricanes and sent them to 6 OTU. When they returned 32 was posted to Acklington for a rest and Worrall sent the three to 501 at Gravesend.

Gent would claim two 109's during the battle but was killed in a Miles Magister aircraft on the 2nd of January 1941 with 501 near Wells.

Pilot Officer Keith Gillman

Keith Gillman is probably one of the most famous faces of the Battle of Britain. Sadly, it is not for his achievements. He was born in Dover in 1920 and joined the RAF in 1939. After training he joined 32 in May 1940 claiming a 109 in July.

On the 25th July 1940 just off his home-town of Dover he went missing in combat with ME109's. He was never found but a photograph taken of him by a publicity unit that summer was used in many Raf recruiting posters of the period and on the cover of the Picture Post. Many of those reading these items at the time did not know his name or the fact he was missing. His picture is now regarded as one of the iconic images of The Few.

Pilot Officer Douglas H. 'Grubby' Grice DFC

Douglas Grice was raised in Wallasey, Cheshire. He served in the Artists Rifles. Like many others he joined the RAF on a short service commission and after training, joined 32 at Biggin Hill in 1938.

Grice served in France and claimed five victories before being downed by the return fire from a Heinkel 111 on the 8th June. He made a forced landing and found some British soldiers. With another pilot he was given a car and they travelled over 400 miles across France until they returned to the UK.

Grice was awarded a DFC and returned to 32 and Biggin Hill. On the 4th July 1940 he was shot down and landed on the Sandwich Golf Course where an army officer he knew from the Artists Rifles entertained him. He continued flying and made some claims before being shot down again on the 15th August over the sea. He was burned when the fuel tank caught fire, but the saltwater probably helped his healing when he bailed out. He was picked up by a naval boat and taken to hospital.

Later Grice became the Controller at Biggin Hill Control and a Staff Officer at Fighter Command (as a Wing Commander). He was given an MBE and left the service to become a solicitor. He died in March 1988.

Sergeant Bernard Henson

Bernard Henson was born in 1914 and joined on a short service commission in November 1938. He joined 32 in June 1940 and made a couple of claims in July and August 1940.

On the 18th August he was hit by return fire and made a forced landing near Oxted in Surrey with a slight wound. He was transferred to 257 Squadron in September. He was shot down by Adolph Galland of JG26 on the 17th November 1940 and posted as missing. His body was washed up two months later near Dover.

Sergeant William Higgins

Bill Williams was from Derbyshire and joined the RAF in 1938 after training as a teacher. After training he arrived at 32 on the 2nd July 1940. He shot down several aircraft with 32 before being sent to 253 Squadron at Kenley.

On the 14th September 1940 he was shot down by a ME109 over Sittingbourne and was killed.

Flying Officer John Humpherson DFC

John Humpherson was born in Enfield in 1917. He joined the RAF on a short-service commission in 1937 and joined 32 at RAF Church Fenton in August 1937.

In 1939 he served with 607 Squadron flying Gloster Gladiators and moved back to 32 at Wittering in May 1940. He made a few claims and these increased when they returned to Biggin Hill for the Battle of Britain. He re-joined 607 on 23rd August and was awarded a DFC.

In May 1941 he joined the re-formed 90 Squadron at RAF Watton. This was equipped with B17 Flying Fortress aircraft. On the 22nd June 1941, Humpherson and eight others took off on a scientific experiment into high altitude flying. Due to atmospheric conditions, the aircraft crashed with just one survivor. Humpherson was killed.

Pilot Officer John. F. Pain

John Pain was born in Scotland to Australian parents and grew up in Queensland.

He obtained a short-service commission in the RAF and sailed to the UK for training. He joined 32 on the 29th July from 7 OTU at Hawarden. He made several claims over the next three weeks before being shot down on the 18th August. He was wounded and bailed out being admitted to hospital.

In November he joined 249 at RAF North Weald and was sent to North Africa. In January 1941 he joined 261 Squadron on Malta where he made various victory claims. He joined 72 Squadron in the Western Desert before returning to the UK commanding various units as a Squadron Leader.

In late 1944 he resigned his commission and returned to Australia. He changed his name to Booker-Pain in 1972 and died in 1980.

Sergeant Leonard Pearce

Lenoard Pearce was from Harrogate when he joined the RAFVR in August 1938 for pilot training. He qualified as a pilot in June 1939 and was called-up in September 1939. He initially flew Spitfires with 92 Squadron but moved to 32 in early July 1940. He was shot down and slightly wounded in August and upon recovery went to 249 at North Weald. He moved on to 46 and made a forced landing back at Biggin Hill on the 13th October 1940.

He was promoted to Flight Sergeant with 46 Squadron but on the 9th April 1941, he stalled his Hurricane when landing at night and was killed.

Pilot Officer Jan Piotr Pfeiffer (Poland)

Jan Piotr Pfeiffer fled to the UK after Poland fell in 1939. He was 30 years old when he arrived at 32 Squadron on the 3rd August 1940. He flew with 32 but is best known for two crash landings in his first two days. On the 14th September 1940 he was transferred to 257 Squadron at Martlesham Heath.

He then moved to instructing before converting to Mosquitos and joining 307 Squadron at RAF Predannack in Cornwall in 1943. On the 20th December 1943 he was killed with his navigator when their aircraft crashed into the sea. It was believed the aircraft had suffered engine failure.

Sergeant Tony Pickering

Tong Pickering joined the RAF in April 1939 as a Volunteer Reserve pilot under training. When the war started, he went to the FTS at RAF Sealand and on the 27th July 1940, he was sent directly to 32 Squadron. He had no experience of fast monoplanes when he arrived. Together with Sergeants Gent and Whitehouse he was sent by Squadron Leader Worrall to an OUT for advanced training.

He re-joined 32 in August and started operational flying. In December he moved to 601 and a few months in 1941, went as a test pilot to a Maintenance Unit. He was commissioned at the end of 1941 and joined 131 Squadron at Castletown.

He held various ground postings before being posted in early 1943 to the Middle East and became a squadron commander. He was released from the RAF in December 1945 and worked for GEC. He died in March 2016, one of the last of the Few.

Sergeant Karol Pniak (Poland)

Karol Pniak joined the Polish air force in 1928 and flew with various units. In September 1939 before Poland fell, he claimed a Dornier 17 and a JU87 Stuka. He then made his way via Romania to England and joined the RAF. After converting to Hurricanes, he joined 32 Squadron on the 3rd August 1940.

He made several claims while with 32, but on the 24th August, he was shot down and bailed out. He landed heavily injuring his ankle and knee and was admitted into hospital.

In September he joined 257 at Martlesham Heath before moving on to 306 at RAF Tern Hill. He then held various staff and training roles being awarded a DFC in June 1942.

He moved to North Africa to join the Polish Fighting Unit known as Skalski's circus (after its leader Stanislaw Skalski). In 1944 he went to 61 OTU at RAF Rednal. After the war he returned to Poland and was under constant scrutiny by the Communist authorities. In 1956 he contracted tuberculosis and retired. He died in 1980.

Pilot Officer John Proctor DFC*

John Proctor joined the RAF as an apprentice in 1929. He applied for pilot training in 1932 and after training joined 501 Squadron in May 1940 as a Sergeant Pilot. He claimed seven victories over France before returning to the UK. In early July 1940 he was commissioned and joined 32 Squadron. He made three further claims and was awarded the DFC.

In May 1942 he took command of 33 Squadron and 352 in 1944. He stayed in the RAF after the war and received a bar to his DFC during the Korean War. He reached the rank of Wing Commander and left the service in 1957 and moved to South Africa. He died in 1991.

Pilot Officer Jack Rose DFC

Jack Rose from Shooters Hill, London joined the RAF on a short-service commission in October 1938. After trained he was posted to 32 at Biggin Hill in August 1939. In May 1940 he was posted to 3 Squadron and served in France and claimed two and a half victories.

On the 22nd August 1940 he returned to 32 Squadron at Biggin Hill and remained with them until the autumn. He was awarded a DFC in 1942. He then commanded 184 Squadron from 1943 and they converted onto Typhoons. On D-Day he operated over Normandy and then from a strip near Caen.

He then went to the Far East and commanded 113 Hurricane Squadron supporting ground troops against the Japanese. He retired in 1946 as a Wing Commander and joined the Colonial Service. He died in October 2009.

Flight Lieutenant Humphrey Russell DFC

Humphrey Russell attended Marlborough College and joined the RAF on a short-service commission in 1936. After training he joined 32 Squadron at Biggin Hill in October 1936.

He became a flight commander and worked in the Station HQ before returning to the squadron. He was wounded during the Battle of Britain and admitted to hospital. In April 1941 he commanded 32 Squadron before moving to 118 in late 1941. He then commanded 128 in Sierra Leone. He won a DFC in 1944 and commanded 164 (Typhoons) and in May 1944 he was shot down and captured. He was released and retired from the service in 1958 as a Wing Commander. He died in 1983.

Pilot Officer Eugene G. Seghers (Belgium) DFC

He joined the Belgian army before transferring to their air force. After the surrender to Germany he made his way to England and joined the RAF.

He joined 32 Squadron on the 4th August 1940 after converting to Hurricanes. He served with several squadrons making claims through 1941 and became an instructor at 53 OTU and the Central Gunnery School. In July 1944 he was a Flight Lieutenant with 91 Squadron and attacking V1 flying bombs over Uckfield, Sussex. One exploded killing him. He was awarded a DFC.

Pilot Officer Rupert Smythe DFC.

Rupert Smythe was born in Dublin, joining the RAF on a short service commission in 1937. After training he joined 504 Squadron at RAF Digby in September 1939.

In May 1940 he was sent to Hendon to await a posting in France but ended up with 32 Squadron. He flew with 32 over the Dunkirk beaches and through the Battle of Britain making several claims.

Awarded a DFC he was sent to be an instructor at RAF Cranwell and did not return to operational flying. He left the RAF in 1946 as a Flight Lieutenant. No other details are known.

Flight Sergeant Guy Turner

Guy Turner joined the RAF as an apprentice rigger in 1928. He later applied for pilot training and after selection and training joined 32 at Biggin Hill in August 1939. The following month he was promoted to Flight Sergeant. On the 22nd May 1940 he was posted as missing over France but returned two days later.

Shot down during the Battle of Britain he was badly burned and became an East Grinstead 'Guinea pig'. He was commissioned in 1942 and served as an engineering officer. He retired from the service in 1962 as a Squadron Leader. He died in December 1982.

Pilot Officer Boleslaw Wlasnowalski (Poland)

Wlasnowski was a pilot in the Polish Air Force when the German army invaded in September 1939. He shared a victory shooting down a Dorner 17 before fleeing Britain. He joined the RAF and after a conversion course joined 32 at Biggin Hill on the 3rd of August 1940.

He claimed a Dorner 17 and a ME109 before moving on to 607 at Tangmere where he made another claim. He moved to 213 and made a claim for a ME109 damaged. On the 1st November 1940, he was shot down and killed by 109's off Portsmouth.

Sergeant Sidney Whitehouse.

After arriving at 32 Squadron with Sergeants Pickering and Gent he was sent for advanced flying training at Sutton Bridge 6OTU. He returned to the squadron in late August with the others.

He flew throughout the remainder of the battle and into October and November when he was commissioned. In 1941 he became a flying instructor but returned to operational flying with 167 Squadron. In 1944 and 1945 he served in Burma and India and was released in 1946 as a Wing Commander. He died on the 6th January 2015, again one of the last of the Few.

Squadron Leader John Worrall DFC

Worrall joined the RAF in 1930 at Cranwell. He received his commission and was posted to 1 Squadron at RAF Tangmere.

He served in the Middle East and attended a languages course in Peking, China. He joined 32 at Biggin Hill in December 1939 and stayed with them through out the Battle of Britain. He made several claims and was awarded a DFC.

He worked in several Staff posts after the battle and after attending the Raf Staff College in 1945 was posted to command West Malling and Kai Tak in Hong Kong. He retired in 1963 as an Air Vice-Marshal. He died in 1988 while he was living in Spain.

Appendix B

610 Squadron profiles

Pilot Officer Eric S Aldous

Eric Aldous having attended Dulwich College joined the RAFVR in 1938. After pilot training he 610 at Biggin Hill at the end of July 1940. He flew through out August and into September before he was posted to 41 Squadron on the 12th September. He was wounded in combat at the end of the month and after recovery, became a flying instructor.

In August 1941, he joined 615 Squadron flying Hurricanes. On the 16th October 1941, he was lost flying from Manston on an attack against oil storage tanks in Holland. He was 23 years old.

Pilot Officer Frederick J. Aldridge

Born in Ireland he joined the RAF in June 1939. After attending 7 OTU at Hawarden, he converted to Spitfires and joined 610 on 3rd September 1940. He joined 308 Polish Squadron in December 1940 but was posted to fly Tomahawks with 250 Squadron in Palestine in early 1941. Moving on to Libya he saw further action. Later in the war he became a flying instructor in Canada, he left the service in 1947. No further details are known.

Sergeant Stanley Arnfield DFM, DFC.

Stanley Arnfield joined the RAF in 1930 as an apprentice fitter. He served in India before returning to the UK and applying to become a pilot. After training he flew Westland Wallaces, but then in October 1938 he joined 610 Squadron. He flew over Dunkirk and through the Battle of Britain, being shot down and breaking an ankle. He had several claims for victories and after recovery went to Canada as an instructor. He was awarded the DFM and was commissioned in July 1941.

In September 1943 he trained to fly Lancasters and joined the unusual group who had flown single engine fighters and heavy bombers. He flew many operations against Germany and was awarded a DFC. He retired from the RAF as a Flight Lieutenant in 1951 but died of a heart attack in 1954.

Sergeant Aubrey C. Baker DFC

Aubrey Baker joined the RAFVR in 1935. He trained later as a pilot and after training went to 610 at Biggin Hill on the 27th July 1940. With no experience of Spitfires, he was sent to 7 OTU at Hawarden for training.

He returned to 610 on the 12th of August and claimed a ME109 12 days later. He continued to make claims and in 1941 was commissioned. He was then sent to the Middle East joining the famous 112 Squadron in the Western Desert flying Tomahawks. He made further claims and was awarded the DFC in 1942.

He left the RAF in 1946 as a Flight Lieutenant and died in 1978.

Sergeant Cyril Bamberger DFC*

Cyril Bamberger was born in Port Sunlight on the Wirral and obtained an apprenticeship at Lever Brothers the major employer in the area. In 1936 he joined 610 as an aircraft hand and in April 1939 began pilot training. On the 27th July 1940 he returned to 610 at Biggin Hill as a new pilot. However, like Aubrey Baker he had no Spitfire experience and was sent to Hawarden for further training.

He returned on the 12th with Baker and began operational flying.

He flew with 610 throughout the remainder of the Battle of Britain before volunteering for service in the beleaguered island of Malta. He joined 261 Squadron and made several claims over the island in 1941. He returned in June 1941 to the UK as an instructor.

In March 1943 he returned to ops in the Western Desert where he again had several successes and was awarded a DFC. In 1945 he went to the Gunnery School at Catfoss as an instructor and received a bar to his DFC. He left the RAF at the wars end but remained with 610 Squadron as a reservist. In 1952 he was given a permanent commission and worked during the Korean War. He retired in 1959 as a Squadron Leader. He died in February 2011.

Sergeant Robert A. Beardsley DFC

Robert Beardsley came from Charlton and attended John Roan school in Blackheath. He joined the RAFVR and trained as a pilot joining 610 at Biggin Hill on the 27th July 1940. Like Baker and Bamberger, he went off to re-train on Spitfires and returned on the 12th August.

He flew throughout the battle and was awarded a DFC. After time as an instructor he joined 93 Squadron and flew in North Africa. He then joined 222 in 1944 and flew with them during the allied advance across Europe.

He was released from the RAF in 1945 but re-joined and trained to fly jets with 74 Squadron in 1949. He became a Fighter Controller and when he retired in 1970, became a teacher in Suffolk. He died in 2003.

Sergeant Horatio H. Chandler DFM AFC

Horatio Chandler joined 610 as an aircraft hand before under-taking pilot training and joining 501 Squadron flying Hurricanes in Spring 1940. He rejoined 610 at Gravesend on the 30th June and on the 24th July, he shot down a109's off Dover and a Fleet Air Arm Skua in error. The crew escaping. He made several further claims and was awarded a DFM in October 1940. He then became a flying instructor but returned to operations with 65 and 615 Squadrons in 1941 when he was commissioned. He received the AFC in 1943 and was released from the service in 1946. He died in July 2000.

Sergeant Douglas F. Corfe

From Hoylake in Cheshire, he joined the newly establish 610 RAuxAF Squadron at Hooton Park in 1936. He began pilot training when he joined the RAFVR in 1938 and qualified as a pilot. He initially flew Hurricanes with 73 Squadron in France in 1940, but on the 25th July, he re-joined 610 at Biggin Hill.

On the 10th September 1940 he joined 66 Squadron at Kenley but was shot down and injured near Canterbury. After he recovered, he was sent to Malta with 229 Squadron. He joined 229 on the island and a month later he was in combat neat St Paul's Bay and was jumped by four ME109's. He tried to dodge between the hills but was hit by ground fire and hit the hills exploding. He was killed instantly. At the time of his death in April 1942 he was 23.

Pilot Officer Kenneth H. Cox

Ken Cox joined the RAFVR in 1937 and trained as a pilot. He joined 610 Squadron on the 27th July 1940 having been commissioned. He was heavily engaged in combat during the Battle of Britain and made several claims. On the 28th August 1940, he was shot down and killed. His Spitfire crashed at Stelling Minnis.

Squadron Leader John Ellis DFC* OBE CBE

John Ellis joined the RAF in 1936 and after pilot training he joined 66 Squadron and then 213. Upon the out-break of war, Ellis joined 610 at Wittering and flew as a flight commander over the Dunkirk beaches. He claimed three victories over the evacuation beaches and numerous claims during the Battle of Britain. He took command of 610 at Biggin Hill and was awarded a DFC.

In 1941 he became a flying instructor and was awarded a bar to his DFC. At the end of the year he went to the Middle East as a Wing Commander at Khartoum. In April 1943 he commanded the Qrendi wing at Malta and flew offensive operations over Italy.

On the 13th June 1943 he was shot down and captured. He went to Stalag Luft III and was Roger Bushell (Big X's) deputy. He was repatriated at the end of the war and stayed in the RAF. He retired in 1967 as a Group Captain and died in 2001.

Sergeant Peter Else

Else joined the RAFVR and started pilot training in 1938. He was called up on the out-break of the war and after training joined 72 Squadron at RAF Church Fenton.

On the 6th June 1940 he was posted to 610 Squadron due to their high losses over the Dunkirk beaches. He made one claim during the Battle of Britain before he was shot down breaking an arm in the process. His arm was amputated below the elbow and he was discharged from the service.

He returned to his original job at Marshalls in Cambridge but started test flying Tiger Moths. He stopped flying in 1946 and became an engineer. He died in 1991.

Flying Officer Frederick Gardiner DFC

While at Cambridge he joined the University Air Squadron before gaining a RAFVR commission in 1938. He was also an accomplished glider pilot. With the outbreak of war, he was called-up and after pilot training converted to Spitfires and joined 610 Squadron on the 16th June 1940.

On the 28th August he was shot down and wounded. He remained with 610 Squadron before taking up several appointments in development work. He then instructed new Army glider pilots in 1943 before converting to Beaufighters and joining operations in 254 Squadron. He was awarded a DFC and became squadron commander. He ended as a Squadron Leader and emigrated to Vancouver dying in 2003.

Sergeant Bernard G.D. Gardner

Born in 1916 he joined the RAFVR in 1937 as an Airman under training. He was called up on the 1st September 1939 and after training joined 610 Squadron at Biggin Hill on the 27th July 1940. He claimed three ME109's destroyed in August but had to make a forced-landing with a badly wounded arm.

When he recovered, he flew a Blenheim with a signals unit but was shot down and killed by friendly anti-aircraft fire on the 28th June 1941.

Pilot Officer Donald M. Gray

He joined the RAFVR in 1938 and under-went pilot training. He was called-up and joined 610 Squadron at Biggin Hill on the 27th July 1940. He shot down a ME109 on the 24th August 1940, but crash landed himself having been wounded.

He returned to the Squadron while it was based at Acklington in Northumberland, but he was killed in a flying accident on the 5th November 1940.

Sergeant Ronald Hamlyn DFM

He joined the RAF in 1936 as a direct entry pilot. On the outbreak of war, he joined 72 Squadron at Church Fenton and after Dunkirk joined 610 Squadron at Gravesend.

He made several claims during the Battle of Britain and was awarded a DFM in September 1940. He was commissioned in January 1941 and joined 242 Squadron. He then joined 275 Air Sea Rescue Squadron at RAF Valley on Anglesea. He later served as an advisor to the USAAF and then at the Air Ministry in 1944. He retired in 1957 as a Squadron Leader. He died 1991.

Flying Officer Geoffrey Keighley OBE

Geoffrey Keighley was a Yorkshire man and a manager at Harrods pre-war. He joined 610 Squadron in 1939 and trained as a pilot. On the 31st of May 1940 he was shot down by return fire from a Dornier over the Channel off Dunkirk and rescued by a fishing boat and the Navy.

He was shot down and wounded on the 20th July 1940 and upon recovery posted to 616 Squadron. He then worked in the operations room at RAF Usworth near Sunderland and was awarded an OBE in 1945. He left the RAF as a Wing Commander in 1946 and died in 1966.

Flying Officer Peter Lamb AFC

Lamb was born in 1914 and joined 610 Squadron in early 1938. During the Battle of Britain, he made several victory claims and left the squadron in October 1940. He was awarded an AFC in 1943 and ended up as a Squadron Leader. After the war he re-formed and commanded 610 Squadron at Hooton Park. He died in 1969.

Pilot Officer Peter Litchfield

Peter Litchfield joined the RAFVR in 1937 and after training he was commissioned and joined 610 Squadron. On the 18th July 1940 he was shot down and killed. His body was never recovered; and he is remembered on the Runnymede Memorial.

Sergeant Edward Manton

Edward Manton came from Cheshire and joined the county's squadron (610) in 1936 as an aircraft hand. He applied for and started training as a pilot and after training, he rejoined 610 at Biggin Hill on the 27th July 1940. However, he had no experience of Spitfires and was sent away for further development. Shortly after returning he was shot down on the 29th August and was killed near Mayfield, Sussex.

Pilot Officer Claude Merrick DFC

Claude Merrick joined the RAFVR and after training and commissioning, joined 610 Squadron at Biggin Hill on the 27th July 1940. Like many of his colleagues he was sent off to an OTU to get more experience. He returned to 610 squadron on the 14th August; but was shot down on the 24th and wounded.

After further training he flew Albemarles and on the night of D-Day flew paratroopers into Normandy. He was awarded a DFC and made acting Squadron Leader. He left the RAF in 1946 as a Wing Commander and died in October 1984.

Sergeant William J. Neville

Neville was an engineer in Sunbury on Thames when he joined the RAFVR in 1938. He started pilot training and after OTU he joined 610 at Biggin Hill on the 27th July 1940. On the 8th August he made a forced landing and three days later went missing off Calais. His body was never recovered.

Pilot Officer Stanley Norris DFC*

Stanley Norris joined the RAF on a short service commission in 1937. He joined 29 Squadron at Debden and in September 1939 joined 66 Squadron at Duxford. A month later he joined 610 at Wittering.

He fought over Dunkirk and through the Battle of Britain making several claims and being awarded a DFC. He then became an instructor before going to Malta with 126 Squadron at Takali. He then became the Squadron Leader of 243 Wing in North Africa, before going to 11 Squadron in Burma.

He became a Wing Commander and was awarded a bar to his DFC. Returning to the UK he remained in the RAF leaving as a Wing Commander in 1947. He then served as a King's and Queen's messenger. He died in 1991.

Sergeant Claude A. Parsons

Claude Parsons like many of his colleagues joined the RFVR and started pilot training. He was trained on Hurricanes but transferred to 610 Squadron on the 15th June 1940. On the 9th July he accidently shot down a Skua naval fighter, the crew surviving.

He made several claims and joined 66 Squadron in September 1940 with whom he continued to score. He was promoted to Flight Sergeant. However, on the 8th November 1941 he was shot down and killed off the Dutch coast. His body has never been found.

Pilot Officer Constantine Oliver Pegge DFC*

Pegge joined the RAF on a short-term commission in 1938. After his pilot training he joined No. AACU but crashed a Hawker Henley at Farnborough in November 1939.

In May 1940 he converted to Spitfires and joined 610 Squadron at Gravesend. He made several claims during the Battle of Britain and in May 1941 he became an OTU flying instructor. He was awarded a DFC and a bar later in the war.

He commanded 610 Squadron in late 1941 and other squadrons. He became a Squadron Leader and stayed in the RAF after the war flying Gloster Meteors. He was with the Central Fighter Establishment in May 1950 when he crashed into the Wash and was killed.

Sergeant Norman H. Ramsay DFC

He joined the RAFVR in 1939 and started pilot training. He joined 92 Squadron in May 1940 but moved on to 610. He made on claim for a ME110 and moved to 222 Squadron in September 1940.

He made various claims and was commissioned in 1941 and became an instructor before moving to Malta in early 1943. He was awarded a DFC and stayed in the RAF post war. He retired as a Flight Lieutenant in 1962 and went to live in New Zealand. It is not known if he is still alive, but if he is, he would be 100 years old in July 2019.

Pilot Officer Brian V. Rees

Brian Rees was from Caernarvon and joined the RAF on a short service commission in 1938. He converted to Spitfires in May 1940 and joined 610 Squadron on the 16th June. He made several victory claims, but very little is known of his service history after the Battle of Britain. In 1944 his name is missing from RAF personnel lists and it is assumed he left for unknown reasons. He died in 1979.

Squadron Leader Andrew T. Smith

Andrew Smith came from the well to do Fulwood Park merchants residential district of Liverpool. He attended Cambridge University and joined 610 Squadron in 1936 with a commission. Over Dunkirk he made two claims and took command of the squadron when the leader was killed.

On the 25th July 1940 he was coming into land at RAF Hawkinge in a damaged Spitfire after combat. He stalled and crashed being killed.

Flight Lieutenant Edward B. Smith DFC

Smith came from Formby near Liverpool and was educated at King William College on the Isle of Man. He joined 610 Squadron in 1936 and was given a full commission in August 1939. He made several claims over Dunkirk and the Battle of Britain, but on the 12th August, he was shot down and fished out of the sea by the navy. Suffering burns he was admitted to hospital and received the DFC.

After recovering he became a flying instructor and in June 1943, he became a member of the Air Staff in North Africa. After the war he worked near Liverpool and died in September 2013.

Sergeant John R. Tanner

John Tanner came from Enfield and joined the RAF as an apprentice in 1931. He later became a pilot and joined 610 Squadron at Gravesend in July 1940. He failed to return from a flight over the Channel on the 11th August 1940. His body was washed up near Calais where he is now buried.

Flying Officer William H.C. Warner

Warner was born in New Brighton near Liverpool and joined 610 Squadron in May 1937. He was called-up in August 1940 and flew with them during the Battle of Britain. He went missing on the 16th August 1940 off Dungeness. His body has never been found.

Pilot Officer Frank Webster

Frank Webster joined 610 Squadron in late July 1940 but like many pilots was sent off to OTU for further training on Spitfire. He was commissioned. He flew his first operation sortie on the 24th August but two days later he was badly damaged by a ME109 and crashed in flames while trying to land at Hawkinge. He was killed in the resultant crash.

Sergeant Peter H Willcocks

Peter Willcocks and joined the RAFVR in 1938. After pilot training he joined 610 Squadron at Biggin Hill on the 27th July 1940. On the 10th September he joined 66 Squadron at Kenley. He made two forced landings and was wounded. Then on the 11th October he crashed while landing in poor visibility but survived. On the 28th November 1940 he collided with another Spitfire and was killed over Edenbridge, Kent. The other pilot 'Dizzy' Allen survived. Peter Willcocks was just 20 years of age.

Flying Officer Douglas Wilson

Douglas Wilson came from Northern Scotland and obtained a civilian pilots licence. He joined 610 Squadron in 1936 and he was called-up in August 1939. Wilson shot down to ME109's during the Battle of Britain and survived the war as a Wing Commander. He died in July 1985.

Appendix C

79 Squadron profiles

Sergeant Henry A. Bolton

Henry Bolton came from Hartlepool and joined the RAFVR in 1939. He was called up and trained as a pilot joining 79 Squadron at Acklington in July 1940. The squadron moved south to Biggin Hill and he was severely damaged in combat on the 31st August. As he tried to make a forced landing he crashed and was killed. He was 21.

Pilot Officer Leofric Trevor Bryant-Fenn DFC

Bryant-Fenn was working for an aircraft company when he obtained a short-service RAF commission in 1938. He qualified as a pilot and eventually ended up as a pilot at 79 Squadron on the 29th June 1940.

He made several claims at Biggin Hill but was wounded in combat on the 1st September. He did not return from hospital until 1941. In 1942 he converted to Mosquitos again making claims while with 264 Squadron. He was awarded a DFC and went o Burma and the Far East. He remained in the RAF post war and retired as a Group Captain in 1968. He died in 1988.

Flight Lieutenant Rupert F. Clerke DFC

Was educated at Eton and Cambridge. He joined the University Air Squadron and obtained a permanent commission in 1937. After pilot training he joined 32 Squadron, before arriving at 79 in July 1940.

He made several claims before he left and converted to Mosquitos on No. 1 Photo Reconnaissance Unit. He continued to fly Mosquitos on long range trips. In 1942 he went to 157 Squadron at Castle Camps and shot down a JU88. He was given command of 125 Squadron and made other claims before being awarded a DFC. He remained in the RAF after the war and retired as a Group Captain. He died in 1988.

Pilot Officer Douglas G. Clift

Douglas Clift joined the RAF on a short service commission in1939. He under-went pilot training and joined 79 Squadron at Manston in November 1939. When the squadron went to France in May 1940, he went with them and made several claims. He returned to the UK and during the Battle of Britain he made other claims before leaving 79 in March 1941. He then became an instructor before volunteering for the Merchant Shipping Fighter Unit (MSFU). Using fighters catapulted from merchant ships he would be expected to shoot down aircraft such as Fw. 200 Condors. He did not make any further claims and ended up in the Far East.

After the war, he stayed in the RAF and worked as an adviser to the Iranian Air Force. He retired as a Squadron Leader in 1974 and died on New Year's Eve 2008. Surprisingly he was never decorated.

Squadron Leader John Heyworth AFC

Heyworth was educated at Rugby school where he excelled at cricket and rugby. He attended Edinburgh, with the intention of becoming a medical doctor. However, in 1931 he joined the RAF on a short-service commission and started pilot training. By 1934 he was with 54 Squadron and an accomplished pilot taking part in the Hendon air pageant. He moved to 504 Squadron where he was graded as an exceptional pilot. He therefore became a test pilot.

He was re-called to the RAF and went on a Spitfire conversion course and had the ignominy of crashing it on landing. By July 1940 he was with 222 Squadron at Kirton in Lindsey as a supernumerary Squadron leader. He then joined 79 as their commander and made two claims before the squadron moved down to Biggin Hill. He made further claims while leading the squadron through the Battle of Britain and took them in 1941 to Pembrey were he made a further claim.

In 1941 he returned to Rolls Royce as a test pilot and worked on testing new jet engines. He was awarded an AFC in 1946 after being released as Wing Commander from the RAF. He died in 2010.

Pilot Officer Herbert K. Laycock

Herbert Laycock joined the Raf on a short-service commission and started training as a pilot. He joined 616 Squadron on the 20th September 1939.

He flew over Dunkirk before joining 79 squadron and heading to Biggin Hill. He then moved on to 87 Squadron in October 1940 at Exeter.

He converted to Beaufighters and flew with 603 Squadron in Libya and then over Greece. He became Squadron leader and continued to fly operationally. He was forced to crash land his Beaufighter after an engine caught fire in August 1943 (Beaufighters were known to be difficult to keep aloft on one engine); and both Laycock and his observer were badly burned and captured. Both men were reported to have died a week later in a hospital for prisoners at Phaleron in Greece.

Pilot Officer Paul Mayhew

Paul Francis Mayhew attended Haileybury School and then Christ Church at Oxford. He was a member of the University Air Squadron and then joined the RAFVR as a pilot under training. He ended his training by converting to Spitfires but was sent to 32 Squadron on Hurricanes. On the 11th July 1940 he joined 79 Squadron at Acklington and moved south with them to Biggin Hill. He made several claims before the squadron moved on to Pembrey in September. On the 29th of that month he was with several other aircraft who intercepted Heinkel III's over the Irish Sea. After assisting in shooting one down, he ran short on fuel and force landed in neutral Ireland. He was interned and tried to escape in January 1941. Finally, in June 1941 he escaped and managed to get to Northern Ireland. He re-joined 79 Squadron and became a flight commander. In February 1942 he stalled his aircraft on landing and died in hospital.

Flying Officer Morris

No other details are known.

Pilot Officer George Nelson-Edwards DFC

Nelson Edwards attended Shrewsbury School and then Brasenose College, Oxford. He was a member of the University Air Squadron and called-up for service in September 1939. After attending OTU he joined 79 Squadron at Acklington on the 20th July 1940.

On the 9th August he shared a Heinkel III shot down off Sunderland. He moved south with the squadron and was involved in numerous battles making several claims. In 1941 he became a flying instructor and in June 1942 became the CO of 93 Squadron which was re-forming at RAF Andreas on the Isle of Man. The squadron went to North Africa where he made several claims and was awarded a DFC.

He was then given several staff appointments as an acting Wing Commander. He left in 1945, only to re-join in 1946. He eventually retired in 1960 as a Wing Commander and ran a pub. He moved to Cyprus and died there in 1994.

Pilot Officer Brian R. Noble

Brian Noble was born in 1916 and joined the RAFVR in May 1938 for pilot training. After being called up, he joined 79 Squadron at Biggin Hill in June 1940. He made several claims but was shot down and wounded on the 1st September over Biggin Hill. Having suffered burns, he attended the East Grinstead plastics unit under Achibald McIndoe. He was released from the RAF at the wars end but re-joined and became a Fighter Controller. He retired in 1969 as a Wing Commander and died in 1990.

Pilot Officer Thomas C. Parker OBE

Thomas Parker joined the RAF in 1937. He flew with various squadrons, before joining 79 in early 1939. He was given a short-service commission in September 1939 and went with the unit to France in May 1940.

He returned to the UK with 79 and flew throughout the Battle of Britain in many actions. He continued flying throughout the war and remained in the RAF operating jets post the wars end.

He retired in 1962. He is believed to have since died. He was awarded an OBE.

Pilot Officer George C. Peters

George Peters was from Sussex and joined the RAF in 1938 on a short service commission. After flying training, he joined 79 Squadron at Biggin Hill at the start of August 1940. He made claims while at Acklington and after returning to Biggin Hill before the squadron moved to Wales. In late September 79 attacked a number of Heinkel 111's over the Irish Sea and Peters was reported as missing. Some Hurricanes had run short of fuel and he may have ditched in the sea. However, he was reported as missing and his body was washed ashore in Ireland where he is buried.

Pilot Officer Donald Stones DFC*

Donald 'Dimsey 'Stones is probably the best known 79 Squadron battle of Britain pilot. He joined the RAF on a short-service commission in June 1939 and under-went pilot training. In January 1940 he joined 32 Squadron but moved on to 79 in March.

He got his nickname from the child's book 'Dimsie' as he turned up at breakfast one morning with a copy of the book sticking out of his pocket.

He flew over France and Dunkirk and was awarded a DFC in June 1940. He flew with 79 through the Battle of Britain and was slightly injured on the 1st September 1940. Having made numerous claims, he became in instructor in December 1940.

He then flew over Malta as part of their Night Fighting Unit (MNFU) he made victory claims over Malta and received a bar to his DFC. He then went on to the Far East commanding 155 Squadron, but

Became embroiled in an argument with a provost Officer and Court Martialed. He was found guilty and reverted to Flight Lieutenant for using bad language and reprimanded. He lost command of 155.

After a break he was given command of 67 Squadron and made claims against Japanese aircraft. On the 15th May 1943 he was wounded and send home. In March 1945 a Colerne another officer was messing about with a detonator when it exploded and caused Stones to lose an eye.

He undertook various Colonial service roles after the war but continued to fly as a civilian. He died in 2002.

Pilot Officer Owen Tracey

Nothing is known of this pilot.

Sergeant John Wright

John Wright came from Glasgow and joined the RAF in 1935 as an aircraft hand. He applied for pilot training and started to train. He was posted to 79 in July 1940.

He damaged a couple of enemy aircraft during the Battle of Britain, but on the 4th September 1940, he was wounded by return fire and force landed in Surbiton in Surrey. He was taken to hospital but died. He was 24 years old.

Appendix D

72 Squadron profiles

Sergeant Howard J. Bell-Walker OBE

Howard Bell-Walker came from Birmingham. He joined the RAFVR in 1939 and trained as a pilot. He converted to Spitfires after initial and advanced training and joined 64 Squadron at Leconfield in August 1940. He then moved to 72 Squadron on the 11th September.

Twice in September 1940 he was shot down, the second time being hospitalized. In November he returned to 64 Squadron and then 602 in early 1941. On the 12th August 1941 he was part of an escort for a 'Circus' over France and was shot down again. He was wounded and bailed out to captivity. After the war he remained in the RAF and was awarded an OBE for work in the Engineering branch. He retired in 1967 as a Squadron leader and moved to Ontario, Canada. He died there in 1999.

Pilot Officer Brown

Nothing is known about this pilot.

Pilot Officer Herbert R. Case

Herbert Case joined in 1936 as an airman under training. He was called up in September 1939. After training he was commissioned and converted to Spitfires with 64 Squadron.

On the 20th September 1940 he moved to 72 Squadron. He was killed on the 12th October 1940 when his aircraft crashed at Capel-le-Ferne near Folkstone. For many years, the cause of death was unknown but years later an army officer's wife wrote to Case's mother stating that he had been killed in combat with ME109's.

Squadron Leader Anthony R. Collins

Tony Collins joined the RAF in 1930 on a short-service commission. He trained as a pilot and in 1930 was with 30 Squadron in Mosul, Iraq. In June 1940 he underwent a refresher course at 6 OTU and was sent to command 72 Squadron at Acklington. When the squadron moved South, he was wounded on the 2nd September over Herne Bay. On the 5th October he left 72 and went to 46 Squadron. He left the RAF in 1955 as a Wing Commander. He died in February 1976.

Pilot Officer Ivor Cosby DFC

Ivor Cosby joined the RAFVR and trained as a pilot. He joined 13 Army Co-operation squadron and went with them to France in 1940. He returned with the squadron and volunteered for fighter pilot training. He went to 610 Squadron on the 3rd September 1940 but moved to 72 on the 20th also at Biggin Hill. On the 4th November he moved to 222 at Hornchurch and 602 on the 11th, November.

On the 28th December 1940 he joined 141 Squadron flying Defiant night fighters. He remained with them until 1943 when he became an instructor. He returned to ops with 264 Squadron in September 1943 and made several victory claims. He was awarded a DFC and stayed in the RAF flying Mosquitos with 96 Squadron in 1946. He retired as a Wing Commander in 1974 and died in 1994.

Flying Officer Paul J. Davis-Cook

Paul Davis-Cooke attended Shrewsbury School and Trinity College at Cambridge University. He joined 610 Royal Auxiliary Air Force in 1937. He trained as a pilot and on the 8th January 1940, he joined 613 at RAF Odiham. In August he volunteered for Fighter Command and after converting to Spitfires re-joined 610 at Biggin Hill on the 3rd September. He joined 72 at Biggin Hill on the 20th September. He was shot down and killed by 109's near Sevenoaks on the 27th. Eyewitnesses claimed he was shot in his parachute as he bailed out and landed dead. Whether this is true is unknown. He was 23 years old.

Pilot Officer Thomas D. H. Davy DFC

Thomas Davy was born in China and spent a lot of his childhood shuttling between the two countries. In October 1938 he obtained a short-service commission in the RAF and joined 35 Squadron at Cottesmore in Rutland. He then joined 98 and 150 Squadrons flying Fairey Battles in France in 1940. He was lucky to survive the decimation of the Battle squadrons. On the 12th of May he was the sole survivor of a flight of six aircraft. He was awarded a DFC.

He then transferred to Fighter Command and joined 72 Squadron at Biggin Hill on the 28th September. By January 1941 he was a flight commander with 315 Polish Squadron and a Flight Lieutenant. He joined the Merchant Shipping Fighter Unit (MSFU). He was killed on the 13th September 1942 during an exercise. He is buried in Anfield cemetery Liverpool.

Sergeant Basil Douthwaite

He joined the RAF as a pilot under training in 1938 and joined 72 Squadron May 1940. He flew over Dunkirk shooting down a Stuka and a 109 later, on the 1st September. Ten days later he was wounded over Gravesend and made a forced landing. He was commissioned in September and claimed a Heinkel 111 in November. It is believed he became an instructor and survived the war, leaving as a Flight Lieutenant in 1945. He died in 1996.

Pilot Officer RD Elliott

No details are known of this pilot.

Flying Officer Thomas Elsdon DFC

Born in Dundee he joined the RAF College at Cranwell. He joined 72 Squadron in 1937 at Church Fenton. He made several claims in 1939, over Dunkirk and during the Battle of Britain. He was badly wounded on the 7th September. He was awarded a DFC in October 1940 but did not return to action until mid-1941.

He took command of 136 Squadron and took it to India and Burma where he saw considerable action before returning to the UK in 1944. He stayed in the RAF post-war and received an OBE. He retired as a Group Captain in 1959. He died in 2003. His son, Wing Commander Nigel Elsdon was killed flying Tornados during the first Gulf War in 1991.

Sergeant John S. Gilders

John Gilders was born in Deal, Kent. He joined the RAFVR in 1938 and trained as a pilot. He joined 72 Squadron in June 1940 and moved to Biggin Hill with them in September.

He made several claims during their time at Biggin Hill but on the 19th October, they moved to Leconfield and he moved to 616 Squadron at Kirton in Lindsey. On the 26th November he joined 41 Squadron at RAF Hornchurch. On the 21st February 1941 his Spitfire flew into the ground at Chilham, Kent. His body was not recovered, and the landowners refused to allow an excavation. Eventually in 1994 a new landowner allowed the body to be recovered and he was given a full military funeral.

Sergeant Norman V. Glew

Norman Glew joined the RAFVR and trained as a pilot in 1938. He joined 72 at Acklington in June 1940 and moved with them to Biggin Hill. He made a couple of claims before moving to 41 Squadron in November 1940. He then went to Malta but flew on to Egypt and joined 260 Squadron. He was commissioned in August 1941. He flew across the Western Desert and joined 229 Squadron on Malta in 1943. He became an acting Squadron Leader and took command of 1435 Squadron in March 1944. On the 17th May 1940 he was killed in a Hurricane during a mock combat with a Spitfire.

Flight Lieutenant Edward Graham

Edward Graham attended Wellington School and joined the RAFVR in 1934. In 1935 he was released and obtained a short service commission. In 1937 he joined 72 Squadron at Tangmere flying Gloster Gladiators before converting to Spitfires. He became a flight commander and flew with 72 over Dunkirk and into the Battle of Britain. On the 15th August 1940 he was with the squadron when they attacked the large-scale bomber force heading towards Newcastle. He made several claims over the coming weeks. On the 21st September at Biggin Hill, he took command of the squadron when Squadron leader Collins was ill. He led them into 1941. In 1942 he became station commander of RAF Acklington and went to India. He left the RAF in 1958 as a Wing Commander and settled in Australia. Having born been in 1911, he is believed to have died or he would now be 108 years old!

Sergeant Malcolm Gray

Gray joined the RAFVR in July 1938 and trained as a pilot. He was called up on the 1st September and joined 72 Squadron in June 1940. He flew with them until the 5th September when he was shot down and killed at Elham Park Wood, Kent. He was just 20 years of age.

Pilot Officer Dennis Holland

Dennis Holland learnt to fly while he was still young, 17 to be precise. He became a civilian instructor, but he was called-up in September 1939. As a very experienced pilot he excelled and after being commissioned he joined 72 in early 1940 on Spitfires.

In September he made three victory claims, but on the 20th, he was shot down near Sittingbourne. He baled out but was seriously wounded and died soon after arrival at hospital.

Sergeant Maurice Lee

Maurice Lee was an apprentice aircraft engineer when he joined the RAFVR as a Sergeant in 1939. After pilot training, he joined 72 at Biggin Hill on the 15th September 1940. He claimed a Heinkel 111 before transferring in October to 421 Flight at Gravesend. He shot down a 109 but was wounded and crash landed. Lee was known as a good poor weather pilot and would often undertake the weather check flights. However, on the 31st December 1940 he crashed and was killed, trying to land at Biggin Hill in poor weather. He was 21 years old.

Sergeant Arthur C. Leigh DFC, DFM

Arthur Leigh joined the RAFVR as a pilot under-going training in 1939. He converted to Spitfires and joined 64 Squadron at RAF Leconfield in September 1940. He moved to 72 on the 11th of October and then to 611 at Acklington in November.

He made several claims during the summer of 1941 and was awarded the DFM. He then became an instructor and a ferry pilot before returning to ops with 56 Squadron at RAF Manston flying Typhoons. He was awarded a DFC, but on the 9th September 1943, he was hit by flak and had to bale-out over the Channel. He was picked up by an air sea rescue launch. He continued flying and stayed in the RAF after the war. He was released in December 1945 and died in 2004.

Pilot Officer Alec Lindsay

Lindsey was a RAFVR pilot and after training joined 72 Squadron on the 11th September 1940. He was also commissioned. He became an instructor in 1941, before going to Malta to join 185 Squadron in August 1942. He was killed over Malta on the 23rd October 1943, due to friendly anti-aircraft fire hitting his Spitfire. He is buried on the island.

Pilot Officer John P. Lloyd AFC

John Lloyd like so many of the others joined the RAFVR in 1939 and started pilot training. He was commissioned in July 1940 and joined 64 Squadron at Leconfield. He then moved to 72 Squadron on the 11th September 1940. He made a couple of victory claims, but he was damaged and seriously wounded on the 18th September near Dover. He was awarded an AFC and returned to operations with 21 Squadron flying Mosquitos. On the 8th August 1944 he took off for an Intruder flight over Normandy but crashed due to an unknown cause. He was captured with his navigator. He was released in 1945 as a Squadron Leader. He died in 1971.

Pilot Officer Ernest E. Males

Ernest Males came from London and joined the RAFVR in 1939. He was commissioned and sent to 72 Squadron in June 1940. Males made several victory claims during the Battle of Britain and was shot down once. On the 27th September 1940, he was shot down over Sevenoaks by ME109's and killed.

Sergeant Norman Norfolk DFC

Norman Norfolk joined the RAF as a trainee pilot in June 1936. He was with 72 Squadron at Leconfield in late 1939. He was heavily engaged during the Battle of Britain with 72 and made several claims. He was commissioned and received a DFC. He left the RAF in 1945 and died in March 2005.

Pilot Officer James O'Meara DSO, DFC*

James O'Meara joined the RAF on a short service commission in 1938. He trained as a pilot and joined 64 Squadron in 1939. He flew over Dunkirk and into the July stages of the Battle of Britain making a high number of victory claims. He was posted to 72 Squadron at Biggin Hill on the 20th September 1940. He continued to claim victories and was awarded a DFC. He joined 421 Flight at Gravesend and was with them when they became 91 Squadron in 1941. He was awarded a bar to his DFC and re-joined 64.

He continued after a rest and joined 234 as a supernumerary in 1943. He then commanded 131 Squadron and was awarded a DSO. He retired in 1959 as a Squadron Leader and died in 1974.

Sergeant Neil Morrison

Neil Morrison joined the RAFVR and after training served with 54 Squadron at Catterick in September 1940. He moved to 72 on the 4th October and then on to 74 on the 26th. He flew with them in October and November 1940; but on the 24th February 1941 he was posted as missing.

Flying Officer Oswald Pigg

Oswald Pigg came from Newcastle upon Tyne and joined the RAF on a short service commission in 1937. He joined 72 Squadron late in 1937 at Church Fenton. On the 2nd June he shot down a JU87 over Dunkirk, but he was wounded in the process. On the 15th August he claimed a ME110; but on the 1st September he was shot down and killed at Pluckley, Kent.

Sergeant Ronald E. Plant

Ronald Plant came from Coventry and joined the RAFVR in 1939 as an airman under pilot training. In May 1940 he joined 72 Squadron at Acklington. He was dispatched to 7 OTU to gain further experience on Spitfires before he returned on the 15th July 1940.

After a few weeks with 72, he moved to 616 in September. In November he moved to 603 at Hornchurch. On the 21st he collided with a Heinkel 111 which crashed killing its crew. Sadly, Plant crashed with his Spitfire and was killed at Widdenham.

Sergeant Maurice H. Pocock MID

Maurice Pocock joined the RAFVR in 1938. In June 1939 he joined 72 Squadron. He was still with 72 during the start of the Battle of Britain he damaged two enemy aircraft before he was wounded and taken to Preston Hall hospital outside Maidstone.

In 1941 he stayed with 72 and was one of the fighters scrambled to intercept Rudolf Hess when he flew a ME110 to the North of England and into Scotland. In November 1941 he became an instructor and became a Warrant Officer. He then went to North Africa with 93 and then 152 Squadrons. He moved on to Beaufighters and was mentioned in dispatches in 1944. He left the RAF in 1946 as a Flight Lieutenant and died in 1995.

Pilot Officer Peter D. Pool

Peter Pool joined the RAFVR in 1937 and trained as a pilot. He was commissioned in August 1940 and joined 266 Squadron. On the 3rd October he joined 72 Squadron at Biggin Hill but was shot down in flames on the 11th over Sittingbourne. He baled out wounded and was taken to hospital. He was promoted to Flight Lieutenant, but after treatment having resumed flying; he was killed on the 19th August 1942. He was at the time with 610 Squadron and shot down while supporting the ill-fated Dieppe landings. His body was never found.

Pilot Officer Norman Robson

Norman Robson was joined the RAF and after training joined 72 at Church Fenton in October 1938. He was still with them at the start of the Battle of Britain and made several claims in August and September 1940.

In November 1940 he became a flying instructor and had an uneventful remainder of the war. He attained the rank of Squadron Leader post war but was killed in a flying accident at near Middle Wallop in 1954.

Sergeant William T. E. Rolls DFC, DFM

Bill Rolls joined the RAFVR in 1938. After pilot training he joined 72 Squadron on the 19th June 1940. When the squadron moved south, he started to make several victory claims. He was awarded a DFM in November 1940 and then became an instructor.

In October 1941 he resumed operations with 122 Squadron and was commissioned. He made several further claims before flying off HMS Furious to Malta in July 1942. He became a flight commander with 126 Squadron and continued to score. After breaking his leg, he was sent home and received a DFC.

He remained in the RAF until 1975 with various ground postings. He died in July 1988.

Pilot Officer Scoreton

No details are known.

Flying Officer Desmond Sheen DFC*

Desmond Sheen was an Australian who joined the RAF and 72 Squadron in 1940. He had been a cadet in the RAAF but came to the UK in 1937 to join the RAF. He was shot down twice in the Battle of Britain once on the 31st August when he came down in his parachute and was confronted by a young army officer with a revolver. The officer was suspicious of his darker blue RAAF uniform, but was soon treated to a garden party where he sat with guests watching the battle above. Four days later he was shot down again, this time he was lucky to survive when he became pinned against his fuselage. He managed to get free and opened his chute just before he landed in some treetops.

He remained with 72 making several claims and became its commander in 1941. He received a DFC and a later bar to it. He left the RAF in 1949, but then re-joined on a permanent commission as a Flight Lieutenant. He flew Vampire jets as well as later Spitfires and went to RAF Leuchars as a Wing Commander. He ended as a Group Captain and retired in 1971. He worked for BAC. He died in the summer of 2001.

Sergeant Robert Staples

Robert Staples was an aircraft apprentice when he applied to join the RAF. He was accepted and after pilot training he joined 72 Squadron at Church Fenton in 1937.

He flew with the squadron throughout the Battle of Britain but was involved in a fatal collision with another Spitfire on the 5th October 1940 in which Pilot Officer Sutton was killed. In March 1941 he became an instructor and was commissioned in January 1942. He retired from the RAF in 1948 as a Flight Lieutenant and died in 1986.

Flight Sergeant Jack Steere AFC.

Originally from Wallasey, he became a Halton apprentice in 1927 and served on seaplanes. He also served on HMS Glorious before training to be a pilot and joining 23 Squadron at Biggin Hill in 1935.

After postings to other units he joined 72 Squadron in 1939 and flew over Dunkirk. He flew throughout the Battle of Britain making several claims and became an instructor and a Warrant Officer. He received an AFC and stayed in the RAF leaving in 1961 as a Squadron Leader. He died in 1998.

Pilot Officer Norman Sutton

Norman Sutton was born in Yorkshire but played rugby pre-war in St. Helens where he also worked for the renowned Pilkington glass factory. He joined 611 Squadron as an airman in 1939 before training to be a pilot.

He was commissioned in August 1940 after his training and re-joined 611 Squadron. On the 29th September he was posted to 72 Squadron at Biggin Hill. On the 5th October he accidentally collided with Sergeant Robert Staples and was killed. He was buried in St Helens cemetery.

Sergeant Patrick H. Terry

Sergeant Terry joined the RAF on a short service in January 1939 and trained to be a pilot. He went to 19 and 111 Squadrons, but in September 1939 after the war had started, he resigned his commission and re-joined as a Sergeant Pilot in 1940. The reasons behind this are unknown. On the 3rd October he joined 72 Squadron before moving on to 603 Squadron. On the 5th of November 1940 he was shot down and injured by a ME109 over Canterbury. He subsequent RAF service is unknown, but he died in 1974.

Flying Officer John W. Villa DFC.

John 'Pancho' Villa was born in London. He joined the RAF on a short service commission in 1937 and went to join 2 AACU at Lee on Solent. In May 1940 he joined 72 Squadron and he shot down a JU87 Stuka over Dunkirk. He went to Biggin Hill with the squadron where he made several claims and was awarded a DFC.

In October he was posted to 92 Squadron at Biggin Hill and continued to claim aerial victories. In June 1941 he became a flying instructor and went on to command 65 Squadron as well as 504 and 198. He had increasing problems with his sinus and left the RAF in 1946 as a Squadron Leader.

He became a civilian transport pilot flying in the Berlin airlift and across the Mediterranean. He died in the Isle of Man in 1983.

Sergeant John White DFM

John White came from Lanarkshire and joined the RAFVR. He then joined 72 Squadron at Gravesend in June 1940. He served through-out the Battle of Britain and force landed at Eynsford with an injured leg on the 7th September. He made several more claims in September and by the end of the year was awarded a DFM.

In June 1941 he joined 73 Squadron in North Africa. Only a few days after arrival he was killed when after a strafing mission, he was damaged and spun into the ground at Sidi Bari. He was 25.

Sergeant Archie Winskill KCVO, DBE, DFC*

Archie Winskill came from Penrith in Cumbria. He joined the RAFVR and after training, he joined 54 Squadron at RAF Catterick. On the 3rd October 1940 he joined 72 Squadron at Biggin Hill but moved two weeks later to 603 Squadron. In 1941 he joined 41 Squadron but was shot down near Calais in August. He baled out and hid in a farmer's barn. An escape line managed to get him to Gibraltar, and he returned to Britain, in November 1941. He was then commissioned.

No longer allowed to fly over French territory he went to North Africa commanding 232 Squadron. He was awarded a DFC and a bar after several victory claims in North Africa. He remained in the RAF after the war and was made CBE. He became an Air Commodore and captain of the Queen's Flight in 1968. He was knighted in 1980 and died in 2005.

Pilot Officer Douglas Winter

Douglas Winter came from South Shields and joined the RAF in 1929 an apprentice air-fitter. He applied for pilot trained and eventually joined 72 as a Sergeant Pilot in October 1939.

He was commissioned on the 1st April 1940 and served over Dunkirk. He made several victory claims during the battle, but was killed on the 5th September, when he bailed out too low near Elham, Kent. He was buried at South Shields and was 26 years old.

Appendix E

92 Squadron profiles

Pilot Officer Anthony Bartley DFC*

Tony Bartley was born in India and attended Stowe school. He learnt to fly at the civilian West Malling airfield in 1938 and joined the RAF on a short service commission in 1939. After training he joined 92 Squadron in October 1939.

He flew with 92 over Dunkirk and throughout the Battle of Britain making several victory claims. He was awarded a DFC and went to 74 Squadron in March 1941. He then became a flying instructor and test pilot on Spitfires with Jeffrey Quill.

In February 1942 he returned to operation with 65 Squadron as a flight commander. In July 1942 he commanded 111 Squadron in North Africa where he again had success. He was awarded a bar to his DFC and went to the United States to test aircraft and give lectures. In 1945 he was sent to the Far East, but Japan surrendered. Post war he married the film star Deborah Kerr and moved to Hollywood where he became a film producer. He died in 2001.

Pilot Officer John Bryson

John Bryson was a large man who came from Canada where he had been a Mounted Policeman (Mountie). For some reason he had left the police and came to England to join the RAF on a short service commission in 1939.

He joined 92 Squadron in October 1939 and was soon in action. He was shot down and killed by 109's on the 24th September 1940. He managed to land his aircraft with one leg virtually severed. He passed out and did not regain consciousness at North Weald where he landed. He was 27.

Flying Officer John F. Drummond DFC.

Drummond came from Blundellsands near Liverpool. He joined the RAF on a short service commission in 1938 and joined 46 Squadron. He went with them to Norway in May 1940. He made several claims over Norway, but was evacuated, but not with the squadron aboard HMS Glorious. As a result, when the carrier was sunk, he escaped. He was awarded a DFC.

He joined 92 Squadron on the 5th September 1940 at Biggin Hill and was soon engaging the Luftwaffe. He made several victory claims, but on the 10th October, he collided with Pilot Officer Williams. He was injured but when he baled-out he was too low and killed. He was 21 and buried at Thornton in West Lancashire.

Pilot Officer Harry Edwards

Edwards was born in Manchester but moved with his family to Canada. In January 1939 he received a commission in the RAF and joined 92 at Tangmere in October 1939.

He scored victories over Dunkirk and was still with the squadron in September 1940. He was killed on the 11th September when he was shot down by ME109's; but his body was not discovered until the 7th October in a wood near Smeeth, Kent. He was buried at Hawkinge cemetery.

Sergeant Peter R. Eyles

Peter Eyles joined the RAF as an apprentice in 1932. He then applied for pilot training and joined 92 Squadron at RAF Tangmere in October 1939.

He was in action over Dunkirk and in the Battle of Britain, but he was shot down and killed by Major Werner Molders of JG51 on the 20th September. He crashed into the Channel and his body was never recovered.

Sergeant ETG Firth

No details known.

Sergeant Ronald Fokes DFC, DFM.

Ron Fokes joined the RAFVR as a pilot under training in 1937. In January 1940 he joined 92 Squadron at Croydon. He made claims over Dunkirk and stayed with the squadron during the Battle of Britain. He was awarded a DFM in November 1940. After becoming an instructor and being commissioned, he returned to operations. He became a test pilot in 1942 before joining 93 Squadron on Typhoons.

He received a DFC in 1944 and was promoted to Squadron Leader commanding 257 Squadron. Flying Typhoons on the 12th June 1944, he was hit by flak and crashed near Caen. He baled out too low and was killed.

Pilot Officer Frederick N. Hargreaves

Fred Hargreaves joined the RAF on a short service commission in June 1939. He joined 92 Squadron in March 1940 and flew with them throughout the summer. He was lost on the 11th September 1940 off Dungeness. He was believed to have crashed into the Channel.

Sergeant Ralph Havercraft AFC

Havercroft joined the RAFVR in 1937 and after converting to Spitfires with 41 Squadron he was called up in September 1939. He was sent to 604 Squadron and Blenheims but on the 14th March 1940 he joined 92 Squadron.

In May and throughout the summer of 1940 he made several claims, he then became a test pilot and was commissioned. He was awarded an AFC in 1949 and retired in 1963 as a Wing Commander. He died in 1995.

Pilot Officer Robert Holland DFC

Robert Holland entered the RAF College in in 1938. He was granted a permanent commission and joined 92 Squadron in October 1939.

He made several claims over France and Dunkirk with 92, he was shot down on the 15th September 1940, near Ashford and was injured. A month later he was back in action and making more victory claims. He was awarded a DFC in November and in early 1941 joined 91 Squadron.

He became an instructor and then went to India with 607 Squadron where he shot down a Japanese Oscar fighter. He remained in the RAF and was killed in a flying accident when his Vampire collided with another from 233 OCU on the 17th November 1954.

Sergeant Donald Kingaby DFM DSO**

Donald Ernest Kingaby, was born in 1920 in London. He joined the RAFVR in April 1939 and under-went pilot training. He went to 5 OTU Aston Down and after converting to Spitfires joined 266 Squadron at Wittering on 24th June 1940.

Kingaby damaged two Ju88's and a Me110 on 12th August. He was wounded in the hand on the 18th and did not fly in combat again before he was posted to 92 Squadron at Biggin Hill on the 25th September 1940.

While with 92 he damaged Messerschmitt 109's on 27th and 30th September, shot down a Me109 and probably another on 12th October. He destroyed another on the 15th, he then shared a Me110 on the 20th, a Dornier 17 on the 24th; while damaging a 109 on the 25th. He continued with a 109 destroyed on 1st of November and shot down three more and probably another on the 15th. He then shot down a 109 on the 1st December.

Don Kingaby was awarded the DFM in December 1940 and was described in many newspapers as 'the 109 specialist'.

In 1941 he destroyed another eight Me109's and probably another four; with two damaged. He was awarded a Bar to the DFM in July 1941 and a second Bar in November 1941; being the only man do so.

In early November 1941 he became an instructor at 58 OTU Grangemouth and was commissioned. He returned to ops in March 1942 with 111 Squadron at Debden. He moved on to 64 Squadron at Hornchurch in April 1942.

On 2nd June 1942 he damaged a Fw190 and destroyed one on the 30th July. Don Kingaby was posted to 122 Squadron at Hornchurch in early August as a Flight Commander and took part in the actions over Dieppe where he destroyed a Dornier 217.

Don Kingaby was made Squadron Leader in November 1942 and continued to make claims into 1943. He was awarded the DSO in March 1943 and promoted to Acting Wing Commander, leading the Hornchurch Wing. In September 1943 he was posted HQ Fighter Command. He then led in April 1944 a Spitfire Wing, which would provide low-level cover for the Overlord invasion forces. He claimed his final victory on the 30th of June 1944, when he shared a Me109F.

After Overlord he was given command of the Advanced Gunnery School at Catfoss and remained there until the end of the war.

He was granted a permanent commission after the war and was awarded an Air Force Cross in June 1952. He retired from the RAF in 1958 as a Squadron Leader. He died on the 31st December 1990 in Massachusetts, USA. His ashes were brought back to the UK and interred at Bromley Hill cemetery, Kent near Biggin Hill. In 1993 his widow unveiled a memorial to him in the chapel at Biggin Hill.

Flight Lieutenant Brian Kingcombe DFC, DSO

Charles Brian Fabris Kingcombe was born in Calcutta on 31st May 1917 and educated at Bedford. He entered the RAF College Cranwell in January 1936 as a Flight Cadet. Soon after he began his pilot course, he was seriously injured in a car accident.

A RAF medical board told him he would never fly again as he was expected to suffer permanent double vision. But after months in hospital his resilience, will and strength paid off and he rejoined his course. He joined 65 Squadron at Hornchurch on 30th July 1938 and was still serving with it in 1940.

On 27th May Kingcombe joined 92 Squadron at Northolt as 'A' Flight Commander.

He claimed two He111's destroyed and another probably destroyed on 2nd June, shared in destroying Ju88's on 10th and 24th July, probably destroyed a Me109 on 9th September, destroyed a He111 on the 11th, damaged two Me109's on the 14th, damaged a Do17 on the 15th and shared a Ju88, probably destroyed a He111 and damaged another on the 18th.

Kingcombe destroyed a Me109 on the 23rd, damaged a Ju88 and a Me109 on the 24th, got a probable Do17, damaged another, shared a Ju88 and damaged two others on the 27th, destroyed a Me109 on 11th October, destroyed two more and damaged a third on the 12th and destroyed another on the 13th.

On 15th October Kingcombe was shot down in combat with Me109's. He baled out, wounded, and was admitted to the Royal Naval Hospital at Chatham. His Spitfire, X4418, crashed at Wybornes Farm, High Halstow. Kingcombe was awarded the DFC on the 25th October 1940. He re-joined 92 Squadron on the 23rd December 1940 after recovering.

On 16th June 1941 he probably destroyed a Me109 and on 24th July destroyed another. Kingcombe was posted away in August to 61 OTU as a Flight Commander. He returned to operations in February 1942, taking command of 72 Squadron at Gravesend.

He damaged a Fw190 on 15th April and got a probable Me109 on 27th May. In late June 1942 Kingcombe was promoted to Acting Wing Commander, to lead the Kenley Wing. On 27th August he damaged a Fw190.

He was posted in late 1942 to Charmy Down, where the Fighter Leaders School was being formed; and he was awarded the DSO in December 1942.

In May 1943 Kingcombe was posted to Malta, to lead 244 Wing, which flew in support of the Eighth Army in Sicily and Italy. After the invasion of Italy, he was promoted to Acting Group Captain.

Kingcombe went on a course to the RAF Staff College Haifa in October 1944 and in March 1945 became SASO at 205 (Heavy Bomber) Group. The group was equipped with Liberators and he flew occasionally as a waist-gunner over northern Yugoslavia. He remained in Italy after the wars end, then moved to Egypt, where he was mostly concerned with repatriating troops to the UK.

After the war he held various staff appointments and instructed at RAF Staff College before being invalided out of the RAF on 26th January 1954 as a Wing Commander, retaining the rank of Group Captain. His war service had taken a toll on his health and he had contracted tuberculosis.

After leaving the RAF, he set up a London garage and car hire business. In 1969, he set up *'Kingcombe Sofas'*, an enterprise which involved the employment of Devon boat builders to craft sofas to each customer's requirements. Brian Kingcombe died on 19th February 1994.

Squadron Leader Robert Lister DFC MID

Robert Charles Franklin Lister was born in 1913 and went to Cheltenham College. He entered RAF Cranwell in 1932 and won the Groves Memorial Prize in 1934. He graduated and joined 13 (Army Co-operation) Squadron at Netheravon in July 1934. A year later he went to 20 (Army Co-Operation) Squadron at Peshawar and in 1937, he was supporting the Army, operating in the mountains of Waziristan against tribesmen. He was awarded the DFC in August 1938 for gallantry in operations in Waziristan and was Mentioned in Despatches in February 1938.

He returned to the United Kingdom and went to the Central Flying School for an instructor's course, after which he went to 10 FTS at RAF Tern Hill. In January 1939 he was made Adjutant of 614 Squadron, Auxiliary Air Force at Cardiff.

In late 1939 Lister crashed on take-off due to an engine failure and fractured his spine. He was in plaster for nine months and was given grounded with a desk job at the Air Ministry.

With the war in full swing he was cleared for flying duties in August 1940 and asked for a posting to Fighter Command. He was posted to 7 OTU Hawarden to convert to Spitfires and then took temporary command of 41 Squadron at Hornchurch on 8th September.

He lasted six days before he was shot down on the 14th whilst flying at the rear of a squadron formation in Spitfire R6605. He baled-out slightly wounded in the arm. On the 22nd, he was sent to 92 Squadron as a supernumerary, but took command when the CO was burned in an accident.

On 24th September, 92 Squadron was scrambled to be part of a 'Big Wing' of three squadrons. Time was wasted and it met a formation of nine Ju88's with a 100+ Me109 escort, head-on and slightly below. After a general break Lister, in X4427, found himself alone and being circled by some nine Me109's. He was eventually hit by a cannon shell in the bottom of the cockpit and wounded in both legs. He went into a spin, managed to get back to Biggin Hill but had only one flap working, causing him to go out of control into a skidding diving turn which fortunately took the Spitfire into a valley below the level of the airfield. Lister regained control, made a landing without flaps and stopped ten yards short of a wood at the far end.

After long hospital treatment Lister was declared medically unfit for flying duties in 1941 and posted to the Operations Room at Biggin Hill as Controller. In 1942 he became SASO at HQ 219 Group at Alexandria and in 1943 became CO 209 Group at Haifa.

From September 1944 until July 1945 Lister was on the staff at Air HQ Eastern Mediterranean, after which he commanded RAF Amman, Jordan until March 1946, when he was posted back to the UK.

Lister commanded various bases in the UK and retired on 31st October 1954 as a Wing Commander, retaining the rank of Group Captain. He died in 1998.

Pilot Officer Lewis

Nothing known

Pilot Officer John W. Lund

John Wilfred Lund was born in May 1919 at Norton in Yorkshire. He was educated at Kingswood School near Bath and then Oriel College, Oxford where he read History. He was a member of the University Air Squadron and was called up on 18th November 1939.

Lund was posted to FTS Cranwell on 1st January 1940, before going on to No. 1 School of Army Co-operation at Old Sarum in June. He was sent to 5 OTU Aston Down on the 10th and after converting to Spitfires he joined 611 Squadron at Digby.

On 2nd July 1940, Lund shared in the destruction of a Dornier 17 and shared another on the 21st of August. He was posted to 92 Squadron at Biggin Hill on the 2nd October 1940. He was shot down by Me109's on the 15th and crashed into the sea off Bee Ness Jetty and rescued from the River Medway.

John Lund was killed on the 2nd October 1941 with 92 Squadron, aged 22 while carrying out a low-level Rhubarb operation over Northern France. As they were returning across the English Channel, they were attacked by Fw190's and all three Spitfires were shot down. Lund was reported missing and is commemorated on the Runnymede Memorial.

Sergeant Jack Mann DFM

Jack Mann was born in Northampton in June 1914 and educated at St. James School.

He joined the RAFVR in 1938 as an Airman under Pilot training and did his weekend flying at 8 E&RFTS Woodley. He was called up on the outbreak of war and posted to 3 ITW at Hastings in December.

'Jacky' Mann went to 9 FTS Hullavington and then to 5 OTU Aston Down to convert to Spitfires. He joined 64 Squadron at Kenley on 27th July 1940.

He made his first operational sortie on the 29th July and on 5th of August he destroyed a ME109. On the 8th he probably destroyed another two 109's and one more on the 11th.

Mann was slightly wounded on the 16th of August and made a force-landing at Hawkinge. He was slightly injured again, this time on the ground when Kenley was bombed on the 18th August, but he re-joined the unit a week later.

Jack Mann was sent to 92 Squadron at Biggin Hill on the 12th of September and two days later he damaged a 109 was wounded again. He was placed sick.

He moved to 91 Squadron in 1941 and shot down a ME109 west of Cap Gris Nez. In the engagement, his Spitfire, P7783, was severely damaged and he was badly burned when he made a crash-landing at Mongeham, Kent. He underwent plastic surgery at East Grinstead, becoming a Guinea Pig and was awarded a DFM.

He then went to No. 1 ADF at Hendon and became a Warrant Officer, before being commissioned in July 1942. He then flew transport flights across the Atlantic before leaving the RAF in 1946 as a Flight Lieutenant.

He became an airline pilot and a Chief Pilot for Middle East Airlines in Beirut where he lived.

In 1989 Jacky Mann was kidnapped in Syrian-controlled West Beirut. His captors, local militia groups demanded the release of Arabs jailed in Britain. He was an elderly man and held in solitary confinement and chained to a radiator. He lost three stone in weight before being release in 1991. He was returned to the UK for medical treatment before moving with his wife 'Sunny' to live in Cyprus where he died in 1995. Before his death he was awarded a CBE.

Pilot Officer Robert McGowan

Robert Henry McGowan was born in 1916 in Liverpool. He joined 611 Squadron before the war as an air mechanic and later became an airman under pilot training. He was commissioned and posted back to 611 Squadron in August 1940; before converting to Spitfires at No.7 OTU at Hawarden near Chester.

On the 6th of September he was posted to join 92 Squadron at Biggin Hill. On the 8th McGowan was shot down by ME109E's and wounded, but he managed to bale out. He was admitted to Faversham Cottage Hospital. He was then transferred to the RAF Hospital at Halton and went on to the RAF Convalescent home at Torquay in October 1940.

McGowan re-joined 92 Squadron in late November 1940 and was posted to 15 FTS at RAF Lossiemouth. From there he went to CFS in March 1941 for an instructor's course. He then moved on to Moose Jaw, Saskatchewan, Canada as an instructor.

Keen to return to operations in 1944 he returned to the UK and was a Lancaster pilot with 189 Squadron. He was killed on the 22nd December 1944 on a raid on Politz. The aircraft and crew were lost without trace.

Sergeant Morris

Nothing is known

Pilot Officer Roy Mottram

Roy Mottram was born in March 1917 and joined the RAF on a short service commission in August 1939. After training he joined 92 Squadron at Croydon on the 26th April 1940.

On the 15th September he claimed a Heinkel 111 destroyed and a Dornier 17 damaged. On the 18th he crashed at Hollingbourne after being shot down by a 109. Mottram was taken to Orpington Hospital with slight burns.

Back on ops within two days he shared a Heinkel 111 and on the 26th he claimed a probable 109.

Roy Mottram was killed in August 1941 while flying with 54 Squadron. He was shot down in a Spitfire while escorting Bristol Blenheims on a Circus operation to Lille. He is buried in Merville Communal Cemetery, France.

Sergeant Trevor Oldfield

Trevor Guest Oldfield was born in April 1919 in London and joined the Royal Auxiliary Air Force in 1938. He initially served as an air mechanic at RAF Kenley. He then became an armourer and was called up for war service un 1939. Oldfield then applied for an underwent pilot training and converted onto Spitfires in August 1940.

After conversion he was sent to 64 Squadron in early September 1940, but quickly on to 92 Squadron at Biggin Hill.

Just before midday on the 27th of September, the squadron was scrambled shortly after 14:45, Oldfield and nine others intercepted Junkers 88's and their high-flying Messerschmitt fighter escorts. Oldfield had crashed on to Hesketh Park in Dartford.

Sergeant Kenneth Parker

Kenneth Bruce Parker of Worthing, Sussex was born in May 1915 and joined the RAFVR in 1938. He worked as a chief clerk for the London Assurance Company.

Parker was called up on the 1st September 1939 and he joined 64 Squadron at Leconfield in September 1940. He moved on to 92 Squadron at Biggin Hill on the 24th.

On the 15th of October Parker was shot down and killed in combat with Messerschmitt 109's over the Thames Estuary. His Spitfire crashed into the sea. Parker's body was washed up on Terschelling island off the Dutch coast and he is buried in the cemetery.

Pilot Officer A. John Pattinson

Aberconway John Sefton Pattinson was born in Chelsea, London in 1918. His father having been killed in action seven months previously. Pattinson joined the RAF on a short service commission in December 1937 and was posted to 5 FTS, at RAF Sealand in 1938. He then joined 25 Squadron at Hawkinge flying Gloster Gladiators.

By July 1940 Pattinson was with 23 Squadron at Collyweston, flying Blenheim twin engine fighters. With a shortage of fighter pilots, he converted to Spitfires and was posted to 92 Squadron at Biggin Hill in early October. On his first sortie on October 12th, he was shot down and killed by 109's over Hawkinge. He was just 21 years of age.

Flight Lieutenant James Paterson MBE

James Alfred Paterson was born at Chatton in the district of Gore, Southland, New Zealand on the 16th October 1919 on his family farm.

He was a soldier in the Otago Mounted Rifles, Territorial Army and in 1937 he applied for a RNZAF short service commission. He was accepted and began pilot training. Paterson was awarded his wings in December and sailed for the UK.

Paterson was posted to 82 Squadron at Cranfield in June 1938 and at the outbreak of war, he went to 71 Wing in France, flying Magisters on reconnaissance patrols. In late 1939 he joined 226 Squadron at Rheims and in May 1940 he was detached to special duties.

After Dunkirk, Paterson went with 226 Squadron, but he volunteered for Fighter Command and converted to Spitfires before joining 92 Squadron at Pembrey.

On the 24th of July, Paterson shared in the destruction of a Junkers 88 and another in August. He then shot down a ME110 in September. The same day he was shot down by ME109's and baled out, with his clothes on fire and badly burned about the face.

Paterson insisted on flying again before he could see properly and on the 27th of September he took off and was shot down in flames by 109's near Maidstone. He is buried in Biggin Hill plot at Star Lane Cemetery, Orpington, Kent. He was awarded a posthumous MBE in January 1941 for his outstanding services in France in May 1940.

Squadron Leader Phillip Sanders DFC

Phillip James Sanders was born on the 1st of May 1911 in Brampton, Derbyshire and educated at Cheltenham College and Balliol College, Oxford. He joined the RAF with a direct-entry permanent commission as a University Entrant in March 1936. He was trained at 5 FTS Sealand and he joined 1 Squadron at Tangmere in October 1936.

Sanders was posted to RAF Hornchurch in August 1939 for operational duties. He took command of 92 Squadron at Northolt on 25th May 1940 with whom he destroyed two Heinkel 111's over the Dunkirk beaches.

On the 9th of September he destroyed another He111 and probably a 109. On the 11th he destroyed a 109 and a Heinkel 111 and probably another 109. On the 15th of September, he shot down a Dornier 17 and 109 on the 20th.

However, after this latest combat he headed back to Biggin Hill with a damaged Spitfire. He had oil on his uniform and his batman tried to remove it with petrol. This ended in a terrible accident when Sanders lit a cigarette and promptly ignited his sleeve. He suffered minor burns and was taken to hospital.

He flew no more operational sorties with 92 before he was posted to HQ 11 Group in October 1940. He was awarded a DFC in November 1940.

In 1942 he went to the USA as a fighter test pilot at Wright Field, Dayton, Ohio before returning to the UK where he joined the staff of HQ 84 Group, remaining there until the end of the war. He stayed in the RAF after the war, retiring in 1962 as a Group Captain. He then worked for the Ministry of Defence in a civilian capacity, retiring in 1976.

Sanders died on 11th January 1989.

Pilot Officer Cecil Saunders

Cecil Henry Saunders was born in July 1911 at Forest Hill, South East London. He joined the RAF on a short service commission and after his initial training he moved on to 14 FTS Kinloss.

Saunders joined 92 Squadron at Croydon on the 20th April 1940 and claimed a probable Heinkel 111 and a share in another on the 4th July. On the 9th of September he was in combat over Biggin Hill and made a force-landing at Midley, near Rye. Injured in the process, he was admitted to the RAMC Hospital at Brookland, with shrapnel wounds in his leg.

On the 11th of October, Saunders re-joined 92 Squadron. It took him some time to score again, but on the 26th of October he damaged 109, while on the 29th he shared a 110. On the 1st of November he shot down a rare Ju87 Stuka and damaged another 110. His claims of victories continued into 1941, but in May 1941, Saunders was posted to 74 Squadron at Gravesend as a Flight Commander.

Cecil Saunders joined 145 Squadron in the Western Desert in late July 1942. And claimed a probable 109 and an Italian Mc.202. He was awarded a DFC in December 1942 and was posted to 71 OTU Port Sudan.

He continued in various staff roles throughout 1944 and 1945, before commanding 145 Squadron in July/August 1945. He retired from the RAF in May 1958 as a Wing Commander and died on the 1st of September 1992.

Pilot Officer Thomas Sherrington

Thomas Baldwin Aloysius Sherrington was born at Ayr on the 26th of March 1917 He joined the RAF on a short service commission in early 1939. After completing his training, he arrived at the 11 Group Pool at St. Athan on the 20th of November 1939. He converted on to Hurricanes and was sent to No. 2 Ferry Pilot Pool on 21st December.

In March 1940, Sherrington was posted to 92 Squadron at Croydon. He made a number of claims in September and October 1940; before being posted to 53 OTU Heston in February 1941 as an instructor. He was then promoted and became to commanding officer of 4 Squadron at 61 OTU.

He was released from the RAF in 1947 as a Flight Lieutenant and went to live in the USA where he died in 2008.

Flight Sergeant Charles Sydney

Charles Sydney, of St Mary Cray, Kent, was born in July 1915 in St. Pancras and joined the RAF in 1931 as an aircraft apprentice. He later volunteered for pilot training and joined 19 Squadron at Fowlmere in August 1940. He moved to 266 Squadron at Wittering and quickly on to 92 Squadron in September.

He was shot down and killed on the 27th of September at Walton-on-Thames in Spitfire, He was buried at the Biggin Hill plot of the St Mary Cray Cemetery, Orpington, Kent.

Pilot Officer Donald Stanley

Donald Arthur Stanley of Muswell Hill, Middlesex was born in 1921.

He joined the RAFVR in 1939 and started pilot training. He joined 64 Squadron at RAF Leconfield in September 1940. He was killed on the 25th of February 1941 with 611

Squadron, believed to have shot down by Major Molders of JG51. His body was never found, and his name is on the Runnymede Memorial.

Flight Lieutenant John W. Villa DFC.

John 'Pancho' Villa was born in London. He joined the RAF on a short service commission in 1937 and went to join 2 AACU at Lee on Solent. In May 1940 he joined 72 Squadron and he shot down a JU87 Stuka over Dunkirk. He went to Biggin Hill with the squadron where he made several claims and was awarded a DFC.

In October he was posted as a flight commander and a flight lieutenant to 92 Squadron at Biggin Hill and continued to claim aerial victories. In June 1941 he became a flying instructor and went on to command 65 Squadron as well as 504 and 198. He had increasing problems with his sinus and left the RAF in 1946 as a Squadron Leader.

He became a civilian transport pilot flying in the Berlin airlift and across the Mediterranean. He died in the Isle of Man in 1983.

Pilot Officer Trevor 'Wimpey' Wade AFC

Trevor Sidney Wade was born in January 1920 and educated at Yardley Court School and Tonbridge School in Kent. He joined the RAFVR in 1938 and was called-up on the outbreak of war. He received a commission in April 1940.

On the 21st of May, Wade was posted to 92 Squadron at Croydon. On the 28th of July in poor weather conditions on a night patrol over Swansea Bay, he was forced to bale out over Exeter.

On the 19th of August, Wade shared a Junkers 88, but his Spitfire was hit by return fire and he made a forced landing on Lewes racecourse. The aircraft overturned and Wade was trapped upside down in the cockpit but fortunately the aircraft did not catch fire.

He fought throughout the autumn and into December 1940 making several claims; and these continued into 1941. He was posted in June 1941 to join 123 Squadron at RAF Turnhouse in Scotland.

He was awarded the DFC in July 1941 and joined 602 Squadron at Kenley in September 1941. He was shot down on the 17th but was uninjured. He then became a flying instructor.

In late 1943 Wade was appointed OC Flying at AFDU, testing the performance of captured enemy aircraft. For this, he was awarded the AFC in September 1944.

In early 1945 Wade went to the USA to test captured Japanese fighters and to gain experience on new American types coming a member of staff on the renowned magazine Aeroplane.

In late 1947 Wade was offered the job of assistant test pilot at Hawker Aircraft and started to test fly the new Hawker jets. After a spell in the USA on an exchange scheme, he returned to Hawkers and resumed test flying, but he was killed on the 3rd of April 1951 at Ringmer, Sussex, whilst testing the P1081 experimental aircraft.

Pilot Officer Bill Watling

William Charles Watling was born in Middlesborough in 1920 but moved to Guernsey with his family.

He joined the Royal Air Force and attended the RAF College, Cranwell in September 1939, but his training course was suspended with the outbreak of war and he joined the RAFVR to train as a pilot at Cranwell. When his training was completed, he was given a permanent commission in July 1940 and posted to 92 Squadron at RAF Pembrey. He converted onto Spitfires at No. 5 OTU at Aston Down before returning on the 2nd of August 1940.

On the 2nd of September he was shot down in combat over East Guldeford near Rye, Sussex and baled out, but he was badly burned on the face and hands. He spent nearly two months recovering and returned to flying in November. He claimed a probable ME109 on the 2nd of November and damaged another on the 1st of December.

Watling died on the 7th of February 1941. He was part of a section of two Spitfires which took off from RAF Manston for a morning weather test. The visibility was extremely poor, and he flew into high ground near Deal. Watling was buried in the Biggin Hill plot of St. Mary Cray Cemetery, Orpington, Kent.

Pilot Officer Geoffrey Wellum DFC

Geoffrey Wellum was born in Walthamstow on the 14th of August 1921. He joined the RAF on a short service commission and began his initial training on the 14th of August 1939.

Wellum joined No. 6 FTS Little Rissington before joining 92 Squadron at RAF Northolt in May 1940. He was to become one of the youngest pilots in the Battle of Britain.

On the 11th of September 1940 Geoffrey Wellum shot down a Heinkel He111, and shared a Junkers 88 two weeks later. After the battle he damaged two ME109E's on the 2nd of November and a third on the 17th.

He remained with 92 Squadron into 1941 and damaged 109 in June and probably shot one down in July followed by a confirmed victory. He was awarded the DFC in August 1941 and posted as an instructor to 52 OUT at RAF Aston Down.

In February 1942 Wellum was sent to 65 Squadron at RAF Debden as a Flight Commander and posted to Malta in July. He flew with 1435 Flight from RAF Luqa but became ill and was sent back to the United Kingdom to recover. After a lengthy break he became a test pilot at Gloster Aircraft, testing the new Typhoon.

Geoffrey Wellum retired from the RAF in June 1961 as a Flight Lieutenant. He became a commodity broker in London. His autobiography called 'First Light' was published in 2002. Sadly, he died in July 2018.

Pilot Officer Desmond Williams

Desmond Gordon Williams was born on the 12th of July 1920 in Shropshire and attended Victoria College in Jersey. He joined the RAF on a short service commission and started his training in January 1939.

Des Williams joined 92 Squadron at RAF Tangmere in October 1939. The squadron were at the time flying Bristol Blenheim's, but they soon traded them in for Supermarine Spitfires in March 1940.

William's was soon in action over the Dunkirk beaches and claimed a ME110 destroyed and two others probably destroyed. On the 2nd June he shot down a Heinkel 111 over Dunkirk.

claimed a probable Heinkel 111 on the 10th of July and a shared JU88 on the 14th of August. He continued to claim throughout the following weeks and into October.

Des Williams was killed on the 10th of October 1940 when he collided with Flying Officer Drummond while they attacked a lone Dornier 17 near Tangmere. Williams was just 20 years old and buried in London Road Cemetery, Salisbury.

Flight Lieutenant Allan Wright DFC* AFC

Allan Richard Wright was born in Teignmouth, Devon on the 12th of February 1920 and educated at St. Edmunds College. He entered the RAF College Cranwell in April 1938. With the outbreak of war, he was enlisted as an airman and started pilot training. He was granted a permanent commission on the 23rd of October 1939 and joined 92 Squadron.

The squadron was equipped with Blenheims, but he converted with the rest of the unit to Spitfires and flew over Dunkirk. Over Dunkirk on the 23rd of May 1940, Wright shot down a ME110, possibly another and damaged a third. The next day he claimed a probable Heinkel 111 and on the 2nd of June he shot down a ME109E.

Wright continued to fly with 92 throughout the Battle of Britain. On the 14th of August he shared a Heinkel 111; and on the 29th he shot down another this time at night over Bristol. On the 11th of September he shot down a Heinkel 111 and a probable ME109E. He continued to make steady claims for the next few weeks.

With his experience and ability, Wright was made the 'B' Flight Commander on the 27th of September as an Acting Flight Lieutenant. To celebrate he shot down a JU88 and shared a Heinkel 111, while also damaging a Dornier 17 and two more Junkers 88's.

On the 30th of September he shot down two Messerschmitt 109E's, but he was damaged by 109 off Brighton and wounded in the thigh by splinters. He made a forced landing at Shoreham and was taken to Southlands Hospital.

He was awarded the DFC in October 1940 and after returning to combat shot down a 109 near Dover on the 6th of December 1940.

Wright remained with 92 Squadron into 1941 and on the 16th of May he shared 109; making similar claims in the following days. He was awarded a Bar to his DFC in July and posted as an instructor to No. 59 OTU at Crosby-on-Eden in Cumberland. In September 1941 he was sent to HQ 9 Group, to work on air fighting tactics and on to HQ Fighter Command.

In February 1942, Wright was made the Chief Instructor at the Pilot Gunnery Instructor School, then forming at CGS Sutton Bridge. In October 1942 he was sent to train USAAF squadrons about to be posted to the UK.

Wright returned to the United Kingdom and went on a night fighter course at No. 54 OTU Charter Hall in December 1942. He was posted to the renowned 29 Squadron at RAF West Malling in March 1943 as a Flight Commander. He shot down a Junkers 88 on the 3rd of April 1943.

Various staff postings followed, and he went to the Army Staff College Camberley in August 1944 before gaining an AFC in September 1944.

Wright remained in the RAF post war and held a number of positions including one at the Air Ministry. He converted onto jet fighters and became Wing Commander Flying at RAF Waterbeach flying Hunter and Javelin aircraft.

After two years in the Far East and a further two at HQ Fighter Command he was appointed to command the Ballistic Missile Early Warning Station at Fylingdales on the North Yorkshire moors.

He retired on 12th February 1967 as a Wing Commander and moved to North Devon. He died on the 16th of September 2015.

Appendix F

74 Squadron profiles

Flying Officer Roger John Eric Boulding

Roger Boulding joined the RAF on a short service commission in 1938. He trained as a pilot and joined 98 Squadron and then 148 Squadron flying Fairey Battles in November 1939.

In August 1940 during the height of the Battle of Britain he volunteered for single seat fighter training and after conversion joined 74 Squadron at Kirton in Lindsey. He made several claims but none while at Biggin Hill during the battle.

In 1941 he was shot down during a sweep over France and was captured ending up in Stalag Luft III.

After the war he returned to service flying Lancasters and then Vampire jet fighters in the Middle East. He retired as a Wing Commander in 1966 and died in March 1993.

Pilot Officer Peter Chesters

Peter Chesters was born in April 1919 at Thorpe Bay, Essex. He attended Haileybury College in Herefordshire and was a keen sportsman and a good shot representing the school at Bisley in 1935.

Chesters had a keen interest in flying and would attend RAF Rochford at the weekends where he would talk with the pilots. This led in 1939 to him joining the RAFVR for pilot training. He converted onto Spitfires and joined 74 Squadron on the 29th of September 1940.

He started flying combat sorties in early October and many practice flights under the tuition of the Malan and other senior pilots. On the 15th of October, 74 Squadron moved back to Biggin Hill.

On the 27th October Chetsers shot down his first victory which became an unusual incident as recounted in the text of this book...the 109 having to force land at Penshurst airfield and Chesters landing next to him and fighting with the pilot.

Chesters remained with the squadron into November 1940 and he often flew as Sailor Malan's wingman.

In late 1940 Chesters was wounded in the leg by a 109 over Chatham. He parachuted to earth and came down in the mud at Conyer Creek in Essex. However, he began to sink due to the weight of his clothing and flying equipment. He was luckily assisted by a local who pulled him from the mud and took him home for a hot bath and a drink. The local community believed he had actually stayed with the Spitfire to ensure it did not hit the village and they wrote to Biggin Hill praising Chesters for this. He remained in hospital for treatment, he soon returned to the squadron.

Chesters was back in action in 1941 making a number of combat sorties but no specific claims.

In April 1941 he shot down a ME109E of 2/JG51 piloted by Feldwebel Friedrich Maoller. The 109 crashed with its pilot at Frost Farm, St Nicholas at Wade, Kent. Chesters then made the fatal mistake of attempting a victory roll over RAF Manston but crashed onto the parade ground and was killed.

Peter Chesters is buried near the family home at the Sutton Road Cemetery, Southend-on-Sea, Essex.

Pilot Officer Bryan V. Draper

Bryan Vincent Draper was born in 1016 in Barry, South Wales. He joined the RAFVR in April 1938 as an air man under pilot training. He was called up at the start of the war and converted to Spitfires before going to the No. 11 Group Pool at RAF St Athan.

He joined 74 Squadron on the 17th of February 1940 and was soon in action during the Dunkirk withdrawal and the Battle of Britain making several victory claims.

On the 20th of October his aircraft was badly damaged over south London and he made a forced landing with a seized engine.

After the Battle of Britain, he claimed three JU87 Stuka's destroyed and a ME109E damaged on the 14th of November. He was awarded a DFC on Christmas Eve 1940 and was posted away to the Central Flying School on an instructor's course. After this he instructed at the RAF College Cranwell and in Canada.

He was promoted to Flight Lieutenant in March 1942 and converted to Mosquitos, before joining 45 Squadron at Kumbhirram in India in February 1945. The squadron flew attack missions against the retreating Japanese army in Burma; but on the 28th of February 1945 he was conducting a bombing attack when his aircraft broke up in the air near Mandalay. Sadly, the wooden Mosquitos which were held together with glue did not like the tropical damp conditions and a number came apart in the air.

Bryan Draper and his navigator Warrant Officer James were both killed and are buried in the Taukkyan War Cemetery at Rangoon.

Flight Lieutenant Johnny Freeborn DFC*

Johnny Freeborn was born in Yorkshire on the 1st of December 1919 and attended Leeds Grammar School.

He joined the RAF and started his training on the 17th of January 1938. He was granted a commission and started his flying training in mid-1938. He then joined 74 Squadron at RAF Hornchurch in October 1938.

Freeborn was involved in one of the first friendly fire incidents of the war when on the 6th of September 1939, he was scrambled with other members of the squadron to investigate a reported bandit. They attacked and attacked what they thought were ME109's and shot down two of them killing the pilots. Sadly, they were in fact Hurricanes of 56 Squadron. They shot down two, killing one of the pilots. The incident became known as 'The Battle of Barking Creek' and Johnny Freeborn and another pilot were sent for Court Martial on the 7th of October 1939. The two pilots were however acquitted and returned to flying duties.

In May 1940, Freeborn made a number of victory claims and during the Battle of Britain, he made a number of claims. He was awarded a DFC in August 1940.

He was given temporary command of 'A' Flight on the 8th of August when Sailor Malan was given command of the squadron; and this was made permanent a week later. He continued to make victory claims throughout the rest of 1940 and in February 1941 he was given a bar to his DFC.

He was rested and sent on an instructor's course at No. 57 OUT in June 1941. In January 1942, he was posted to the Training Command of the USAAF at Selma, Alabama, as the RAF Liaison Officer. He then moved on to Eglin Field in Florida where he tested aircraft such as the Mustang and the Thunderbolt.

He returned to Europe in December 1942 and given command of various stations. In February 1943 he joined 602 Squadron at Perranporth as a supernumerary leading the squadron on bomber escort missions.

In June 1943 Freeborn was given command of 118 Squadron at Coltishall before going to No. 61 OTU at Rednal and then No. 57 OTU at Eshott. He then moved to Italy to be Wing Commander Flying of 286 Wing.

At the end of the war Freeborn left the RAF in 1946 as a Wing Commander. He then worked as a director for Tetley Walker before living in Spain. He returned to the United Kingdom and died in August 2010.

Sergeant John Glendinning

John Glendinning hailed from County Durham and like many pilots became a member of the RAFVR. He was called up at the start of the war and after training he joined 54 Squadron at Catterick. He then moved to 74 Squadron at Biggin Hill in late October 1940 and made a number of claims in November and December 1940.

On the 12th March 1941 he was shot down over Dungeness by Major Werner Molders and killed.

Sergeant Clive Hilken

Clive Geoffrey Hilken was born in September 1919 in Hull. He joined the RAFVR before the war and was called up, converting to Spitfires and joining 74 Squadron in August 1940 at the height of the Battle of Britain.

In mid-October 1940 the squadron moved to Biggin Hill. Hilken was shot down on the 20th of October over south London and he baled out wounded. He was admitted to Orpington Hospital.

He returned to the squadron in 1941, but he was shot down again on the 21st of April and had to bale out. He was uninjured and continued with 74 Squadron.

On the 27th of June 1941 he was shot down and wounded near St. Omer in France and taken prisoner. After hospital treatment he spent the rest of the war in a prison camp. He was liberated in 1945 and left the RAF later in the year as a Warrant Officer.

He then became a teacher and was head teacher of the school at RAF Geilenkirchen in Germany. He died on the 30th of June 2005.

fSergeant Thomas Brian Kirk

Thomas Brian Kirk was born in 1919 in Thirsk, North Yorkshire and joined 608 Squadron, Royal Auxiliary Air Force as an air mechanic. He was later selected for pilot training and once completed, he joined 74 Squadron in late August 1940. Within weeks he made his first victory claim, when he shot down a ME110 on the 11th of September.

In mid-October Kirk was shot down over Maidstone. He managed to bale-out, but he was severely wounded and was admitted to Preston Hall Hospital in Maidstone in a critical condition. Sadly, he died of his injuries some ten months later on the 22nd of July 1941, aged 22. He was taken home by his family and buried at St Oswald's church, East Harlsey, Yorkshire.

Squadron Leader Adolph Geysbert Malan (Sailor) DFC* DSO*

Adolph Gysbert Malan was born in Wellington, South Africa on the 3rd of October 1910. In February 1924 he became a cadet on the South African training ship General Botha before joining the Union Castle Steamship Line three years later.

Malan joined the Royal Navy Reserve in February 1932 and was given a commission as a Sub-Lieutenant in June 1935. In late 1935, Malan applied for a short service commission in the RAF, was duly accepted. He soon acquired the name 'Sailor' for obvious reasons a name which stuck with him. He started flying training and joined 74 Squadron in December 1936.

He became a flight commander in March 1939 and made a Flight Lieutenant. With the on-set of war he was soon in action over the Dunkirk beaches destroying and probably destroying a number of German aircraft. At the end of the evacuation he was awarded a Distinguished Flying Cross in June.

On the night of the 18th/19th of June, Malan proved his flying abilities when he shot down two Heinkel 111's and considerable feat in a Spitfire.

When the Battle of Britain started, he made steady claims leading his section and then the squadron when he was made Squadron Leader. He was awarded a bar to his DFC in July 1940. Further victories followed and he became one of the most renowned pilots in Fighter Command.

When the Battle of Britain ended, Malan continued commanding the squadron and received a Distinguished Service Order for his command in December 1940.

In 1941 Fighter Command went on to the front foot and started making sweeps across France. Malan continued to make claims and became the Wing Commander of the Biggin Hill Wing. He became a major air tactician and leader controlling the battle and managing his squadrons and young pilots.

He was awarded a bar to his DSO in July 1941 and in August sent to rest as a Chief Flying Instructor at No. 58 OUT at Grangemouth. Two months later he was sent to the USA to lecture the USAAF on Luftwaffe tactics and air fighting.

In later 1941, 'Sailor' Malan was posted to Sutton Bridge to command the Central Gunnery School; but on the 1st of January 1943 he returned to his beloved Biggin Hill as Station Commander. He could not stay away from operational flying and often flew on sweeps but scored no further victories. Biggin Hill went from strength to strength and claimed its 1,000th victory in May 1943.

Sailor Malan left the station in October 1943 and took command of 19 Fighter Wing, 2nd TAF on 1st November. In March 1944 he took command of 145 Wing which was made up of three Free French squadrons. He flew with them on D-Day.

Malan attended the RAF Staff College in 1945 but left the service and returned home to South Africa with his young family. Sadly, he became ill in the 1960's with Parkinson's disease and died on the 17th of September 1963.

Malan was seen by many as the chief RAF fighter pilot and his 'Ten rules of air fighting' was published and hung in every fighter squadron including many US fighter squadrons. The rules were still to be found in to the 1950's at many stations.

Sergeant Neil Morrison

Neil Morrison joined the RAFVR in September 1937 for pilot training. He was called up on the 1st of September 1939 and went to No. 7 OUT at Hawarden. He converted to Spitfires and joined 54 Squadron at Catterick in September 1940.

Morrison moved on to 72 Squadron at Biggin Hill on the 4th of October and then on to 74 Squadron on the 26th of October. He made a couple of victory claims in late 1940 and shot down a ME110 in 1941; but on the 24th of February he went missing and his body washed was up on the beach at Lydd-on-Sea, three months later.

Flight Lieutenant John C. Mungo-Park DFC*

John Colin Mungo-Park was born in Wallasey, Cheshire in 1918 and educated at Liverpool College. He joined the RAF on a short service commission in 1937 and was sent to No. 10 FTS at RAF Tern Hill. He then went on to the Anti-Aircraft Co-operation Unit at Lee-on-Solent.

In September 1939, Mungo-Park was posted to 74 Squadron at RAF Hornchurch and made his first claim over Dunkirk with a share of a Henschel 126.

When the Battle of Britain started, he made a number of claims and these continued throughout the period of the battle. He was awarded the DFC in November 1940 and became a Flight Lieutenant.

In March 1941 he took command of the squadron when Malan was posted. He led 74 on sweeps over France and continued to make victory claims. However, on the 27th of June 1941 he was shot down and killed. He is buried in Adinkerke Military Cemetery, Belgium.

He was awarded a posthumous bar to his DFC in July 1941.

Flying Officer William H. Nelson DFC

William Henry Nelson came from Montreal in Canada. He joined the RAF on a short service commission in March 1937. After training he went to 10 Squadron at Dishforth, North Yorkshire flying Whitley bombers. He took part in the squadrons first war mission with a leaflet drop on Germany on the night of the 8th/9th September 1939. Making several other trips he was awarded the DFC in June 1940.

The shortage of fighter pilots led to Nelson volunteering for fighter training and he converted to Spitfires at Sutton Bridge. He was transferred to 74 Squadron at RAF Hornchurch on the 20th of July and a few weeks later started to make victory claims.

Having survived the Battle of Britain he was killed on the 1st of November 1940, when 109's hit him over Dover. His aircraft was not seen to crash, and his body was never recovered.

Flying Officer Alan Leslie Ricalton

Alan Leslie Ricalton was born on the 21st of January 1914 in Northumberland and joined the RAF in 1938. He initially trained as a bomber pilot and was sent to 142 Squadron at Andover which was equipped with Fairey Battles.

In 1940 the squadron was in France and when the Blitzkrieg began 142 Squadron made attacks on the advancing German units at Sedan. The squadron had heavy losses but Ricalton survived and continued back with the unit to RAF Waddington.

When Fighter Command needed more pilots Ricalton volunteered and was posted to 74 squadron at Kirton-in-Lindsey in August. He does not appear to have attended a Spitfire OYU and did his conversion on the squadron.

When 74 Squadron moved to Coltishall in early September Ricalton tackled with the Luftwaffe and claimed two ME110's damaged. When they moved to Biggin Hill he made a number of combat flights with them, but he was shot down by Messerschmitt 109's over the Thames Estuary. He crashed in his Spitfire at Hollingbourne, Kent. He was buried in Sittingbourne Cemetery.

Sergeant John Alan Scott

John Alan Scott was born in 1918 in West London. He joined the RAFVR in 1939 and was called up on the outbreak of war. After converting to Spitfires, he joined 266 Squadron at RAF Wittering. Shortly afterwards he joined 611 Squadron at Tern Hill and then 74 Squadron at Biggin Hill on 23rd October 1940.

Scott was only on the squadron four days when he was shot down and killed by ME109's over Maidstone on the 27th of October 1940. His Spitfire crashed at Dundas Farm, Elmsted near Ashford. He is buried in the Alperton Burial Ground, Wembley.

Sergeant Wilfred Malcolm Skinner DFM

Wilf Skinner came from Gloucester and joined the RAFVR pre-war but became a full-time RAF pilot. In June 1940 he joined 74 Squadron at Hornchurch and was with the squadron when they flew and fought over Dunkirk.

Skinner made various claims throughout the Dunkirk campaign and later during the Battle of Britain. He was with the squadron when they moved to Biggin Hill, but he made no further claims until November.

He was awarded a DFF, commissioned and became an instructor in 1941, before re-joining 74 Squadron. He was shot down in July 1941 on a sweep over France and spent the rest of the war as a prisoner of war, including a stint in the infamous Stalag Luft III. He died in 2003.

Sergeant Harold John Soars

Harold John Soars was born in July 1918 and joined the RAFVR in 1938 for pilot training. He was called up and after converting to Spitfires sent to 74 Squadron at Kirton-in-Lindsey on the 21st of August 1940.

Soars made a number of combat flights but made no victory claims. He was shot down on the 1st of by a 109 at Dover and admitted to the Victoria Hospital in Folkestone. When he recovered, he re-joined 74 Squadron.

Little is known of his further war service, but he was promoted to Warrant Officer in May 1942 and commissioned the following October. He left the RAF as a Flight Lieutenant in 1947 and served with the RAFVR. He died in 1975.

Pilot Officer Robert L. Spurdle DFC*

Robert Lawrence Spurdle was born in Wanganui, New Zealand in 1918. In 1939 he obtained a short service commission in the RNZAF.

Acter his initial training, he was sent for light bomber pilot training but was held up due to illness. With war in Europe he was sent to the UK and he was sent to No. 7 OTU at Hawarden in August 1940. He then 74 Squadron at Kirton-in-Lindsey on the 21st of August.

Spurdle was soon in combat and made a few claims in September and October, but he had to bale out on the 22nd of October.

He remained with the squadron and continued making claims throughout the remainder of 1940 and into 1941. In April 1941, Spurdle was posted to 91 Squadron at RAF Hawkinge. He was then sent to the Merchant Ship Fighter Unit at Speke airport in Liverpool. After training on catapulted Hurricanes, he made two trans-Atlantic trips without incident.

Spurdle returned to 91 Squadron in early 1942 and made further claims during sweeps over France. He was awarded the DFC in August 1942, before being posted to Malta. He was however declared to be operationally tired and was sent to 116 Squadron on anti-aircraft co-operation duties.

In November 1942 Spurdle returned to New Zealand and the RNZAF. He then flew fighters in the Soloman Islands and claimed two Japanese aircraft as destroyed.

Spurdle returned to the UK in March 1944 and he joined 130 Squadron at Lympne. He then almost immediately moved to 80 Squadron at RAF Hornchurch and command of the squadron in July. In September 1944 the squadron was operating from an airfield in Holland and Spurdle made further victory claims in December 1944.

He was sent to HQ 83 Group in January 1945 and awarded a bar to his DFC.

Spurdle was then sent to work as a forward air controller with the 11th Armoured Division in Germany. When the war ended, he was sent Catfoss for an instructor's course but transferred to the RNZAF in the autumn. He died in there 1994.

Pilot Office Harbourne Mackay Stephen DSO, DFC* CBE

Harbourne Mackay Stephen was born in Elgin, northern Scotland in 1916. He joined the RAFVR in April 1937 and learnt to fly. He was given a six-month attachment with the regular RAF and converting to Hurricanes he joined 605 Squadron at Tangmere as a Sergeant-Pilot.

He was with the squadron when the war started, and his attachment became more permanent.

In March 1940 Stephen was airborne with the squadron when they had their first war time contact with the enemy. They managed to damage a German bomber and returned home.

Stephen was commissioned in April 1940 and sent to join 74 Squadron at Hornchurch. He was in combat over Dunkirk and made a number of victory claims. During the Battle of Britain, he made steady claims and became one of the squadron's leading pilots.

He was awarded the DFC on the 27th of August 1940 and a bar in November 1940. A DSO followed in December 1940.

In January he was sent to RAF Turnhouse and No. 59 OTU as the Chief Flying Instructor, but this was changed, and he went to test aircraft at Farnborough.

In June 1941, Stephen went to Portreath to form 130 Squadron. He then took over as Squadron Leader with 234 Squadron at Warmwell and made a number of victory claims. He was then sent the Far East in 1942.

Stephen commanded 166 Fighter Wing and went to HQ 224 Group, Fighter Ops and then to Air Command South East Asia.

He was released from the RAF in 1945 as a Wing Commander and worked in the newspaper industry. He also commanded 602 Squadron Royal Auxiliary Air Force from 1950 to 1952. To add to his DSO and DFC he was awarded a CBE in 1985.

He died in August 2001.

Pilot Officer Peter St John

Peter Cape Beauchamp St. John was born on the 25th of May 1917. In 1935 while working as an Estate Agents clerk in London, he joined the Territorial Army as a Sapper, in the Royal Engineers.

He later joined the RAF on a short service commission and after flying training he joined 87 Squadron at RAF Debden in July 1938.

He then converted to Spitfires and was then posted to 74 Squadron at Hornchurch on 20th April 1939.

He fought over Dunkirk and into the Battle of Britain with 74 Squadron making a few claims. He became ill in August and was sent to Princess Mary's RAF Hospital, Halton. He was deemed unfit for flying until the end of the month when he returned to action. He claimed further victories, but he was shot down and killed on the 22nd of October. He is buried in St Mary's churchyard, Amersham.

Pilot Officer Henryk Szezesny DFC KW* VM

Henryk Szczesny was born in Warsaw on the 27th of March 1910 and joined the Polish Air Force in 1931. He served as a fighter pilot and in September 1939, he shot down two Heinkel 111's, probably shot down a Dornier 17 and damaged another before he was wounded.

He escaped via Romania where his wounds were treated before making his way to England and the Polish depot in Blackpool.

He was commissioned in February 1940 and after extra pilot training he converted to Spitfires joining 74 Squadron at Hornchurch in early August 1940.

He was soon in action and became known as Henry the Pole or sneezy due to his surname. He claimed a Dornier 17 and a Messerschmitt 110 before making further claims in September and early October.

He remained with 74 when they went to Biggin Hill, but he did not make any further claims until December before moving on to 257 Squadron and then 242 and 302 Squadrons.

He received a number of awards including a DFC in October 1941 and made more combat claims.

On the 28th of December 1942 he was made Squadron Leader Flying at the Polish Wing, based at Northolt. He continued operations and on the 4th of April 1943 he was shot down near Paris and captured. He was sent to Stalag Luft III.

After the war he returned to the UK and remained in the RAF. He became a fighter controller and retired as a post war Flight Lieutenant in 1965. He died in 1996.

Appendix G

Battle of Britain top scorers of Biggin Hill (while operating from the airfield):

N.B. Official figures may not correspond with the contents of the book

32 Squadron

Tony Barton

11 August 1940	ME109E destroyed	Dover
16 August 1940	2x ME109E's destroyed	South South East of Biggin Hill
18 August 1940	Junkers 88	Btwn Biggin Hill & coast
24 August 1940	ME109E damaged	Folkestone
25 August 1940	Henshel 126 damaged	Mid Channel

Peter Brothers

19 July 1940	ME109E destroyed	Dover
20 July 1940	ME109E destroyed	Mid Channel
29 July 1940	ME109E destroyed	Kent coast
16 August 1940	ME110 destroyed	Kent
18 August 1940	Dornier 17 destroyed	Biggin Hill
18 August 1940	ME109E destroyed	Canterbury
22 August 1940	ME109E destroyed	Folkestone
24 August 1940	ME109E destroyed	Dover

Mike Crossley

20 July 1940	½ share ME110 destroyed	SE of Dover
20 July 1940	ME109E destroyed	Near Dover
25 July 1940	ME109E unconfirmed	SE of Dover
12 August 1940	2x ME109E's destroyed	Deal-Dover area
15 August 1940	2x Junkers 88's destroyed	Near Portsmouth

15 August 1940	Dornier 17 destroyed	Croydon
15 August 1940	½ share Dornier 17 destroyed	Croydon
16 August 1940	ME109E destroyed	4 miles north Folkestone
16 August 1940	JU88 & ME110 destroyed	Sevenoaks, Kent
18 August 1940	JU88 and ME109 destroyed	Ashford & Canterbury
18 August 1940	Dornier 17 damaged	Near Ashford
25 August 1940	Do. 17 & ME109E destroyed	Off Cap Griz Nez

Alan Eckford

18 August 1940	Dornier 17 destroyed	Biggin Hill
18 August 1940	ME109E destroyed	Canterbury
26 August 1940	Heinkel 111 damaged	Thames area

John Flinders

15 August 1940	ME109E destroyed	Caterham, Surrey
18 August 1940	2x ME110's destroyed	2 miles North of Canterbury

Peter Gardner

11 August 1940	ME109E Damaged	Dungeness
12 August 1940	ME109E & Dornier 17 destroyed	Deal area
15 August 1940	Junkers 88 destroyed	SE of Croydon
16 August 1940	ME109E destroyed	East of Goodwin Sands

William Higgins

20th July 1940	ME110 destroyed	English Channel
12 August 1940	ME109E destroyed	Off Dover
24 August 1940	ME109E destroyed	Folkestone

John Humpherson

20 July 1940	JU 87 Stuka destroyed	South of Dover
12 August 1940	ME109E probable	South of Canterbury

15 August 1940	Junkers 88 destroyed	Thorney Island airfield
15 August 1940	ME109E probable	2m SE of Croydon

John Pain

15 August 1940	Junkers 88 damaged	Croydon
15 August 1940	ME109E probable	Croydon
16 August 1940	Junkers 88 destroyed	Biggin Hill airfield area
16 August 1940	Junkers 88 probable	Biggin Hill airfield area
18 August 1940	Dornier 17 destroyed	
18 August 1940	Dornier 17 probable	

Karol Pniak

12 August 1940	ME109E destroyed	Dover-Manston area
15 August 1940	ME109E destroyed	Near Croydon
15 August 1940	Dornier 17 probable	Near Croydon
18 August 1940	2x ME109E's destroyed	North of Canterbury
22 August 1940	1/3 share Dornier 17 damaged	
24 August 1940	ME109E probable	Near Dover

John Proctor

20 July 1940	½ share ME110 destroyed	12 miles SE of Dover
20 July 1940	ME110 destroyed	Off Folkestone
12 August 1940	ME109E probable	% miles SW of North Foreland
25 August 1940	ME109E destroyed	South of Dover

Rupert Smythe

19 July 1940	ME109E unconfirmed	5 miles South of Dover
12 August 1940	Dornier 17 destroyed	Off coast Deal – Dover
14 August 1940	ME109E destroyed	NW of Hawkinge
20 August 1940	Dornier 17 damaged	Thames Estuary area.

Boleslaw Wlasnowski

15 August 1940	ME109E destroyed	Off Harwich, Suffolk
18 August 1940	Dornier 17 destroyed	Biggin Hill area
18 August 1940	ME109E destroyed	Chatham area

610 Squadron

John Ellis

24 July 1940	ME109E destroyed	10 miles South of Dover
24 July 1940	ME109E destroyed	8 miles North of Margate
25 July 1940	ME109E destroyed	Off Folkestone
25 July 1940	2x ME109E's destroyed	Off Dover
12 August 1940	ME109E destroyed	Dungeness
12 August 1940	ME109E probable	Dungeness
16 August 1940	Junkers 88 damaged	Dungeness
18 August 1940	Heinkel 111 destroyed	Biggin Hill
18 August 1940	ME109E destroyed	Biggin Hill
26 August 1940	ME109E destroyed	Folkestone
27 August 1940	Heinkel 111 destroyed	Folkestone

Ronald Hamlyn

14 August 1940	ME109E damaged	Dover
24 August 1940	Junkers 88 destroyed	Dover
24 August 1940	4x ME109E's destroyed	Dover to Gravesend area
26 August 1940	ME109E destroyed	Dover
26 August 1940	ME109E probable	Dover
28 August 1940	ME109E destroyed	Dover-Deal area

| 30 August 1940 | ME109E destroyed | Between Ashford & Biggin Hill |

Peter Lamb

24 August 1940	ME109E destroyed	Near Dover
26 August 1940	Dornier 17 destroyed	Between Deal - Dover
29 August 1940	ME110 destroyed	Between Tunbridge Wells - Rye
30 August 1940	Heinkel 111 destroyed	North of Ashford, Kent

Stanley Norris

24 July 1940	ME109E unconfirmed	
25 July 1940	2x ME109E's destroyed	Over English Channel off Dover
29 July 1940	1/3 Dornier 17 damaged	Off Dungeness
14 August 1940	2x JU87 Stuka's destroyed	South Coast
14 August 1940	JU87 Stuka damaged	South Coast
24 August 1940	ME109E destroyed	20 miles N. of Isle of Sheppey
29 August 1940	ME110 Probable	15 miles S. of Tunbridge Wells

Claude Parsons

24 July 1940	½ Dornier 17 destroyed	Off Cap Griz Nez
25 July 1940	ME109E destroyed	4 miles South of Dover
14 August 1940	JU87 Stuka damaged	South of Folkestone
18 August 1940	Dornier 17 probable	South East of Biggin Hill

Constantine Pegge

12 August 1940	2x ME109E destroyed	Hawkinge and Dover
18 August 1940	ME109E destroyed	Biggin Hill- Dungeness
18 August 1940	Heinkel 111 damaged	Biggin Hill – Dungeness
24 August 1940	ME109E probable	North of Gravesend
28 August 1940	ME109E destroyed	Dover – Deal area

29 August 1940	Dornier 17 damaged	Mayfield, Sussex
30 August 1940	Heinkel 111 destroyed	Dungeness

Edward Smith

24 July 1940	ME109E destroyed	10 miles South of Dover
24 July 1940	ME109E unconfirmed	10 miles NE of Margate
24 July 1940	V-156 Vindicator damaged	Margate
25 July 1940	ME109E destroyed	SE of Dover
29 July 1940	1/3 Dornier 17 damaged	10 miles South of Dungeness
11 August 1940	Heinkel 59 seaplane destroyed	3 miles off Calais

79 Squadron

Rupert Clerke

6 September 1940	Junkers 88 probable	3 miles SE of RAF Kenley
27 September 1940	1/3 Heinkel 111 destroyed	Kent
27 September 1940	1/3 Heinkel 111 probable	Kent

George Nelson-Edwards

6 September 1940	Junkers 88 damaged	English Channel
27 September 1940	1/3 Heinkel 111 destroyed	English Channel
27 September 1940	1/3 Heinkel 111 probable	English Channel
29 September 1940	Heinkel 111 probable	English Channel

Thomas Parker

28 August 1940	¼ Heinkel 59 destroyed	Mid Channel
4 September 1940	2x ME110's damaged	Brooklands, Surrey

Donald Stones

31 August 1940	Dornier 17 destroyed	Newchurch

31 August 1940	Dornier 17 probable	Newchurch
1 September 1940	Dornier 17 damaged	Biggin Hill
4 September 1940	ME110 Probable	Beachy Head, Sussex
7 September 1940	Dornier 17 Probable	Biggin Hill
7 September 1940	½ Junkers 88 Probable	Biggin Hill

72 Squadron

Thomas Elsdon

1 September 1940	2x ME110E's destroyed	10 miles SE of Croydon
4 September 1940	2x ME110's destroyed	Tenterden- Tunbridge Wells
7 September 1940	ME109E destroyed	Maidstone area.

Joseph O'Meara

27 September 1940	Dornier 17 damaged	Near Sevenoaks
29 September 1940	Junkers 88 destroyed	Near Biggin Hill???
29 September 1940	Junkers 88 probable	Near Biggin Hill???

William Rolls

2 September 1940	ME110 destroyed	Maidstone
2 September 1940	Dornier 17 destroyed	Maidstone
4 September 1940	2x JU86's (ME110's) destroyed	Ashford / Tunbridge Wells
11 September 1940	Dornier 17 destroyed	Maidstone
11 September 1940	Dornier 17 Probable	Maidstone
14 September 1940	ME109E destroyed	West of Canterbury
14 September 1940	ME109E damaged	Brenchley
20 September 1940	ME109E destroyed	Between Ashford Canterbury

Desmond Sheen

4 September 1940	ME110 Probable	Tenterden – Tunbridge Wells

John 'Pancho' Villa (includes claims with 72 & 92 squadrons)

1 September 1940	ME109E probable	Gatwick, Sussex
1 September 1940	ME109E damaged	Gatwick, Sussex
2 September 1940	ME110 Destroyed	Herne Bay
2 September 1940	ME110 Probable	Herne Bay
2 September 1940	ME110 damaged	Herne Bay
4 September 1940	ME110 destroyed	Tenterden-Tunbridge Wells
4 September 1940	ME110 Probable	Tenterden-Tunbridge Wells
7 September 1940	Heinkel 111 Probable	East of Rochester
10 September 1940	½ Dornier 17 destroyed	Nr East Grinstead, Sussex
14 September 1940	½ Heinkel 111 destroyed	20 miles S of Eastbourne
15 September 1940	2x ME109E's destroyed	Dungeness – Faversham
15 September 1940	Dornier 17 destroyed	Biggin Hill
15 September 1940	½ Heinkel 111 destroyed	Dartford area
27 September 1940	Heinkel 111 destroyed	Croydon – Brighton area
28 September 1940	ME109E destroyed	North of Hastings
11 October 1940	Dornier 17 destroyed	Thames Estuary
20 October 1940	1/6 ME110 destroyed	E. Tunbridge Wells-Maidstone
25 October 1940	ME109E destroyed	South West of Maidstone
29 October 1940	ME110 destroyed	15 miles SSE of Rye, Sussex

John White

2 September 1940	Dornier 17 destroyed	Near Maidstone
7 September 1940	Heinkel 111 Probable	East of Rochester
7 September 1940	Dornier 17 damaged	
11 September 1940	Dornier 17 destroyed	Nr Cranbrook
11 September 1940	Dornier 17 Probable	Nr Cranbrook

14 September 1940	½ Heinkel 111 destroyed	Dartford area
15 September 1940	½ Heinkel 111 destroyed	NE of Maidstone
15 September 1940	Heinkel 111 destroyed	
23 September 1940	ME109E Probable	Near Canterbury

92 Squadron

Brian Kingcombe

9 September 1940	ME109E Probable	Canterbury- Biggin Hill
11 September 1940	Heinkel 111 destroyed	Dungeness
14 September 1940	2x ME109E's damaged	Canterbury
15 September 1940	Dornier 17 damaged	Hornchurch
18 September 1940	½ Junkers 88 destroyed	Off Isle of Sheppey
18 September 1940	Heinkel 11 probable	Southend area
18 September 1940	Heinkel 111 damaged	Southend area
24 September 1940	Junkers 88 damaged	Rochford- Maidstone
24 September 1940	ME109E damaged	SE of Dover
27 September 1940	Dornier 17 damaged	Maidstone
27 September 1940	Dornier 17 Probable	Maidstone
27 September 1940	2x Junkers 88 damaged	Sevenoaks area
11 October 1940	ME109 destroyed	South of Dungeness
12 October 1940	2x ME109E destroyed	Mid-Channel / Cap Griz Nez
12 October 1940	ME109E damaged	NW of Margate
13 October 1940	ME109E destroyed	Ashford area of Kent

Tony Bartley

14 September 1940	Dornier 17 damaged	Kent
14 September 1940	ME109E damaged	Canterbury

15 September 1940	Dornier 17 destroyed	Hornchurch
15 September 1940	Dornier 17 Probable	Hornchurch
18 September 1940	Dornier 17 destroyed	Biggin Hill to Gravesend area
27 September 1940	Junkers 88 destroyed	Biggin Hill area

John Drummond

11 September 1940	ME109E Probable	10 miles NW of Dungeness
23 September 1940	ME109E destroyed	Tonbridge towards Chatham
24 September 1940	ME109E Probable	Maidstone
24 September 1940	ME109E damaged	Maidstone area
24 September 1940	Junkers 88 damaged	Maidstone area
27 September 1940	1/3 ME110 destroyed	Sevenoaks – Westerham
27 September 1940	Junkers 88 destroyed	High Halden
30 September 1940	ME109E Probable	Brighton
5 October 1940	ME109E destroyed	Dungeness
5 October 1940	Henschel 126 destroyed	Dungeness

Ronald Fokes

10 September 1940	½ Dornier 17 destroyed	10 miles SW of Biggin Hill
15 September 1940	Dornier 17 damaged	Canterbury-Maidstone areas
24 September 1940	Junkers 88 probable	Maidstone area
30 September 1940	ME109E Probable	Biggin Hill- Beachy Head
15 October 1940	2x ME109E's destroyed	Mid Channel & Ashford, Kent
15 October 1940	Heinkel 111 destroyed	Mid Channel
26 October 1940	ME109E destroyed	South East of Tunbridge Wells

John Villa (see 72 Squadrons list)

Robert Holland

15 September 1940	ME109E Probable	Canterbury area

| 15 October 1940 | ME109E Probable | SE of Ashford, Kent |
| 26 October 1940 | ME109E destroyed | Nr Tunbridge Wells |

Donald Kingaby

27 September 1940	ME109E damaged	Biggin Hill area
30 September 1940	ME109E damaged	Lewes, Sussex
12 October 1940	ME109E destroyed	Rochester area
12 October 1940	ME109E Probable	Rochester area
15 October 1940	ME109E destroyed	Mid Channel
20 October 1940	1/6 ME110 destroyed	East of Tunbridge Wells
24 October 1940	Dornier 17 destroyed	20 miles East of Deal
25 October 1940	ME109E damaged	English Channel

Desmond Williams

11 September 1940	Heinkel 111 destroyed	Dungeness-Rye area
15 September 1940	2x Dornier 17's damaged	Dungeness
15 September 1940	½ Dornier 17 destroyed	West of Hornchurch
15 September 1940	Heinkel 111 destroyed	Hendon area
29 September 1940	Dornier 17 damaged	Maidstone-Canterbury area
30 September 1940	Dornier 17 Probable	Hawkinge area
4 October 1940	Junkers 88 damaged	English Channel

Trevor Wade

10 September 1940	½ Dornier 17 destroyed	SW of Biggin Hill
11 September 1940	Heinkel 111 destroyed	Maidstone
15 September 1940	ME109E Probable	Maidstone area
18 September 1940	ME109E damaged	Folkestone area
20 September 1940	ME109E damaged	Dover
22 September 1940	Dornier 17 destroyed	Lewes, Sussex

12 October 1940	ME109E destroyed	Rochester area
12 October 1940	ME109E Probable	Rochester area
12 October 1940	ME109E damaged	Rochester area
26 October 1940	ME109E Probable	Tunbridge Wells
29 October 1940	ME110 Probable	East Grinstead

Allan Wright

11 September 1940	Heinkel 111 destroyed	East London
11 September 1940	ME109E Probable	Folkestone
14 September 1940	ME109E damaged	Tunbridge Wells
15 September 1940	ME109E Probable	Canterbury
19 September 1940	Junkers 88 Probable	Dover area
26 September 1940	Dornier 17 destroyed	Tenterden
27 September 1940	½ Heinkel 111 destroyed	Sevenoaks area
27 September 1940	Dornier 17 damaged	As above
27 September 1940	Junkers 88 destroyed	As above
27 September 1940	2x Junkers 88 damaged	As above
30 September 1940	ME109E destroyed	Redhill airfield
30 September 1940	ME109E destroyed	South of New Haven

74 Squadron

'Sailor' Malan

17 October 1940	ME109E Probable	North of Ashford, Kent
22 October 1940	ME109E destroyed	South of Maidstone.

Bryan Draper

17 October 1940	ME109E destroyed	Gravesend area
17 October 1940	ME109E probable	Gravesend area

| 20 October 1940 | ME109E Probable | Btwn Maidstone & Dungeness |

John Mungo-Park

20 October 1940	ME109E Destroyed	Maidstone area
22 October 1940	ME109E Probable	Maidstone – Hastings area
27 October 1940	ME109E Damaged	South of Maidstone
28 October 1940	ME109E Damaged	Maidstone area
29 October 1940	2x ME109E's Destroyed	East Grinstead area.

William Nelson

17 October 1940	ME109E Destroyed	Gravesend – Maidstone area
27 October 1940	ME109E Destroyed	South of Maidstone
28 October 1940	ME109E Destroyed	East Grinstead

Robert Spurdle

| 29 October 1940 | ME109E Probable | South of Kenley |

Harbourne M. Stephen

20 October 1940	ME109E Destroyed	Sevenoaks – Dungeness area
20 October 1940	ME109E Probable	Sevenoaks – Dungeness area
27 October 1940	ME109E Destroyed	South of Maidstone.

141 Squadron

| 16 September 1940 | Junkers 88 Destroyed (claimed as a Heinkel 111) | Over sea |
| 16 September 1940 | Junkers 88 Probable (claimed as a Heinkel 111) | Over sea |

Appendix H

Roll of Honour of Pilots killed while operating from Biggin Hill during the Battle of Britain:

18th July 1940 10:00am	P/O P. Litchfield	610 Sqn	English Channel
20th July 1940 6:00pm	Sub. Lt. G. Bulmer	32 Sqn	Channel off Dover
25th July 1940 3:40pm	SQL A. Smith	610 Sqn	Crashed Hawkinge
11th Aug. 1940 11:30am	Sgt. J. Tanner	610 Sqn	Channel off Calais
11th Aug. 1940 11:30am	Sgt. W. J. Neville	610 Sqn	Channel off Calais
16th August 1940 5:15pm	Flt. Lt. W. H. Warner	610 Sqn	Off Dungeness
25th August 1940 7:00pm	P/O K. Gillman	32 Squadron	Over Channel
26th Aug. 1940 12:40pm	F/O F. K. Webster	610 Sqn	Crashed Hawkinge
28th August 1940 5:00pm	P/O K. H. Cox	610 Sqn	Stelling Minnis, Kent
29th Aug. 1940 4:00pm	Sgt. E. Manton	610 Sqn.	Hurst Green, Sussex
31st August 1940 6:35pm	F/O E. J. Wilcox	72 Squadron	Dungeness, Kent
31st August 1940 4:00pm	Sgt. H. A. Bolton	79 Squadron	Crashed Kenley
1st Sept 1940 11:15am	F/O O. Pigg	72 Squadron	Pluckley, Kent
5th Sept 1940 2:45pm	P/O D. C. Winter	72 Squadron	Elham, Kent
5th Sept 1940 2:45pm	Sgt. M. Gray	72 Squadron	Eastern Kent
11th Sept 1940 4:15pm	P/O F. N. Hargreaves	92 Squadron	Dungeness, Kent
11th Sept 1940 7:00pm	P/O H. D. Edwards	92 Squadron	Smeeth, Kent
20th Sept 1940 10:20am	P/O D. F. Holland	72 Squadron	Canterbury, Kent
20th Sept 1940 11:35am	P/O H. P. Hill	92 Squadron	Dungeness, Kent
20th Sept 1940 11:35am	Sgt. R. Eyles	92 Squadron	Dungeness, Kent
24th Sept 1940 9:00am	P/O J. S. Bryson	92 Squadron	North Weald airfield
27th Sept 1940 9:40am	P/O E. E. Males	72 Squadron	Sevenoaks, Kent

27th Sept 1940 9:40am	P/O P. Davies-Cooke	72 Squadron	Fell dead Hayes, Kent.
27th Sept 1940 9:20am	Flt. Lt. J. Paterson	92 Squadron	Farningham, Kent
27th Sept 1940 9:40am	F/Sgt. C. Sydney	92 Squadron	Kingston Upon Thames
27th Sept 1940 3:20pm	Sgt. T. G. Oldfield	92 Squadron	Hesketh Park, Dartford
9th Oct 1940 12:50pm	Sgt. E. T. G. Frith	92 Squadron	Near Ashford, Kent
10th Oct 1940 8:15am	P/O D.G. Williams	92 Squadron	Tangmere airfield
10th Oct 1940 8:15am	F/O J. Drummond	92 Squadron	Tangmere airfield
12th Oct 1940 9:20am	P/O H.R. Case	72 Squadron	Folkestone, Kent
12th Oct 1940 4:40pm	P/O A.J. Pattinson	92 Squadron	Hawkinge, Kent
15th Oct 1940 10:00am	Sgt. K. B. Parker	92 Squadron	Medway River
17th Oct 1940 3:40pm	F/O A. L. Ricalton	74 Squadron	Hollingbourne, Kent
19th Oct 1940 ???	Sgt. L. C. Alton	92 Squadron	Marden, Kent
22nd Oct 1940 3:30pm	F/O P. C. St. John	74 Squadron	Nutfield, Surrey
27th Oct 1940 9:00am	Sgt. J. A. Scott	74 Squadron	Maidstone, Kent

Sources Used in this book:

UK National Archives: Squadron Operations Record Book's and individual pilot combat reports: These contain public sector information licensed under the Open Government Licence v3.0.

Luftwaffe combat records

RAF AI (1)k POW interrogation reports

Intelligence reports Lw.KBK-Gefechtsbericht 18.8.1940

Books

'The Battle of Britain: The Hardest Day' by Dr Alfred Price, published by McDonald & Janes 1979.

'Dimsie' by Donald Stones, published by Wingham Press in 1991.

'Poles in Defence of Britain' by Robert Gretzngier, published by Grub Street books in 2001.

'The JG26 War Diary' by Donald Caldwell, Grub Street books 1996.

'Smoke Trails in the Sky' by Tony Bartley, published by Crecy books in 1997.

'A Willingness to Die' by Brian Kingcombe, published by Tempus books 1999.

'Battle of Britain Day' by Dr Alfred Price, printed by Sidgwick & Jackson Ltd. In 1990.

'Spitfire Attack' by William Rolls, printed by William Kimber books in 1987.

'Sailor' by Phillip Kaplan, printed by Pen & Sword books 2012.

'First Light' by Geoffrey Wellum, Penguin Books 2003.

'Hurricane Squadron Ace' by Nick Thomas, printed by Pen & Sword books in 2014.

'Sky Tiger' by Norman Franks, printed by Crecy books in 1980.

'RAF Fighter Command Losses 1939-1941' by Norman Franks printed by Midland Publishing in 1997.

'RAF Fighter Command victory claims of WW2 1939-1940' by John Foreman, printed by Red Kite books in 2003.

'Biggin on the Bump' by Bob Ogley printed by Froglets publishing 1990.

'Battle of Britain 'Then & Now' by Winston G. Ramsey, published by After the Battle.

bbm.org.uk website

About the Author

M S Morgan is a relatively new writer who has served 30 years as a senior detective in the British Police. He has an extensive knowledge of the RAF, especially during the Battle of Britain. Using his knowledge and investigative skills, he had compiled a detailed diary of the events around Biggin Hill – Britain's most famous fighter base in the Battle of Britain.

This chronological history of the station during the battle is concise and seeks to link combat claims to losses. By scouring the official records, he has identified and in some cases; disputed previously held claims about victories and victims. With an open mind he examines the evidence, utilising records, Combat reports, biographies and other material to present a detail diary of the events during the summer of 1940.

Anyone with an interest with an interest in military aviation will find this an interesting read.

This is part of a series of books written by M S Morgan with the others detailing in a similar manner the squadrons of Gravesend during the Battle of Britain and also the night fighters of West Malling from 1941-1943. A future volume on Kenley is currently under way. In addition, he has written about RAF encounters with UFO's and the American War of Independence.

He lives in Kent, England with his wife.

One Last Thing...

If you enjoyed this book or found it useful, I'd be very grateful if you'd post a short review on Amazon. Your support really does make a difference and I read all the reviews personally, so I can get your feedback and make this book even better.

Thanks again for your support! MSM.

Printed in Great Britain
by Amazon